DAVID KEMBER

action LEARNING *and* *action* RESEARCH

IMPROVING THE QUALITY OF
TEACHING & LEARNING

ACTION LEARNING AND ACTION RESEARCH

Improving the quality of teaching and learning

David Kember

with contributions from his associates

Tak Shing Ha, Bick-har Lam, April Lee, Sandra Ng, Louisa Yan and Jessie C K Yum

KOGAN
PAGE

First published in 2000

Kogan Page Limited
120 Pentonville Road
London
N1 9JN
UK

Stylus Publishing Inc
22883 Quicksilver Drive
Sterling
VA 20166-2012
USA

British Library Cataloguing in Publication Data

A CIP record for this book is available from the British Library.

ISBN 0 7494 3113 X

Typeset by JS Typesetting, Wellingborough, Northamptonshire
Printed and bound in Great Britain by Biddles Ltd, Guildford and King's Lynn

Contents

Contents

Foreword

The appearance of this book is very timely. Universities all over the world are undergoing massive traumas as the full implications of managerialism are being felt. Public funding is being cut to the bone, student numbers are increasing, and the quality of undergraduate teaching is under serious threat. Quality assurance mechanisms appear to those in the front line to be yet another source of debilitation, rather than a means of maintaining the quality of their teaching. Alternative, and economically viable, ways of addressing teaching quality are urgently needed.

Enter Kember and his action learning team. Kember started by helping teachers in his own institution to improve their teaching through action research. The results were so encouraging that in 1994 he applied for a cross-institutional grant of HK $13 million, which funded the Action Learning Project (ALP). He called for applications from tertiary teachers in all the (then) seven tertiary institutions in Hong Kong, offering funds and a support structure for teachers to carry out action research into their own teaching. Fifty projects were funded. This book provides an overview of the ALP: the theory and practice of action research, why the term 'action learning' was used rather than 'action research', both self-monitored and external evaluations of the project, and the lessons to be learned from the ALP itself.

The project was by all accounts very successful. Almost all project directors judged that their own teaching had improved, they were more reflective about their teaching, and most judged that their students' learning had improved (with hard evidence in some cases). There were frequent spin-offs to departmental teaching generally, and many project directors got brownie points out of the publications emerging from the project. Amazingly, a few departmental heads deemed educational research not to be 'real' research, and disallowed such publications in promotion and contract renewal exercises! But most did, creating an important and much-needed means by which a concern with improved teaching also benefited the teacher's research record. This is particularly important in universities where good teaching is paid lip service only, the reward system in the event recognizing only research activity, in grants and publications.

The most important contribution of this publication, however, is to the general quality assurance and quality enhancement debate, which Kember conceptualizes in a comprehensive framework that embraces quality, conception of teaching and learning, and cost-effectiveness. The almost universal way of addressing teaching quality is to use top-down bureaucratic measures: external validation of all teaching programmes, with vast amounts of committee and paper work, with ownership of their programmes removed from those most closely involved in design and delivery, the teachers themselves. This does not 'assure' teaching quality. As Kember points out, this model was used in the UK and in Australia in the then polytechnic and advanced education sectors respectively. When they all became universities in the early 1990s, common evaluation procedures were introduced across both these and the existing universities, thus making it possible to compare the teaching quality of institutions where programmes were self-developed and those where quality had been 'assured'. The university sector won hands-down, with few exceptions, most being in the more smug of the Australian 'sandstone' universities.

Quality *enhancement* comes about bottom-up, from teachers driven by a genuine desire to improve their teaching. But what is the most effective model for doing that? Workshops are commonly used and are good in context, but their effect may not last. Developmental projects are undertaken by teachers themselves, but how do academics lacking educational research and evaluation skills suddenly start designing successful projects? The University Grants Commission in Hong Kong financed 231 Educational Development Grants to teachers on the basis of their proposals, of which only 44 (19 per cent) produced a report. No doubt there could have been many unreported benefits, but that success rate is not encouraging. However, the UGC in its wisdom also financed the 50 ALP projects, of which 47 (94 per cent) produced reports (two staff had gone elsewhere). In short, the action learning infrastructure, including the provision of 'critical friends' to help in the development of projects, saw projects through to a conclusion, most of which were successful in bringing about some improvement to teaching. Well over one hundred tertiary teachers, and probably thousands of students ultimately, were involved in the projects. Not a bad return for an outlay of one million pounds sterling, particularly when you compare that with the prodigious expense, both financial and emotional, of the bureaucratic bludgeon of quality assurance measures. (Of course, as Kember points out, quality assurance is imposed for political not educational reasons.)

Asian institutions have a reputation for rigid expository teaching. This is certainly not true of Hong Kong now. In ten years, I saw tertiary teaching in Hong Kong change from highly traditional and rigid, to a general consciousness at individual and institutional levels of the need for innovative, student-centred teaching, and where all tertiary institutions have staff development centres whose role is more than the provision of educational technology training. This is a remarkable transformation, in which the Action Learning Project played an important role. Ironically, during the same period, Australian and British universities went precisely in the reverse direction.

It would be too much to hope that those who need to read this very clearly written book will do so. It is an excellent introduction to action learning, with impressive demonstrations that it can work, but more importantly, it has very strong and important messages for universities all over the world. Simply, the managerial quality assurance model is not cost-effective, and is not working. As Kember and his team demonstrate, there are cheaper and educationally far better ways to go, both to assure and to enhance the quality of university teaching.

John Biggs
Advisory Professor at the Hong Kong Institute of Education
and formerly Professor of Education at the University of Hong Kong

Acknowledgements

The material in this book was to a large extent based upon the experiences of the Action Learning Project. This was a very large project with a lot of people involved, so many people need to be acknowledged and thanked.

The enthusiasm and hard work of the participants in the projects meant that there were a lot of successful projects to report. The many students in the courses they taught also made a major contribution by being willing to try something new and providing immense amounts of feedback. The members of the management committee provided valuable advice on the best way to venture into the unknown.

The University Grants Committee of Hong Kong provided the funding for the project, and should also be given credit for recognizing the importance of activities in teaching development. The Hong Kong Polytechnic University also provided resources for the venture. All of the UGC institutions and their staff deserve credit for being willing to participate in such a way that the initiative was a genuine collaborative venture.

I would also like to thank the associate coordinators. They were thrown in at the deep end at the start of the project, but turned out to be very good at swimming. The associate coordinators for the first round of the project are co-authors for two parts of the book.

An earlier version of Chapter 12 appeared as an article in *Educational Action Research*, volume 5, number 3, and appears here with the permission of the journal editors and the publisher, Triangle Journals.

David Kember

PART A
FRAMEWORK

David Kember

The first part of the book sets the framework by explaining what action learning and action research are and how they compare with other schemes which have been used for assuring the quality of teaching and learning. It aims to provide sufficient information for a teacher to carry out an action learning project concerned with some aspect of his or her teaching, which will have an impact upon the learning outcomes of students enrolled in the course in question.

Chapter 1 provides an introduction to quality schemes in general. It introduces three frameworks for describing and analysing quality mechanisms:

■ The contrast between official policy and what happens in practice, or between *espoused theory* and *theory in use*, using the terminology of Argyris and Schön (1978), forms the first framework.
■ The second is a two-dimensional classification system used to distinguish and classify quality schemes. One dimension distinguishes quality assurance and enhancement schemes with sub-categories for each. The second dimension relates the nature of scheme to the positivist, interpretive and critical research paradigms.
■ The third framework relates quality improvement to the cost of the scheme. This framework is proposed as a means of determining the effectiveness of quality schemes.

The second chapter looks at the characteristics of action research and action learning, and explains why they provide a suitable means for quality enhancement. The mechanism for applying action research to the teaching and learning environment is explained.

Chapter 3 contains guidelines for conducting observation and evaluation, which are important facets of the action research cycle. It describes a number of techniques that have been found useful.

1

Quality in learning and teaching

Higher education has been the subject of increasing criticism in recent years. Daly (1994), for example, reviewed no less than 37 major reports and articles from government agencies, employers and academics themselves detailing faults with higher education in the United States. Critics have been just as vocal in the rest of the world. Partly in response to this chorus of concern, governments have moved to make universities and colleges more accountable for the finance they receive from state coffers.

At the same time many university systems have been making the transition from elite systems, educating only a small well-qualified section of the population, to mass systems educating a much wider portion of the populace. Countries have recognized that their economic competitiveness depends upon having a well-educated workforce able to cope with the pace of technological development.

Funding pressures have intensified the scrutiny of quality. Many governments have been forced to make savings, which have placed restrictions upon government spending. Education, and particularly higher education, has come to be seen as a social service and, therefore, sensitive to budget cuts when the screws are being tightened on public-sector funding.

The increase in student numbers, brought about by a shift to a mass system, rarely seems to have been accompanied by a corresponding funding increase, because of tighter government budgets. Most countries are shifting part of the funding burden from government to student fees. From many parts of the world, though, there have been complaints that universities are being asked to do more with less – and, what is more, to prove that they are doing it well. It is one of life's ironies that, normally, the harder it is to obtain money the more stringent is the review of what has been achieved by spending it.

Concern about the quality of teaching has been particularly strong since many have asserted that teaching has been relegated to a poor second place behind research, because of ever increasing pressure on academics to publish. The outcome has been a worldwide growth in schemes for quality control, assurance and enhancement of learning and teaching.

To look at these schemes it is necessary to have frameworks for describing, classifying and analysing them. The main purpose of this chapter is to introduce three such frameworks:

- The first is Argyris and Schön's (1978) widely cited distinction between espoused theory and theory in use.
- The second, which takes up the majority of this chapter, is a two-dimensional classification system for describing and analysing quality schemes. Along the first dimension, schemes are placed in one of four categories according to their type. The second dimension analyses the nature of the scheme by analogy with the main research paradigms.
- The final framework, for evaluating schemes by assessing quality improvement against the cost of the scheme, is introduced briefly in this chapter and dealt with at length in Chapter 16.

ESPOUSED THEORY AND THEORY IN USE

When looking at organizations, Argyris and Schön (1978) noticed that there was often a mismatch between what the organization said it did and what happened in practice. Policy documents, codes of practice or management statements about procedures could often differ considerably from the way members of the organization operated in practice. The terminology they introduced for the distinction was between espoused theory and theory in use.

Argyris and Schön presented cases, mostly drawn from business organizations, showing the effects of the disparity. In most cases it seems that the management was unaware that practice did not match their policy. The mismatch could then become harmful to the organization, as planning and policy decisions would be based upon assumptions that were not being carried out in practice.

Universities are organizations which commonly have discrepancies between espoused theory and theory in use. They are possibly more prone to such mismatches than many other organizations. Academics have traditionally been used to acting with a degree of autonomy. Central managements have not always found it easy to influence the behaviour and practice of their individual academic staff members.

An area where mismatches between theory in use and espoused theory may be quite common is that of quality schemes. In response to government pressures and the introduction of review procedures, many university managements have introduced new quality schemes, or tightened or extended existing ones. The schemes are documented in policy papers, manuals from registrars' departments, submissions to review panels or the like.

Whether the schemes are universally put into practice according to the documentation may be another matter. The greater the number of people affected by the scheme, the higher the chance of a mismatch. Some may interpret the guidelines or instructions in a way that was not intended. Others may feel that their time and effort is better directed elsewhere and so will avoid, skimp or comply half-heartedly. Opinions on an issue of substance will invariably diverge. Those who find the new system differs from their own beliefs may develop practices that differ in some way from the original intention.

Espoused theory, in the form of policy statements or documents for review panels, will inevitably try to cast the institution in a good light or say what it is believed the panel would like to hear. This does not imply deliberate falsehood, but examples given and cases cited naturally focus upon best practice rather than worst. When describing policy and procedures, the management blueprint is given rather than descriptions of any deviations from the prescribed procedures, which the review document writers might not even be aware of.

An example, with which many will be familiar, concerns statements about the importance of teaching in universities. Many universities now have statements stressing the importance of teaching. It is quite common for there to be a policy of taking into account teaching, as well as research, in appointments, promotions and tenure decisions. It is also quite common for this policy to be ignored or only partially implemented. Individual heads, who were probably themselves appointed because of their research record, may decide that the department's best interests lie in achieving a good research record rather than paying attention to teaching quality. Even when there is a genuine desire to implement the policy, it is not always easy as teaching lacks a readily accepted method of assessing quality, such as research has, in the number of publications. Teaching may be taken into account by ensuring that acceptable standards are met, but research output may then be used to make decisions for promotions and appointments.

The issue at this stage is not to pursue this particularly common mismatch between espoused theory and theory in use. When frameworks are set up for the classification, analysis and evaluation of quality schemes, it is important to note that divergences between policy and practice are common in this area. When analysing and evaluating quality schemes it is, therefore, vital to look beyond the policy documents and public statements. What happens in practice may not match these statements. In analysing and evaluating a quality system it makes no sense to look at something that exists only in a document in a filing cabinet, or the mind of a vice-chancellor. What impacts upon learning and teaching is what happens in practice. This is what should be analysed and evaluated.

CLASSIFYING QUALITY SCHEMES

The second framework is necessary so that the many different measures in existence can be conveniently dealt with, in terms of their overall characteristics. To describe, and more importantly, analyse quality schemes needs some classification system. This section of the chapter introduces a two-dimensional system. One dimension divides schemes between quality assurance and enhancement. This distinction draws upon Elton's (1992) simple approach. He grouped the quality 'A's, namely quality assurance, accountability, audit and assessment, and saw them as concerned with control of both quality and the people who control quality. Quality enhancement was seen as related to the 'E's: empowerment, enthusiasm, expertise and excellence.

Quality assurance

Quality assurance mechanisms are imposed by university management or state regulatory bodies. They concentrate on ensuring that teaching and courses reach some, usually undefined, level of minimum acceptance. Quality control is, therefore, probably a more apt term, but quality assurance is more commonly used, since quality control has unfortunate overtones for academics (Frazer, 1992). In this chapter the term quality assurance is restricted to these imposed threshold measures, though some do use it to encompass all quality schemes, thereby including both quality control and enhancement approaches.

In general most quality assurance schemes or procedures could be described by the following characteristics:

- They are imposed top-down by university managements or, at a system level, by funding or accrediting bodies.
- Participation is compulsory.
- The process is through a review or inspection by a higher authority – though this process is often known by the misnomer 'peer review'.
- The schemes seek to establish that an acceptable standard has been met – though the standard is rarely defined. Some schemes place what is being reviewed into a limited number of qualitative categories.
- Institutions or courses that fail to reach the acceptable standard may be punished by withholding funding or approval of courses. Teachers deemed to be below standard face sanctions such as contract non-renewal or denial of tenure.
- There is rarely a mechanism for offering real rewards to those institutions, courses or teachers performing far better than the minimum acceptable standard. Even where departments or universities are rated

into categories for teaching quality this rarely results in substantial extra funding for those rated highly. This is in marked contrast to research-rating exercises.

Quality assurance systems can be sub-divided into *authorizing* and *reviewing* schemes. Authorizing schemes precede an offering, so exist to certify that appropriate standards will be met before a course is authorized to start or an institution accredited. Reviews take place at intervals to ensure that appropriate standards are being met by teachers, courses and institutions.

Further delineation of quality assurance schemes comes from denoting the type of activity that is investigated. Barnett (1992: 218–20), for example, lists no less than 17 main elements and 26 sub-elements of activities related to teaching and learning, which might be reviewed in a quality audit of an institution. Fortunately the list appears to be hypothetical, as an institution subjected to such a wide-ranging audit would find it a very expensive and time-consuming exercise.

Quality enhancement

While quality assurance seeks to ensure minimum acceptable levels, quality enhancement aims for an overall increase in the quality of teaching. In practice it often encourages the better teachers towards higher quality and more innovative practices, with the expectation of a knock-on or trickle down effect on the majority.

Quality assurance mechanisms are imposed from above, either by university administrations or by external bodies. Quality enhancement initiatives cannot be imposed by regulation so they rely on academics volunteering to participate. While quality control is a top-down approach, quality enhancement tends to be characterized by a more bottom-up orientation. Administrations can offer institutional endorsement, grants for projects, and possibly reward successful participants. Facilitation of quality enhancement initiatives usually tends to be the concern of educational or faculty development units or similar bodies.

Most quality enhancement schemes would have the following character-istics:

- They are usually initiated by bodies such as educational development units or academics themselves. Grants can be awarded by management or accrediting bodies for project-type schemes.
- Participation is voluntary.
- The process is through either attending workshop-type sessions or participating in projects.

- The aim is to improve the quality of learning and teaching. This is often expressed as a striving for excellence, since many schemes of this type attract the better teachers.
- There have been claims that participation in quality enhancement of teaching is effectively discouraged by universities because the time taken by the teaching of quality enhancement is time taken away from research activities, which are rewarded.
- Participation in projects can result in publications, which traditionally are rewarded by universities.

Quality enhancement schemes are then further sub-divided into two categories to cater for the variety of types of schemes and the wide diversity of ways in which they operate. The two categories are workshop-type activities and project-type initiatives, similar to those of the Action Learning Project, featured in this book.

The project category is taken as encompassing a range of initiatives with similar underpinning to the projects supported by the Action Learning Project, but not necessarily identical in all respects. The category includes all project-type initiatives in which academics, often in groups, examine and tackle some aspect of their course with an apparent problem or needing a different approach. Inevitably these projects will last for some time. The projects may be supported by staff from an educational development unit acting in an advisory or facilitative capacity. The initiatives may be isolated, or there may be a broader scheme of grants in place to encourage or initiate such projects.

The other quality enhancement category encompasses workshop-type activities. 'Workshop-type' includes workshops themselves, courses for new staff, mini-courses, newsletters, individual counselling or other forms of advice-giving or teaching-how-to-teach that are essentially instructive in nature. The duration of most of the sessions is considerably shorter than the projects. These workshop-type activities are probably the most common form of quality enhancement measure offered by educational development units (Moses, 1985).

Summary

At this point in its development the categorization of quality schemes has two main categories, quality assurance and quality enhancement. Each of these is sub-divided into two. Quality enhancement is divided into workshop-type and project-type activities. Quality assurance has authorizing and reviewing sub-categories to distinguish measures before or during the operation of the activity or body. Further definition of quality assurance measures is by reference to the type of teaching and learning activity that is examined.

quality assurance		quality enhancement	
authorizing	reviewing	workshop-type	project-type

PARADIGM

The second dimension, for categorizing schemes for quality in learning and teaching, is the paradigm that guides or underpins the approach. This method of classifying schemes is derived from a paper by Graham Webb (1992). Webb restricted his attention to academic or staff development, so the classification was originally only applied to what has been called quality enhancement in this chapter. The framework is also useful with approaches to quality assurance. Webb (1992) classified educational development activities as following positivist, interpretive or critical epistemologies. In Webb (1996) the analysis was expanded.

The categorization seems to provide useful insights into academic development and quality assurance, presumably because many of the actions of academics are framed, probably largely unconsciously, by their epistemological beliefs. Research and teaching are obviously influenced, if not determined, by these beliefs. As these are such a substantial component of the life of an academic, it is inevitable that epistemological beliefs become deeply ingrained and influence other activities, particularly other aspects of university work. It is also possible to ascribe management techniques to the influence of the main paradigms, so altogether the categorization method is perfectly logical.

For those less familiar with the main research paradigms, Table 1.1 summarizes the main characteristics. Attempting to summarize something as broad and deep as a research paradigm within a single column of a table obviously leads to a degree of simplification and generality. The elements in the table do, though, relate surprisingly well to analyses of various quality schemes, which follow.

It should also be understood that, like most classification systems, inter-mediate positions and cases are both possible and common. Some research and some quality schemes fit neatly within one particular paradigm. Others may be intermediate between two or even three paradigms for at least some of the elements used to characterize paradigms in Table 1.1. The triangle representation in Figure 1.1, adapted from Candy (1989), portrays this very well.

Table 1.1 Characteristics of research paradigms

Paradigm	Positivism	Interpretive	Critical
Method	Scientific	Hermeneutics social inquiry	Action research
Technique	Experiment survey	Observation of social situation	Critical discourse
Seeks	Causal explanation universal laws	Understanding meaning	Change emancipation
Position of researcher	Neutral observer	Immersed in social situation	Participant/change agent
Sphere of applicability	Seeks generalizability through random sampling	Sometimes difficult to generalize beyond case	Effect of change may be confined to participants
Influence on subject	Variables manipulated in experiment or held constant statistically	Investigated in natural setting	Aim is to change and emancipate
Verification	Testing hypotheses	Plausible explanation	Consensus among participants

Research projects or quality schemes that are pure examples of a particular paradigm lie at the respective points of the triangle. Those that are intermediate between two paradigms can be placed on the line joining them, at an appropriate point depending upon the degree of character of each paradigm. Projects which have elements of all three, and they do exist, lie somewhere in the middle.

COMBINING THE SCHEMATIC AND PARADIGMATIC CLASSIFICATION

Using the paradigmatic categorization in conjunction with the earlier schematic one results in a two-dimensional grid shown in Figure 1.2.

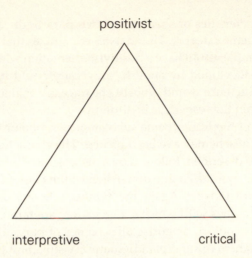

positivist

interpretive   critical

Figure 1.1 Triangle relating paradigms (Candy, 1989)

Elements within the grid are shaded. Heavier shading implies that a scheme under a particular category is more likely to follow the indicated paradigm.

EXAMPLES

Examples of quality schemes are now examined to show where and how they fit into the classification system. In doing this it is necessary to make some assumptions and generalizations about types of schemes. Readers will no doubt be able to think of some versions of a particular type of scheme that have somewhat differing characteristics to 'typical' chosen examples. This is inevitable since different countries, universities and departments have evolved schemes of somewhat differing natures. This is allowed for

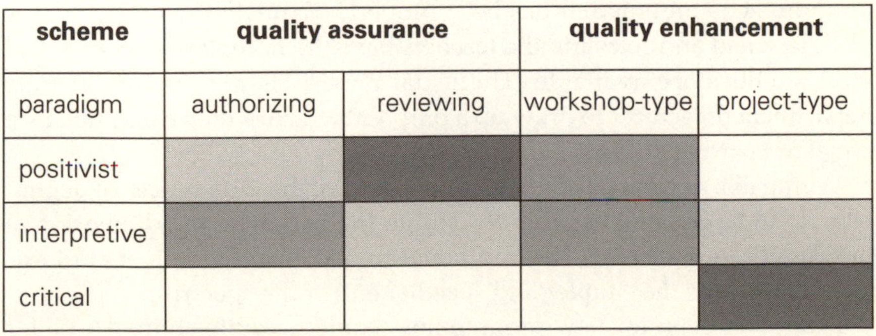

scheme	quality assurance		quality enhancement	
paradigm	authorizing	reviewing	workshop-type	project-type
positivist				
interpretive				
critical				

Figure 1.2 Paradigms of quality schemes

by the varying densities of shadings of two paradigm categories within each quality scheme category. The analysis recognizes that a course review scheme, for example, could have a positivist orientation within one university while that developed by another university could have humanistic leanings. The difference would probably be traceable to management styles and beliefs within the respective institutions.

Within each of the four scheme sub-categories, one or two of the most common types of scheme have been picked. The characteristics of typical programmes are described, followed by a discussion of where they are best placed within the paradigmatic dimension of the classification system in terms of the characteristics. Again, the 'typical' schemes described may be quite different to ones with which some readers are familiar. The point of these examples is not to categorize all schemes of particular types, but to show how the schematic and paradigmatic classification grid can be used as a framework for analysing particular quality schemes.

It should be pointed out that in most cases the proponents or perpetrators of quality systems do not appear to have consciously based their schemes upon the research bases attributed to them. If they did there has been a remarkable conspiracy of silence. It may seem surprising but, for all the quality systems in place, there is remarkably little in the literature showing whether or how any of the approaches were developed from theoretical models, or of research evidence justifying why a particular type of scheme was adopted. In the Preface to his book, which critiques and analyses staff development, Webb (1996) expresses surprise at how little similar or complementary material has appeared.

Programme accreditation

Programme or course accreditation is a mechanism for authorizing quality assurance that has become widespread and almost universal across institutions in many countries. The rationale is to ensure that before a new programme is mounted, it has been properly planned, the curriculum is well designed and relevant, the teachers have the necessary expertise and vital facilities are available. The usual process is for the appropriate department or lecturer to draw up a proposal which is then examined by a panel or board of studies.

Within this general pattern, there are considerable differences of degree, which can be equated to positions within the paradigmatic dimension of the classification scheme. The traditional approach within universities was usually towards the simpler and speedier end of the spectrum.

Proposals, even for new programmes, could be quite short. Those for courses were often about a page in length, consisting of a list of the main topics covered. Evidence about the competence of the staff or facilities would probably not be included, as competence would be assumed. A proposal would then be discussed within the university by a department or faculty board. The whole process could be completed in quite a short period of time.

By contrast, the system for colleges and polytechnics under the former binary system in Australia and Britain was more towards the intensive end of the spectrum. Proposals were expected to be voluminous. Detailed quantitative information was required about facilities and departmental performance indicators. CVs of proposed teachers were included to demonstrate their competence. Greater details about the proposed programme were required, with behavioural objectives specified at both programme and course level.

Examination of the proposal usually proceeded through several stages or committees. Initial committees usually had largely internal membership, though, as the proposal moved up the hierarchy, there would be a preponderance of members external to the department and institution. The final authority resided outside the institution in a body that specified procedures to be followed by all the institutions under its ambit. The whole process could be very time consuming.

Shifting from the traditional model to the more intensive end of the spectrum reflects a parallel shift from an interpretive position to a more positivist one. Evidence required is more quantitative and precise. Course specification is in terms of behavioural objectives. Responsibility for approval is taken away from the intended teachers to an external authority. The whole approach prescribes each step in detail so that everyone follows the standard 'rigorous' procedure.

It has been argued (eg Barnett, 1992; Pratt, 1991) that the more intensive procedures of 'peer review' resulted in more careful and detailed planning and more rigorous examination of it. There is undoubtedly some truth in this argument. However, there is also a cost to greater rigour, which results principally from the extra time involved. The element of a degree of loss of control of their own courses is also felt to be a significant cost by many academics when external review predominates. It is obviously a matter for debate as to whether the extra cost could be justified. Advocates of more stringent procedures would no doubt argue that the less rigorous traditional procedures allowed some proportion of poorly planned courses to proceed unchecked. As with most complex issues, the most satisfactory position is normally one of balance. In this case it would result in a process with sufficient rigour to ensure thorough planning, without incurring unacceptable overheads in excessive timeframes or loss of control. In terms of the paradigmatic framework, it implies an intermediate position.

Evaluation of teaching

Under the quality-assurance review heading, the discussion will concentrate primarily upon the evaluation of teaching, or more particularly instructors, through student feedback questionnaires. Extrapolations can be made to course, programme and departmental reviews as similar principles apply to the paradigmatic classification. Questionnaires are also primary forms of evidence in reviews of teaching at programme or departmental levels, as they are too in staff appraisal schemes.

Reviewing teaching through student feedback questionnaires also takes on several forms, which again can be placed upon a spectrum, or several spectra in this case. Principally, schemes can be formative, or summative and judgemental. They can allow triangulation of multiple evaluation sources or gather data only through a standard questionnaire. They can be voluntary or compulsory. Each of these spectra displays a shift from an interpretive orientation to a positivist leaning.

Schemes with a positivist framework will be examined in more detail as this orientation has become common in universities. Cross (1996) notes that most instructor-evaluation schemes are summative in nature, which is consistent with a positivist attribution. Firstly questionnaires focus upon instructors and their teaching performance. This implies a positivist view of the teaching and learning process. It assumes a delivery model in which the instructor delivers content which is absorbed by the student.

It is compulsory to use a standard questionnaire approved by the university management so that all instructor performance can be measured against a common standard. In some universities the concentration is upon a single overall rating to simplify comparison and judgement. Any other forms of evaluation data are ignored as they lack the precision and object-ivity of the standard quantitative instrument.

Schemes are, therefore, summative and judgemental in nature, usually through an associated staff appraisal scheme. Those staff with a score below some arbitrary figure on an overall teaching rating scale may not have contracts renewed or tenure granted. In most departments, though, this only seems to happen if ratings on that other quantitative measure, the number of refereed publications, is also low.

There are approaches to teaching evaluation that are less firmly entrenched in a positivist tradition. An interpretive dimension can be introduced by having a wider focus to what is evaluated and permitting a range of evaluation techniques. Some universities have moved towards asking staff to compile a portfolio of evaluation data for courses they teach (eg Gibbs, 1992a; Seldin, 1993).

A shift towards the critical paradigm can also be introduced by shifting responsibility for evaluation away from a central body towards the teacher.

In this case the schemes are more likely to be voluntary and initiated by those who wish to better understand and improve their students' learning. A further dimension of the critical influence is present if the purpose of the exercise is towards change and improvement rather than appraisal. It is, therefore, possible for teaching evaluation to have qualities from all three paradigms.

Other types of review, such as course, programme or departmental reviews, can also operate with orientations on spectra from positivist to interpretive. In general the larger the body reviewed the less likely it is that the process will be at the extreme of the positivist pole. The reason for this is that the larger and more complex the operation, the less likely is its operation to be construed as susceptible to judgement by a simple quantitative measure. The UK, though, seems to fly in the face of this generalization by maintaining that it is possible to assess an entire department's research by awarding a single number.

Workshop-type

Moving on to quality enhancement schemes, again there is a sub-division into two categories. Workshop-type activities are dealt with first.

The defining characteristic of a 'workshop-type' activity is that advice or knowledge about teaching and learning is given to lecturers by an educational developer or similar person. The implication is that the educational developer has expertise and knowledge about teaching. The lecturers lack this expertise and learning about it will make them better teachers. It is not surprising that this is the most common form of quality enhancement (Moses, 1985) since it shares an assumption upon which most education is based. The educational developers are normally in the position because they feel that teaching is important, enjoy teaching and are probably good teachers. A natural approach to improving teaching is, therefore, to teach other teachers to teach better.

The variety of types of sessions which fit into the workshop-type category can again be described by a number of spectra. Firstly, the number of people involved can range from just one in individual counselling sessions, through small groups in workshops, to large groups in some arranged programmes. When the advice is dispensed through media, such as newsletters, or through Web sites, the intended audience is presumably substantial. The number who read and, more importantly, take note of the message may be a different matter, though.

A second descriptive spectrum refers to the duration of the event. Individual counselling can last for as little as a few minutes. Seminars traditionally last for an hour or so, while workshops are usually allocated a little longer – up to half a day or perhaps a whole day. In the last few years there has been a growth in the number of courses offered, ranging from intensive courses for new staff lasting a few days, to formal award courses with durations measured in semesters or years.

Attendance at any of these sessions has traditionally been voluntary. The Dearing report in the UK (National Committee of Inquiry into Higher Education, 1997), though, has raised the issue of an element of compulsion, particularly for new staff.

In analysing workshop-type activities on the paradigmatic dimension of the classification scheme, it is pertinent to look at the theoretical underpinning of the advice given and the nature of the activity undertaken. For the nature of the advice given, the paradigmatic classification can be directly equated to the research paradigm from which the advice was derived.

Webb (1992, 1996) believed that positivist prescriptions underpin advice given by educational developers in consultation sessions, workshops on good teaching and courses for new staff. He argued that the certainty and prescriptive nature of the advice derived from positivist research is alluring for an educational developer facing demands for unambiguous advice.

This analysis is undoubtedly correct for many, and probably the majority, of workshop-type sessions. Much teaching advice has been drawn from the instructional design literature, which is itself derived from positivist research. The allure of the instructional design literature is that it gives generic prescriptions for good teaching. Reigeluth describes the outcomes of instructional design (Reigeluth and Stein, 1983: 7):

> The result of instructional design as a professional activity is an 'architect's blueprint' for what the instruction should be like. This 'blueprint' is a prescription as to what methods of instruction should be used when for that course content and those students.

These blueprints or prescriptions underpin many of the crash courses for new teachers or the programmes for teaching or graduate assistants. They are also manifest in the books and workshops that dispense tips for better teaching.

By no means all workshop advice is underpinned by positivism or instructional design. Many educational developers see the limitations of theory based upon prescriptive technical–rational science as they recognize the ill-defined nature of teaching–learning environments. Acceptance of teaching and learning as a messy problem calls into question generic recommendations and suggests instead advice based upon research that recognizes the importance of the context.

For this reason many educational developers base their advice upon research that follows the Student Approaches to Learning tradition.

Approaches to learning have most commonly been categorized into deep and surface (Biggs, 1987; Marton & Säljö, 1976). Students adopting a deep approach seek understanding of material, while those using a surface approach are content with reproducing the material for assessment purposes. The approach adopted by students is, to some extent at least, influenced by the teaching, course, assessment and learning environment. For educational developers this research provides a framework for examining teaching in context.

Another way in which workshop-type activities can be analysed against the paradigmatic dimension is through the type of activity. Workshops, courses, counselling sessions and newsletters that take a didactic approach can be assigned to a positivist influence. It is hard to be didactic about good teaching without making generic prescriptions, which are inevitably positivist in origin.

A natural consequence of a belief in interpretivism and a recognition of the contextual influence upon the quality of learning should be the design of workshop-type sessions which allow participants to reflect upon the context of their own teaching. A more reflective design is also consistent with positioning in the interpretive category because hermeneutics underpins the reflective practitioner approach.

Projects

This book is about project-type initiatives. These may not be identical in all respects to those of the Action Learning Project, but variations on the theme will be discussed at relevant points within the chapters that follow. In particular, smaller initiatives with perhaps one or two projects will be dealt with.

The project-type approach is derived from action research. As such it fits into the critical paradigm. The foundation of the project approach in action research is discussed in some detail in the next chapter so is not elaborated upon here.

It might be noted that the conceptual classification scheme for quality approaches has a very light shading for the interpretive paradigm. This is because my own formulation of the project-type approach utilizes data gathered by interpretive means and techniques during the observation phase of the action research cycle.

SUMMARY OF PARADIGMATIC POSITIONS

The previous section has described a number of typical schemes for improving the quality of teaching and learning. In each case variations upon the nature of schemes have been given which shift the paradigmatic classification of the scheme. To summarize the above discussion and show how they relate together, nine schemes, or variants upon themes, are plotted in Figure 1.3 on the paradigm triangle introduced earlier.

What should be apparent is that underlying beliefs or orientations markedly affect the nature of quality schemes. Variants upon sorts of schemes can appear in quite different zones of the triangle. Their effects on staff and effectiveness in dealing with teaching quality will inevitably be influenced by their position on the triangle. The triangle, therefore, provides a valuable framework for analysing quality systems.

QUALITY VERSUS COST

The two-dimensional framework introduced in this chapter provides a method for describing and analysing quality systems. It is also important to evaluate quality systems.

The framework proposed for this is that of quality improvement versus cost incurred. This seems to be an eminently logical framework. Whatever the type of scheme, the aim of the exercise is to improve the quality of learning and teaching, or ensure that an acceptable standard has been met. Evaluation of a scheme should, then, investigate whether it is meeting its aim and improving quality.

It is inadequate, though, merely to demonstrate that there is an improvement in quality. It must also be shown that the improvement was brought about in an effective manner. It has to be accepted that there is a cost to any quality scheme. It is often not a cost that is clearly or accurately shown in budgets or accounts. This is because the principal component of the costs is usually people's time. The time spent participating in, or complying with quality schemes is time that cannot be dedicated to teaching and research so is, therefore, a very real cost to both the staff themselves and their university.

Any improvements in quality must then be balanced against these costs. Particular systems may improve quality but they are not effective schemes if the cost exceeds the benefits or if some other approach would achieve similar outcomes at less cost. In any institution resources are finite. Those devoted to a particular quality scheme will not be dedicated to teaching, research or some other quality scheme. It, therefore, makes sense to evaluate activities to ensure that resources are devoted to effective ones.

Marginal costs

A further economic concept relevant in the evaluation of quality schemes is marginal cost. Most universities will have some quality systems in place.

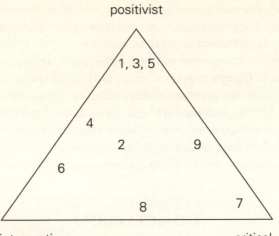

Key

The numbers on the triangle refer to schemes of the following types:

1 Summative instructor evaluation
2 Portfolio evaluation of teaching by the teacher with a view to
   improvement
3 Review of teaching by external inspection
4 Peer review of teaching
5 Didactic workshop giving prescriptive advice
6 Reflective context-based workshop
7 Action research project
8 Action research project using evaluation techniques derived from SAL
   research
9 Action research project by individual to deal with problems in own
   teaching

Figure 1.3 Triangle of quality scheme paradigms (complex analysis)

With the pressure from governments and funding bodies, many must have considered putting more resources into these with the publicly avowed aim of making them more rigorous, so improving quality. When such decisions are made it is appropriate to look at marginal cost increases and marginal returns: that is, the additional increase in quality for the extra cost, usually the extra staff time, which was required.

An important reason for looking at marginal costs and returns is that the law of diminishing returns applies to quality systems as well as in economics. As schemes become more rigorous or intensive, costs continue to rise at much the same rate but the marginal return in quality improvement for each additional unit of cost inevitably decreases, though at different rates for different types of schemes.

It is not easy to measure or estimate either costs or quality returns with any precision. In Chapter 16, an attempt is made to show that it is at least possible to make some qualitative estimates and comparisons. An argument is put forward for the evaluation of quality systems, for it is probably quite common for universities to have quality systems that have reached a level of low marginal returns. If some of the resources were dedicated to different types of measure, the overall quality improvement could be higher for the same cost.

CONCLUSION

This book is about project-type initiatives conducted with an explicit action research philosophy. It might, therefore, be assumed that it argues for quality measures to be positioned in the right-hand corner of the quality assurance and enhancement classification grid. It does advance the case for greater utilization approaches fitting within the critical/project-type classification. However, this should not be interpreted as an argument for quality enhancement through action research projects to the exclusion of other forms of quality assurance and enhancement. Action research initiatives are seen as neither the best nor the only viable approach.

The final part of the book contains an argument that both quality assurance and enhancement are important. A case is made for universities needing both formative and reviewing quality assurance and also both workshop- and project-type quality enhancement. In Chapter 16, it is argued that a good quality system is one that has a balance of approaches.

A good system is one in which the balance has been examined, and unfortunately few institutions do evaluate their quality systems. As a result there must be a suspicion that many are out of balance. In most cases they are probably out of balance towards quality assurance measures, because these are ones which can be imposed top-down by management or funding bodies. If this is the case, it is possible that teaching and learning could be improved by diverting resources towards quality enhancement.

While it is argued that universities should have a balance of quality approaches across the four mode categories, the position with respect to the paradigms is less equivocal. The reader will no doubt have sensed a degree of criticism of quality measures assigned to the positivist paradigm in the earlier section looking at how examples fit within the two-dimensional classification grid.

There are two main arguments against schemes based upon a positivist rationale. The first is that any education scenario is a complex ill-defined issue. Schön (1983) argued that the role of professionals lies in dealing with messy or wicked problems. This undoubtedly applies as much to the academic profession as to any other.

If this position is accepted, then, it is also necessary to accept Schön's corollary that technical–rational approaches to dealing with professional practice are inappropriate. Applying this argument more closely to the content of this chapter, it questions the suitability of testing teaching quality against objectives set by an external agency. The diversity of institutions, missions, courses, students and disciplines makes it hard to justify the appropriateness of applying standard criteria or assessment systems in all cases.

A positivist teaching evaluation scheme will be taken as an example to critique. When a standard teaching evaluation questionnaire is designed it inevitably presupposes both a model and a method of teaching. Kolitch and Dean (1999) examined a typical teaching evaluation instrument and found it consistent with a transmission model of teaching. It was, though, not consistent with a number of other conceptions of teaching, in particular an engaged-critical model which they analysed in detail. Compatibility with a transmission model of teaching leads on to the presupposition that the predominant teaching method will be didactic lecturing. If alternative forms of teaching, such as problem-based learning, peer teaching or project work, are adopted many of the questions on typical teaching evaluation questionnaires become quite meaningless.

As typically happens under the positivist paradigm, the focus is on a very narrow set of variables defined externally. In the case of instructor evaluation questionnaires, the instructor is effectively the only variable seen as pertinent to the entire learning and teaching scenario. Other influences such as the classroom environment, the nature of the relationship between students or the design of the curriculum are factored out of the equation. Other data which might be relevant or informative are ignored because they lack the objectiveness and measurable precision of the standard questionnaire. As a result issues that might be important to students are not addressed if they do not fall within the narrow scope of the selected variables.

The second main argument against positivist approaches to ensuring quality lies in the human dimension inherent in education. The positivist paradigm originated in the natural sciences. Its application to research involving humans has, therefore, been questioned as have theories of management derived from positivist roots (eg Carr and Kemmis, 1986; Stenhouse, 1975).

The danger of positivist approaches is that of de-motivating the staff involved. When standards, review systems and procedures are imposed by management bodies, particularly external ones, there is the chance of teachers feeling that the locus of control is being taken away from them. Further, there can be a perception that the review or inspection system has been put in place because teaching is seen as deficient. If either of these effects operates teaching staff will tend to put less effort and enthusiasm into their teaching with the inevitable result that quality suffers.

In most cases it is likely that any de-motivating effect of positivist quality systems may be small. It is, though, hard to find any evidence of positive motivational effects from positivist quality systems and there is no obvious mechanism for them to occur. Even if rewards are given for good performance these may be perceived as extrinsic motivators and, therefore, have a weak effect.

There is certainly no evidence of positivist approaches to quality assurance having anything like the strong motivational impact provided by some of the projects operating under the Action Learning Project umbrella. Part C of this book shows evidence of high levels of commitment which can surely only be present if the teachers have a strong sense of ownership.

As with the quality methods dimension, it is clear that there is not one paradigmatic approach which can be justified as being superior to all others. It clearly depends upon the context and the aim of the quality scheme. Kuhn (1970) provides a sensible discussion of the basis for choosing paradigms to apply to particular problems. There is an argument, though, for concluding that quality approaches based upon interpretive or critical positions are more likely to be effective in universities than positivist ones. Webb (1992, 1996) discusses the positivist approach to educational and staff development and also has problems with approaches founded upon this tradition.

2

Quality through action learning and research

This book aims to contribute to both theory and practice. It argues that effective quality schemes need to be based upon appropriate theory. This chapter explains what action research and action learning are and argues the case for basing quality enhancement schemes upon them. Essentially it deals with the theoretical basis of action research and shows how it can be used in practice as a quality enhancement mechanism for learning and teaching.

Action research has been widely written about and has found application in diverse fields, including management, social welfare, organizational development and the health sciences. For the application of action research in education, the following general books provide a good grounding: Carr and Kemmis, 1986; Elliott, 1991; McKernan, 1991; McNiff, 1992; Stenhouse, 1975. McGill and Beaty (1995) give a good general treatment of action learning. This chapter will give a relatively short account of the nature of action research, concentrating upon the characteristics that make it appropriate as a mode of quality enhancement in education.

It should be recognized that there are several schools or variants of action research, which vary in the degree to which they are influenced by critical theory. Whichever position is adopted, though, there are characteristics common to action research that collectively distinguish it from research conducted under positivist or interpretive paradigms. It is these common characteristics that the chapter will concentrate upon.

NATURE OF ACTION RESEARCH

The followings definition of the essential components of action research (Carr and Kemmis, 1986: 165–66) would be widely accepted:

It can be argued that three conditions are individually necessary and jointly sufficient for action research to be said to exist: firstly, a project takes as its subject-matter a social practice, regarding it as a form of strategic action susceptible of improvement; secondly, the project proceeds through a spiral of cycles of planning, acting, observing and reflecting, with each of these activities being systematically and self-critically implemented and interrelated; thirdly, the project involves those responsible for the practice in each of the moments of the activity, widening participation in the project gradually to include others affected by the practice, and maintaining collaborative control of the process.

Several major characteristics of action research listed below have been distilled from this definition. In the following text in this section each of these aspects of action research will be briefly discussed. The intention is to firstly amplify the nature of the characteristic for readers unfamiliar with action research. Secondly, the aim is to show why these facets of action research make it appropriate as a vehicle for quality enhancement in education.

Action research is:

- concerned with social practice;
- aimed towards improvement;
- a cyclical process;
- pursued by systematic enquiry;
- a reflective process;
- participative;
- determined by the practitioners.

Action research is concerned with social practice

Firstly, the definition makes it clear that action research deals with social practice. Education is a social practice. In most cases it involves the direct interaction of teachers and groups of students. Even where teaching is through a technological medium there is still the human element in the development and implementation of the learning system and the learners are complex people, rather than receivers or black boxes.

If education is a social practice, then it should surely look towards research derived from a humanistic position, in the most general sense of the term. Many (eg Carr and Kemmis, 1986; Stenhouse, 1975) have argued, along these lines, that positivism, which is probably still the most common paradigm in educational research, was an inappropriate paradigm for education because its methodology was derived from the physical sciences.

Educational issues are also messy or ill-defined problems. To make any progress in dealing with outstanding issues it is necessary to recognize their indeterminate nature and choose an approach designed for such issues. Classrooms are complex arenas; university departments are hives of intrigue and conspiracy. Trying to reach an understanding of issues concerned with teaching and learning, therefore, implies getting to grips with a whole range of human issues such as the attitude of students, the politics within departments and the ethos and environment of the institution.

Technical–rational approaches are unlikely to be successful, as a prime element of their methodology is the narrowing of problems to simple hypotheses by holding other variables constant. This implies ignoring much of the complexity of a teaching and learning system.

Action research is aimed towards improvement

Perhaps the clearest distinction between action research and other modes lies in the attitude to changes to what is being researched. Other paradigms tend to avoid perturbing the subject of their research. Action researchers set out with the avowed intention of improving their practice. Lewin (1952) and Rapoport (1970) both maintain that research should go beyond the production of books and papers to achieving social change.

The very essence of quality enhancement is improvement. Surely, then, schemes to improve the quality of learning and teaching should be derived from a paradigm that embraces change. Understanding a problem, through interpretive work, can be a useful step but solving the problem requires action. Finding a universal law through positivist research is of no help unless there is some means to implement the practical applications derived from the law.

Action research is a cyclical process

Action research is portrayed as a cyclical or spiral process involving steps of planning, acting, observing and reflecting. It is normal for a project to go through two or more cycles in an iterative process. Improvement is brought about by a series of cycles, each incorporating lessons from previous cycles. Figure 2.1 is a portrayal of the action research cycle in its simplest and tidiest form.

Figure 2.1 is similar to the way action research is portrayed in other texts as a series of steps of planning, acting, observing and reflecting within each cycle. Depicting the process in this way follows the normal limitations of modelling and graphically representing complex processes. Producing a diagram which is clear and understandable can create the impression that the facets of the cycle are discrete and always follow in neat sequential steps.

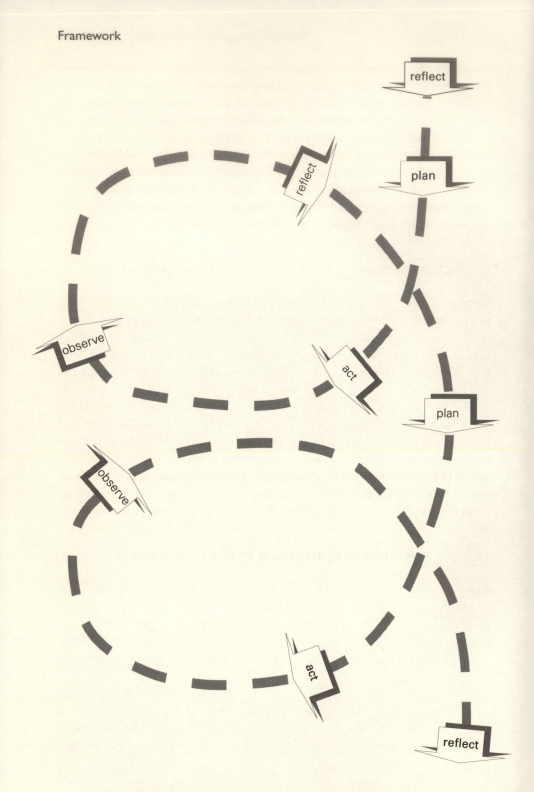

Figure 2.1 Action research as a cyclical process

In practice the process is normally less tidy. The four steps will all be present but there will often be overlaps between them and shifting back and forth. Many projects, and particularly more complex ones, also tend to have multiple spirals as topics and sub-topics emerge.

Cook (1998) amplifies this point in a paper titled 'The importance of mess in action research'. She points out that the initial stages of many projects concentrate upon identifying the problem, because of the ill-defined nature of most of the issues tackled. Projects might have many strands, which could appear chaotic to an outsider. Yet when the final report was written, the need to produce a readable paper in linear form resulted in a description that appears much neater than the way it happened in practice. The process of writing up the work transformed 'bumbling change supported retrospectively by theories' (p 99) into something that appeared logical and clear from the outset.

Even when it is clear what issues are being tackled, the process of carrying out the research is rarely as linear and orderly as it might appear in an initial plan or a final report. Unexpected issues can emerge which cause a change of emphasis. Additional factors might be found to be important, requiring their own subsidiary investigation. Phases of a project can become out of step requiring parallel action. The aim should be that of following an orderly and logical path, but recognizing that diversions and by-ways may be part of the most relevant and effective route.

Action research is pursued by systematic inquiry

Experiences discussed in this book have shown that many teachers take quite naturally to the action research cycle as a logical approach to testing and development. Even those whose academic discipline is grounded in a quite different paradigm can find it quite a straightforward way of solving problems or tackling issues in their teaching. It has a lot in common with the development, testing and refinement cycle used by engineers, for example.

One of the greatest strengths of action research is that it is a quite straightforward practical approach to tackling issues of substance. The methodology is not complex and it does not require the researcher to learn complex and difficult data-gathering or analytical skills. It is, then, within the capabilities of teachers or practitioners to research their own teaching and conduct projects within their own classrooms. There is no need to rely upon outside experts, researchers or external authorities.

It should not be thought that action research is a soft or imprecise mode of research, as rigorous systematic inquiry is just as integral as for other paradigms. The action research cycle incorporates systematic observation and evaluation. Outcomes of systematic inquiry are made public and subjected to normal criteria for scrutiny and acceptance. Action research does, then, contribute to both social practice and the development of theory. Its advocates claim that it brings theory closer to practice.

Action research is participative

The mode has been called participative action research, indicating firstly that it is normally a group activity involving those affected by the topic being investigated. Many would consider it essential that action research be conducted by a group because it is through group discourse that participants become aware of unconscious assumptions or false perspectives. Habermas (1974: 29) warns that there are dangers associated with solitary self-reflection:

> The self-reflection of a lone subject . . . requires a quite paradoxical achievement: one part of the self must be split off from the other part in such a manner that the subject can be in a position to render aid to itself . . . in the act of self-reflection the subject can deceive itself.

Others, however, accept that action research can be an individual problem-solving activity or an individual reflecting on their own practice. This position recognizes the centrality of the reflective process to action research. It recognizes the work of Schön (1983) and followers in describing the thoughts and actions of professionals in their daily practice. The descriptions of reflective behaviour mostly refer to individual professionals.

If individual teachers tackle issues within their individually taught courses using a cyclical, reflective approach, it seems appropriate to conclude that they are conducting action research. If they wish to solve a problem or introduce an innovation, within their own classroom, it is eminently sensible to utilize the methodology of action research to do so. The research may be described as technical action research (Carr and Kemmis, 1986), as it lacks any wider emancipatory character, but if it fits the need then surely it is both legitimate and commendable. While such projects may not affect the beliefs of a broad circle of participants they can, and normally do, cause the individual teacher to reflect upon their own teaching and the beliefs underpinning that teaching. They can also lead to significant improvements in teaching and learning on the course in question.

The term participative is also indicative of the importance placed on the participation of practitioners themselves. A distinction has been made with other paradigms where it is more common for expert researchers to conduct enquiries and hand down their findings and recommendations to those in the field. In application to quality assurance and enhancement, the nature of action research implies a bottom-up character to initiatives, rather than a top-down inspection approach, which is common in quality control systems.

The importance of the involvement of teachers themselves in projects is underscored by the conclusion, drawn in Parts C and E, that the process of engagement is itself a valuable outcome of these initiatives. When conducting an educational action research project, teachers are reflecting upon their own practice as teachers. In the observation or evaluation phase they gather data on their students' learning. When they analyse this they reflect upon the outcomes of their teaching. There can be an enduring impact as many learn to value reflection upon their own teaching as a scholarly activity and acquire the classroom research skills to monitor regularly the quality of learning of their students.

Subject matter

The roles of the practitioner and expert researcher also influence the subject matter of action research. It has been claimed (Carr and Kemmis, 1986; Stenhouse, 1975) that educational researchers following other paradigms commonly concentrate upon theoretical issues, which are of little interest or relevance to teachers. In action research, though, it is the participants or teachers who decide the subject or topic for research.

In the case of educational quality enhancement through action research, the topic is something of interest to the teacher so there is motivation for them to conduct the study. The topic can be some innovation they feel is worth introducing into their teaching. It can be a problem they want to solve or an issue they want to tackle. It can often be a concern that they have been aware of for some time, but which has lain dormant because they were unsure how to tackle it.

THE IMPORTANCE OF PERSPECTIVE TRANSFORMATION

Critical reflection upon practice is an important element of action research for quality enhancement because it is through critical reflection that changes of attitude can occur. Critical theory provides a vehicle by which participants can undergo a process that Mezirow (1981) refers to as perspective transformation. Essentially they need to reach a state of self-realization that enables them to envisage the influence of past assumptions and constraints so as to permit a movement towards actions more consistent with new understandings.

Practices in higher education are often strongly influenced by conventions which academics become so accustomed to that they can become unaware that they are conventions. While some of these unconscious conventions can be beneficial, others may have a negative influence on the quality of teaching and learning. For change to occur it is necessary that those involved realize that their actions are being influenced by unconscious conventions, to make explicit those conventions and to evaluate their worth.

A particularly important deep-seated belief is the teacher's understanding of teaching. Several researchers have observed discrete qualitative categories for conceptions of teaching (Gow and Kember, 1993; Kember and Gow, 1994; Martin and Ramsden, 1992; Pratt, 1992; Samuelowicz and Bain, 1992), and a review (Kember, 1997) found a high degree of commonality between categorization schemes.

Martin and Ramsden (1992) argued that staff development programmes need to embrace the issue of changing the way academic staff conceptualize the teaching of their subjects. A compelling argument in favour of this assertion comes from evidence of the strong relationship between orientations to teaching and the quality of student learning (Gow and Kember, 1993; Kember and Gow, 1994). Two main orientations to teaching were identified: knowledge transmission and learning facilitation. Departments with high mean scores for the knowledge transmission orientation tended to depress the use of a deep approach to learning. Departments more attuned to learning facilitation were less likely to promote a surface approach to learning. By the normal standards of educational research many of the observed correlations were quite appreciable.

This link between teachers' beliefs about teaching, their subsequent actions and student learning outcomes can be widened into a model. This links conceptions of teaching, through teaching approaches, to student learning approaches and learning outcomes. Also included are actual and potential influences upon these constructs: the curriculum design; and institutional and departmental influences. A further component is titled student presage factors. The term 'presage' is taken from the 3P model of student learning (Biggs, 1987) in which the 3Ps are presage, process and product. The student presage factors in this case would include variables like prior knowledge, ability, previous educational experiences and home background. A model with all of these components was formulated in Kember (1997).

The version of that model shown in Figure 2.2 also includes reflection upon practice as a potential influence upon conceptions of teaching. Earlier parts of the chapter have argued that critical reflection during action research projects is a vehicle through which deep-seated beliefs can change. The latter parts of the book present evidence of this happening in practice.

The version of the model shown in Figure 2.2 also has more arrows shown as two-headed than did the earlier version. This is in recognition of the possibility of practice being reflected upon, which subsequently leads to changes in practice. Observation of practice, particularly if conducted systematically, can result in feedback that suggests modifications to the way teaching is conducted and to what is taught.

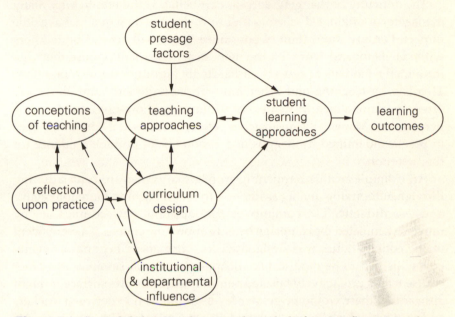

Figure 2.2 A model showing how teachers' beliefs can influence student learning

The model as a whole has not been tested but there have been various pieces of work characterizing elements of the model and establishing the relationship between some elements. The part that has been the most highly researched is that focusing upon students. The three components leading from presage factors to learning approaches to learning outcomes can be seen as a variant of the 3P model of presage, process and product. There is an extensive literature on the model itself (eg Biggs, 1987; Dart and Boulton-Lewis, 1998) and an even wider one on approaches to learning and how they are influenced by the teaching and learning environment (see eg Marton, Hounsell and Entwistle, 1984; Ramsden, 1992 for general treatments).

The evidence of the link between conceptions of teaching and students' approaches to learning, at the departmental level, has been given above. There is also evidence of the relationship at an individual teacher level (Trigwell, Prosser and Lyons, 1997). The mediating role of teaching approaches has also been investigated. Both Kember and Kwan (in press) and Trigwell and Prosser (1996b) have established a relationship between conceptions of and approaches to teaching. It should be noted, though, that the formulations of approaches to teaching were rather different.

Less well investigated are the various potential influences upon teaching approaches and beliefs about teaching. What is clear is that conceptual change is a difficult and lengthy process (Champagne *et al*, 1985; Strike and Posner, 1985).

The difficulty of changing deep-seated beliefs is the reason why many management-originated schemes for improving teaching quality have little impact. For any innovation of substance, there will always be teachers with beliefs inconsistent with the new ideas. They will oppose them, go through the motions or at best half-heartedly introduce the new practices. This is why teaching and other innovations initiated from above are often operationalized in ways that differ from those envisaged by the perpetrators. Many of the mismatches between espoused theory and theory in practice identified by Argyris and Schön (1978) provide evidence for this assertion.

An example of this happening in practice comes from an attempt, through authorizing quality assurance, to make teaching more interactive and less didactic. The committees that approve new courses, in my university, initiated the campaign by only approving courses if a component of the contact hours was designated for tutorials or seminars. Several proposals had to be modified to incorporate tutorial sessions and other course teams pro-actively boosted tutorial hours. On the surface it might appear that there would be greater levels of interaction between teachers and students, which hopefully would go hand-in-hand with enhancements in learning outcomes.

However, observation of tutorial classrooms, subsequent to the approval of the new courses, revealed a rather different outcome. A high proportion of the 'tutorials' that were observed featured very low levels of student participation. They were dominated by exposition from the tutors, who turned the tutorials into mini-lectures. These lecturers had a teacher-centred conception of teaching, which focused upon transmitting knowledge and information.

This case study is far from unusual. Many well-meaning initiatives from heads of department or central management teams end up with unintended outcomes because department members were not persuaded to change deep-seated beliefs incompatible with the innovation.

Employing an action research approach does not guarantee a change in beliefs. Action research projects, though, do at least provide a mechanism for perspective transformation through regular meetings of participants. In these sessions participants reflect upon their experiences with respect to the project topic, which is an aspect of the participants' teaching that they select as being of particular interest or concern. Through discourse within the meetings the perspective of both individuals and the group as a whole can be transformed. As true action research projects need at least two cycles of planning, action, observation and reflection, there is time for perspective transformation to take place.

INTERPRETIVE INFLUENCE

From this initial theoretical justification for action research, it might seem that my approach was developed purely from theory. This was not the case, though, as it would be truer to describe the theoretical formulation as a *post hoc* justification. The initiative evolved to suit a perceived environment within the originating university, and has been adapted and refined in the light of lessons learnt during its operation.

My own involvement with action research evolved from extensive work in educational development in which the principal influence was the student approaches to learning (SAL) tradition, which is probably the predominant approach within the interpretive pretext. The framework of students' approaches to learning was very effective for evaluating the teaching and learning context, and providing interpretation which was readily understood and accepted as pertinent by academic staff.

Within Hong Kong there was particular interest in student approaches to learning because of a phenomenon that became known as the paradox of the Asian student. Anecdotal opinions that Hong Kong students were only capable of rote learning were common, yet there was considerable evidence that the students were high achievers compared to their Western counterparts. Investigation by a number of researchers led to evidence of students employing a learning approach combining memorizing and understanding. The explanation of the paradox was that the perpetrators of the anecdotes had misconstrued visible signs of memorization as evidence of a surface approach when it was commonly part of a search for understanding (Kember, 1996; Watkins and Biggs, 1996).

A cross-university project led to interest in using the methods employed by these researchers to evaluate courses. A combination of use of the Study Process Questionnaire (SPQ) (Biggs, 1987) and interviews showed a range of variables such as workload, assessment, teaching style and curriculum design which were affecting the learning approaches of students and often inducing them to use a surface approach (eg Gow and Kember, 1990; Kember and Gow, 1991). However, the interpretive tradition restricts itself to obtaining understanding while those involved wished to take action to do something to improve what was seen as an undesirable situation. This was why the writer started to look towards the mode of research that embraces the researchers bringing about change.

Coming to action research from a grounding in research into student approaches to learning meant that the early projects, in which I was a full participant, made use of investigative methods commonly used in research into student approaches to learning. Projects in which I was involved had an interpretive character to the observation or evaluation phase of the action research cycle.

Projects supported by the Action Learning Project have had varied topics or foci so the methods of evaluation and observation have necessarily been diverse. Many have included techniques derived from the SAL tradition. In particular there have been examinations of students' approaches to learning and their relationship to contextual variables such as assessment, workload, the learning environment, the programme demands and the curriculum design. That many participants have found these tools of SAL research valuable within their action research projects suggests a logical symbiosis of the interpretive paradigm with the critical paradigm for the purpose of learning and teaching quality enhancement through action research.

ACTION LEARNING AND ACTION RESEARCH

A further pragmatic development through practice occurred with nomen-clature. In looking for a mechanism to bring about changes suggested by the student approaches to learning research, the writer was guided by a literature that referred to action research. We referred to the initial projects of this type, in which the writer participated, as action research projects (eg Kember and Gow, 1992).

After gathering considerable experience of supporting educational action research projects within one university, an opportunity arose to bid for funds for a wider project across several universities. A proposal was prepared for a scheme to support educational action research projects. A member of the university's senior management suggested the word 'research' might cause problems. The adjudicating panel might see the proposal as seeking a research grant – and a very large one at that. If the proposal were interpreted in that way it was unlikely to be successful as the body seeking proposals did not fund research. 'Action learning' was, therefore, sub-stituted for 'action research'.

A benefit of the change was that the word 'learning' appeared and the prime focus of the overall project was to be on student learning. Another benefit was that it provided a good title, the Action Learning Project, for the initiative when the grant was awarded.

The substitution seemed to be quite appropriate, as well as tactically apt, because both action learning and action research were appropriate descriptors for the projects concerned with teaching practices. Both action learning and action research assume that learning results from active experience. Learning and improvements to existing situations come about through iterative or cyclical processes. Initial ideas can be examined in concrete applications. Observation then leads to reflection and the formulation of ideas for improvement the next time the activity is performed.

There appear to be somewhat differing views of the distinction between action learning and action research. Of the two, action research has been written about much more, which is hardly surprising since research normally leads to published outcomes, whereas learning rarely does. Action research is, therefore, quite well defined compared to action learning.

One well-accepted definition of action research was quoted earlier in the chapter. Perhaps the most extensive treatment of action learning is by McGill and Beaty (1995: 21). They do not give a formal definition but their opening description of action learning approximates to one:

> Action learning is a continuous process of learning and reflection, supported by colleagues, with an intention of getting things done. Through action learning individuals learn with and from each other by working on real problems and reflecting on their own experiences.

Comparing this description with the definition of action research by Carr and Kemmis (1986: 165–66), given earlier, the distinction is interpreted as that between learning and research in general. Research is a form of learning which is more systematic and rigorous, and its outcomes are normally made public. The outcomes of learning are usually confined to the individual or fellow members of the learning group or class.

Extrapolating to action research and action learning implies that action research is always a learning process, but a methodical and rigorous form of action learning in which results are published. All action research projects are, then, action learning projects, but the converse does not hold true.

McGill and Beaty (1995: 32) accept that both action research and action learning share the same learning cycle and have many values in common. They also agree that research is not the primary aim of action learning projects, so participants may do little or no data-gathering or research beyond their personal observations and reflections. McGill and Beaty clearly see the focus of action learning lying in the group 'set'. They argue, though, that action research can be an individual activity. This issue was discussed earlier and the conclusion reached that action research by individuals is a legitimate activity. It is, though, probably more common for action research also to be a group activity. Forms of action research more strongly influenced by critical theory are definitely participative group activities, and would also have critical reflection through group discourse as a central activity.

If action learning and action research are seen as the poles of an action spectrum, the projects discussed in this book are closer to the research pole than those described by McGill and Beaty, which concentrate upon participants reflecting upon their actions in set meetings. The main 'data' in their projects are the presentations that set members make at their meetings and the collective critical reflections upon those disclosures. The projects supported by the Action Learning Project used a variety of observation and evaluation techniques discussed in the next chapter. The participants expected to report on their projects and we saw this as an important feature of the overall project as it was a means of disseminating what had been learnt to a wider audience.

As a result of the close relationship between action learning and action research, terminology in this book will slip loosely between the two terms. There are instances, such as these first two chapters, where it is easier to use the term action research, even though action learning is also used in the title, because the literature on action research is more developed.

SUMMARY AND CONCLUSION

This chapter has advocated participation in educational action research projects as a mode of educational development. The characteristics envisaged for this means of quality enhancement are summarized here to characterize this vision of educational action research:

1. Project teams are composed of small groups who share a similar interest or concern. It is also possible for individuals to conduct action research projects within courses they teach.
2. The topic for the project is defined by the participants, to fit within the broad aim of investigating and improving some aspect of their own teaching.
3. Project groups meet regularly to report observations and critique their own practices. This discourse provides for the possibility of perspective transformation.
4. Projects proceed through cycles of planning, action, observation and reflection. At least two cycles are normally necessary to implement and refine any innovatory practices. The time-scale for the cycles is consistent with the extended period necessary for perspective transformation.
5. Evidence of the effectiveness of teaching practices and their influence on student learning outcomes is gathered using interpretive methods.
6. The evidence gathered can be used to convince departmental colleagues, not originally participating in the project, that they too should change their practices and the curriculum.

7. Lessons learnt from the projects can be disseminated to a wider audience through publications. Participants are, therefore, eligible for rewards through the traditional value system of universities.

3

Observation and evaluation methods

The previous chapter has provided a description of what action learning and action research are and how they can be applied to the issues of quality in teaching and learning. The purpose of this chapter is to provide the practitioner with some advice on carrying out an action research project applied to his or her own teaching.

In the Action Learning Project, utilizing a series of action research cycles to implement and refine an initiative did not seem to cause many problems, even though most participants admitted to no previous experience of action research. This may be because it has close parallels to other processes for implementing change or development. Engineers, for example, plan and build a prototype. This is then tested and a refined model is built based upon test data. Several cycles of building and testing prototypes may be necessary before the product goes into production.

The advice given here focuses mainly upon the evaluation and observation phase of the action research cycle. The reason for this was the fact that the project teams supported by the Action Learning Project asked for far more help with evaluation than any other facet of the projects. Of the phases of planning, action, observation and reflection, the support team spent more time, by far, advising on observation than the other three phases put together.

Those who feel a need for advice on the reflection and action phases are advised to read the companion volume, published by Kogan Page, written by McGill and Beaty (2nd edn, 1995) and entitled *Action Learning: A guide for professional, management and educational development*. This book has very detailed guidance on action and reflection through action learning sets. It also provides examples of how to put the guidance into practice in a number of fields.

PURPOSES OF OBSERVATION AND EVALUATION

One purpose of evaluation provides the rationale for the inclusion of observation within a series of action research cycles. If each cycle is to lead to progressive improvement, there needs to be some method for determining what is working well, what needs refining and how it can be improved. This can only come from some form of observation or evaluation of the action during the implementation phase of the cycle.

The participants in the action research projects supported by the Action Learning Project wanted to go beyond evaluation as a diagnostic tool to using it as a means of establishing the effectiveness of their innovation or project. It seems quite natural for anyone to wish to show that their project has been worthwhile and achieved its aims. Evidence of effectiveness is also important if others are to be persuaded to adopt a similar approach. This is important in academic departments, as a revised approach to teaching may have to be more widely adopted if it is to have an impact upon a whole programme.

The participants in the projects were also academics who saw the benefits in writing up their projects for conference papers or journals. For papers to be accepted there was an expectation that they would go beyond description to evaluating the innovation and showing it to be effective. This leads on to the final rationale for evaluation in that it means that lessons learnt from individual projects can be communicated to a wider audience. There would not be much of an audience for mere description, even if it could find a publisher, but evidence that what is being described is educationally effective does make the speaker worth listening to.

Experiment and control – or not?

Before embarking upon a guide to using a range of evaluation techniques, it is worth spending some time discussing the issue of establishing effectiveness. The initial plans of several projects included experiment-versus-control designs as a projected means of showing that a new form of teaching was more effective than a traditional approach. The proposers were usually from disciplines in which experimental or positivistic research was customary.

In most cases these proposers were cautioned that experiment/control methods are hard to deploy in genuine educational innovations introduced into a natural setting and lasting for an extended period such as an academic year. Further, the results are often inconclusive as the experimental conditions are difficult to maintain and statistically significant differences hard to obtain. When this advice was ignored the outcomes usually justified the caution. The reasons are as follows.

The first difficulty lies in ensuring that the experiment and control are genuinely comparable. It is hard to run two classes in parallel with the same content, taught by different methods, with equal conviction and ability. Educational media comparison studies, for example, have been criticized on this basis by a number of writers (eg Levie and Dickie, 1973; Clark, 1983; 1985; Schram, 1977). Clark (1983) suggested that content differences between treatments often confound results. Compelling evidence for this assertion comes from the observation that any positive effects for new media more or less disappeared if the same teacher gave or produced the instruction for each treatment group.

Genuine educational settings are particularly difficult for control/ experiment designs because of the complex array of contextual variables that can interact with the variable under study. It is sometimes possible to control statistically for extraneous variables, but some variables are difficult to measure and factors that were not anticipated can and often do play a part.

Making arrangements for control and experiment groups within a school or university can be difficult. There are likely to be ethical issues as one or more groups accorded different treatment may feel disadvantaged. This happened commonly with the projects under the umbrella of the Action Learning Project. Control groups complained when they did not have access to the newer form of teaching as they felt this might have an adverse effect on their grades. There were also cases of students, supposedly in the control group, who gained access to the experimental material from their friends in the other group.

Normal taught courses last for extended periods such as an academic year or a semester. Designing different teaching programmes, arranging for the separation of groups and holding extraneous variables constant becomes more difficult the longer the trial. It is not surprising, therefore, that many, if not most experiment/control tests are very short in duration. Essentially they are more akin to laboratory experiments than innovations introduced into natural settings. However, shortening the timeframe and resorting to controlled conditions renders the experiment open to the charge of dubious relevance. The validity of findings from artificial laboratory-type experiments for the complex classroom environment has been severely questioned (eg Parlett and Hamilton, 1976). It is paradoxical that the more the innovation is controlled to enhance experimental reliability the greater becomes the discrepancy from the normal classroom setting.

A further criticism of experiment/control designs is that the necessity for keeping conditions constant between treatment groups acts to prohibit the adaptive processes and fine-tuning which usually occur when innovations are implemented (Parlett and Hamilton, 1977: 241–42). It is extremely difficult to foresee all eventualities so successful implementations almost invariably require some modifications to initial plans in the light of experience. Gibbs (1992b) maintains that a process of fine-tuning is essential for a successful outcome to an educational innovation.

This argument is a restatement of the rationale for using a cyclical action learning or action research method to introduce change. Action research aims for the introduction of change and its refinement based upon experience. It was adopted because the experimental methods of the natural sciences were not conducive to this aim. Rather than allowing the research design to dictate the mode of implementation and prohibit fine-tuning, it is preferable to adopt a research approach that fits the investigation to the desired mode of implementation and refinement.

This may mean that the evidence of effectiveness appears less direct than it might with an experiment-versus-control design. The normal procedure is to triangulate data from several of the evaluation techniques described below. These should preferably include multiple sources, the obvious ones being the students, the teacher and colleagues. The intention is to produce a body of evidence that would convince a reasonable person to make a judgement that the project or approach had been effective. In practice this position differs little from the level of proof normally presented in positivist research. Particularly in human or social sciences, the claim that hypotheses are irrefutably proved by experiments is often illusory (eg Labaree, 1998; Schulman, 1988).

Generalizability

A related issue then is the level to which generalization can be made from action research projects. Traditionally, research utilizing action research or naturalistic methodologies has been seen as less generalizable than work of logical positivists. Owens (1982), for example, contrasts the rationalistic and naturalistic paradigms. His conclusion was that generalization was possible with the former but suspect under the latter. Such generalizations, though, are themselves suspect.

It is usually accepted that quantitative studies are generalizable if a random sample was drawn from the population. However, generalizations of quantitative studies are often made to situations that were not part of the statistical population of the original study. For example, it is very common for a sample to be drawn from students in a limited number of schools or universities. Strictly speaking the population is limited to the schools or universities from which the sample was drawn, unless they themselves were selected randomly – which is virtually never the case. It is common, though, for researchers to imply, and readers to accept, that generalizations may be made to schools or universities with similar contexts or characteristics.

The process undertaken is the reader examining the conclusions and the context of the original study and making an intelligent decision on whether the conclusion is applicable in other situations, most particularly the reader's own school or university. Eisner (1991: Ch. IX) argues cogently that the same process of intelligent judgement about generalization applies equally to qualitative research, even for single case studies. He argues that generalization may be made through attribute analysis and image matching as well as through formal inference.

It seems reasonable to treat evidence from action research studies in a similar way. If a particular action research study finds that an innovation works well, it makes eminent sense to recommend others to try something similar if they are facing the same type of issue. The conclusion then is not the type of universal law the positivists strive for. Rather, it follows Stenhouse's (1975: 142) belief that proposals should be presented as provisional specifications to be tested rather than unqualified recommendations.

There is no doubt that the findings from one situation will need to be intelligently adapted to suit the context and circumstances in another. It would also be sensible to follow an action research cycle during the subsequent implementation so that feedback can be gathered and further adaptation made if necessary. The argument is essentially that lessons learnt from one action research project may be utilized by others facing similar issues in related contexts. Intelligent adaptation should be made in anticipation of differences in the context. An action research testing and development process should be utilized for implementation so that a process of fine-tuning can cope with unanticipated differences or difficulties.

EVALUATION AND OBSERVATION TECHNIQUES

The remainder of this chapter is taken up by advice about a number of evaluation and observation techniques that have been found useful within the projects supported by the Action Learning Project.

Reflective journals

Reflection upon practice is an integral part of the action learning or action research cycle. Part C argues that one of the most important outcomes of the projects was that they prompted lecturers to reflect critically upon their teaching and their students' learning. It, therefore, makes sense to start with an aid to reflection.

The most commonly used approach to prompting reflection is reflective writing in a journal. Many individuals find that regularly writing down thoughts about a project or issue is a way of introducing the discipline of critical reflective thinking. Without some conscious procedure it is all too easy to take things for granted, or proceed with the bustle of everyday work without taking the time to stop and reflect.

As well as being a prompt for individual reflection, journal entries can act as the starting points for critical reflection at the regular team meetings of collaborative projects. By sharing observations and reflections it is possible to fine-tune the innovation. Communal reflection commonly leads to deeper insights than the individuals managed by themselves. Sympathetic but critical discussion can also heighten awareness and contribute to changing perspectives.

Reflective journals are not just prompts to reflection, but also sources of data. Reflective journal writing can be thought of as an observation tool. At the end of a project a reflective journal might contain material like:

- initial reflections on the topic of concern;
- the plans that were made;
- a record of actions taken;
- observation of the effects of the actions;
- reflections upon, and personal opinions about, the actions taken and reactions to them;
- results obtained from other observation techniques;
- references for, and notes on, any relevant literature or supporting documents discovered.

A reflective journal should not be equated to a diary or a laboratory record book, but it can contain material that would be kept in either. The distinction between journals and these other documents is that the reflective journal can and should contain personal thoughts and insights. In this respect it differs from most forms of writing about research, or other forms of academic writing for that matter.

Many academics, particularly those from scientific disciplines, find it hard to write in a reflective manner because that means writing down personal thoughts and beliefs. Their training, however, has stressed the need for writing in the third person, citing outside authorities and evidence and avoiding personal bias. They have not only absorbed this lesson well enough to become an academic, but also taught it to their students.

Research reports are often very impersonal documents but this should *not* be the case for an action-learning journal – quite the contrary! It should contain a record of both what the researcher did and what happened, as well as personal thoughts. In it the researcher should regularly and systematically reflect critically on the effects of the project and how it is progressing.

CLOSED QUESTIONNAIRES

Closed questionnaires are ones that constrain the responses to a limited number of responses chosen by the researcher; essentially it is a multiple-choice format. Usually respondents are asked the extent to which they agree or disagree with a given statement. Responses are recorded on a Likert scale, such as the one in Figure 3.1, which ranges from 'definitely agree' to 'definitely disagree'.

A section of a typical closed questionnaire used for course evaluation is shown in Figure 3.1.

The aim of the questionnaire is to obtain your viewpoint on various aspects of this course. The information gathered in this questionnaire will be used to improve the course in future years and guide the development and teaching of other courses.

Please circle the appropriate response to indicate your level of agreement with statements about this course.

SA – strongly agree
A – agree
D – disagree
SD – strongly disagree

1. This course has been run in a well-organized manner.	SA	A	D	SD
2. Material was presented clearly.	SA	A	D	SD
3. The objectives of the course were clear.	SA	A	D	SD
4. I found the course interesting.	SA	A	D	SD
5. The course was relevant to my needs.	SA	A	D	SD

Figure 3.1 Closed questionnaire for course evaluation

Questions should be carefully constructed so the meaning is clear and unambiguous. It is a good idea to trial the questionnaire on a limited number of students before giving it to a whole group.

Closed questionnaires are easy to process and evaluate and can give clear answers to specific questions. However, the questions are defined by the researcher, so they could completely miss the concerns of the respondents. A sensible sequence is, therefore, to draw up the questions after a few exploratory interviews, or include some open-ended questions to give respondents a chance to raise other issues of concern.

Most institutions now have some form of standard teaching question-naire available. These may be of some help in evaluating a project but in most cases the questions will not be sufficiently specific to the particular type of innovation that has been introduced. What might be more helpful are the data banks of optional or additional questions, which are available. These can be used to pick or suggest questions that might be included in a tailor-made questionnaire.

Optical mark readers are available in most institutions for reading responses to questionnaires and compiling a data file for analysis. To make use of an optical mark reader the responses have to be marked on special forms. Designing and printing a form for a tailor-made questionnaire is likely to be prohibitively expensive. However, there are standard forms available for marking responses to typical closed-response questions. The numbered questions are given to the students on one piece of paper. They mark their responses in the numbered positions on the grid of the standard form.

The data from closed-response questionnaires are normally analysed with statistics packages such as SPSS or SAS. Often action learning projects require little more than means and frequencies.

Student learning inventories

Student learning inventories are examples of empirically derived closed questionnaires. There are any number of instruments that purport to measure a wide range of characteristics. Student learning inventories have been highlighted because they examine the quality of learning. In particular they look at the categories deep and surface learning. The inventories can be used to compare groups of students, examine approaches before and after changes to teaching methods, and to examine correlations with other variables.

The Study Process Questionnaire (SPQ) developed by John Biggs (1987) assesses students' approaches to learning. Scores are obtained for each student on deep, surface and achieving approach scales. The SPQ has been widely used in many countries and its cultural applicability widely researched. Detailed accounts of usage of the SPQ are given by Biggs (1987; 1992) and Watkins (1998).

For action learning projects, a suitable way to use the SPQ is to apply it at the start and end of the innovation. Changes in SPQ scores can then be interpreted as a reflection of the teaching and learning context. The results will indicate whether the innovation has encouraged meaningful approaches to learning.

An example of the use of the SPQ is shown in the graph of mean deep approach (DA) scores in Figure 3.2. The lines shown on the graph as RPD1

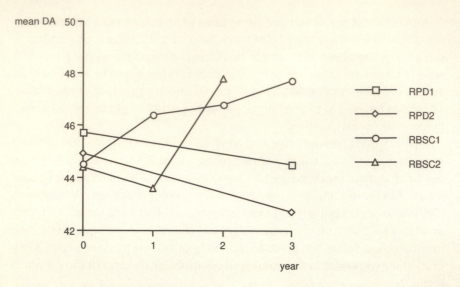

Figure 3.2 Mean deep approach (DA) scores over time using the study process questionnaire

and RPD2 are from applications of the SPQ to the final two intakes to a professional diploma course. The SPQ was completed near the start and end of the course and the results show that use of a deep approach declined as students proceeded through the course, which unfortunately is a common finding in universities.

Following a major action research initiative (McKay, 1995; McKay and Kember, 1997) the professional diploma course was replaced by a BSc course with a very different structure and teaching approach. The attitude of the teaching staff also changed considerably. Evidence of the effectiveness of the changes can be seen from the deep approach scores rising with year of study for the first two intakes to the BSc programme (RBSC1 and RBSC2).

OPEN QUESTIONNAIRES

Open questionnaires have a series of specific questions but leave space for respondents to answer as they see fit. Open questions are, therefore, more likely to find out the views of students but replies are more difficult to analyse and collate. The usual procedure is to search for categories of common responses. An example of an open questionnaire is shown in Figure 3.3. The original left more space after each question.

It is not necessary to have separate questionnaires for open and closed items. The most successful questionnaires often have both open and closed items. The closed-response items target issues that are of particular concern

For the following questions please write as much as you feel is necessary to give a full answer to each question.

(a) What were the best aspects of this course?

(b) How could the course be improved?

(c) Do you have any comments on individual lessons?

Thank you for completing this questionnaire

Figure 3.3 Open questionnaire for course evaluation

or related to project goals. The open-response items can give the students a chance to clarify or respond in more depth. They can also comment on anything else considered relevant.

INTERVIEWS

The format for interviews can be on a spectrum from completely open discussion to tightly structured questions. When gathering feedback from university students it is more efficient to use a questionnaire if the intention is to ask tightly structured questions as the students are capable of interpreting the questions themselves. In higher education, therefore, interviews commonly have a more open or semi-structured format.

Semi-structured interviews have a small schedule of questions to point the interviewee towards an area of interest to the researcher, but then allow interviewees to raise any issues they like within the general topic area. Since interviews give an opportunity for students to raise their own agenda they are useful when issues are open, or at an exploratory stage. Again it is possible to use a combination of techniques by conducting a small number of interviews to discover and define issues for a subsequent tightly structured questionnaire.

Interviews, therefore, provide even more opportunity for respondents to raise their own issues and concerns, but are correspondingly more time-consuming to collect and analyse. Interviews are normally tape-recorded. If detailed analysis (rather than just impression) is required, transcripts have to be produced. The transcripts are normally analysed by searching for responses or themes that commonly occur. Quotations from the transcripts can be used to illuminate or illustrate findings set out in reports and papers.

There are computer programs available to assist with the analysis of qualitative data. One example is the program NUD•IST (QSR NUD•IST, 1997; Richards and Richards, 1991) which has facilities for indexing, text-searching, using Boolean operations on defined index nodes, and combining data from several initially independent studies. This program (and others like it) is worth using if there is a large amount of data in electronic form with multiple variables and constructs. With small amounts of data, such as comments written in response to one or two open-ended questions on a questionnaire, it is normally quicker to use pencil and paper.

CLASSROOM OBSERVATION

As education developed more naturalistic forms of research, a range of techniques was developed for examining what happened in the classroom. The pioneering work with these techniques was almost all in school classrooms, which are probably more interesting than many classrooms in higher education. More recently, though, observation techniques have been used more widely in universities, particularly when non-traditional teaching and learning methods are introduced.

Observation can be conducted by a variety of techniques and with orientations that can be placed on a number of continua. One issue is the degree to which the aims of the observation are pre-defined. Some observations are conducted with a very particular, and perhaps narrow, goal because the teacher or researcher has a very specific issue or problem to find out about. Other observations may set out with a more open framework. If a completely new teaching and learning method is introduced, for example, it may be best to explore openly as it is unlikely to be clear what is worth detailed study.

The observer can also be placed on a continuum with participant to non-participant poles. For action research projects, the most common situation at the participant end of the pole is the teacher observing their own classroom. The degree of movement towards the non-participant end of the spectrum can be seen as determined by the nature of the relationship between the observer and the observed. Some of the Action Learning Project's action research studies employed a research assistant to conduct classroom observations. As these were usually about the same age as the students, they rapidly became accepted as an unofficial member of the class. An intermediate position is when a teacher invites a colleague into the classroom to observe their teaching. After the class the colleague can aid the teacher in reflecting upon pertinent aspects of the teaching. At the non-participant end of the pole would be the school-inspector scenario.

A related continuum deals with the degree of obtrusiveness. If the teacher is acting as a participant observer, the class is unlikely to be aware that observation is taking place. At the other extreme, classrooms can have several camera operators with their associated paraphernalia intrusively filming every action.

Recording

When making classroom observation, some form of recording is often employed because the teacher, and even an observer, may find it hard to note everything that takes place. It is hard for teachers, and particularly novice teachers, to concentrate upon their teaching and simultaneously to act as a dispassionate, reflective observer. The reliability of self-observation can also be questioned.

When making a recording in the classroom there is clearly a trade-off between obtaining a usable record of what takes place and distorting the natural setting and behaviour. Introducing recording equipment into the classroom poses the issue of whether the behaviour of those in the classroom will be affected by the recording process. The more detailed and clear the recording desired, the more obtrusive the equipment and associated staff become. This can clearly be problematic as the purpose of classroom observation is to observe natural behaviour in a natural setting. The most sensible guideline to follow is to use the minimal level of equipment necessary to obtain an adequate recording. Fortunately video cameras have become much smaller over the last few years, so this balance is becoming easier. Experienced practitioners of classroom recording also claim that those who are observed tend to forget about the presence of cameras and observers, and start to behave naturally in a fairly short space of time.

The least intrusive method of obtaining a record of what happens in class is through audio tape recording. Making tape recordings is a way of collecting a complete, accurate and detailed record of discussions in class, conversations in interviews or arguments and decisions at meetings. It is easy to obtain the recording; all it needs is a portable recorder and cassettes. If there are more than a handful of people involved or they are spread around the room it will be necessary to have either several microphones or a sensitive one with a wide acceptance range.

Many evaluation topics require no more than an audio recording, but video is necessary if there is a need to observe actions and expressions. In many cases simply setting up a camera on a tripod at the back of a room can suffice. Movement and action within the classroom and a requirement for detail may necessitate an operator and possibly more than one camera. If the room is large and there are many people speaking, there may be a need to place microphones at strategic points in the room. But remember, the more equipment used, the more likely it is to inhibit discussion or influence people's behaviour.

There are a number of ethical issues that need to be addressed over the use of recordings. The group being taped should decide the purpose of making the recording and the way in which the tapes will be used. If any quotations are made in subsequent reports it is customary to maintain the anonymity of the source.

If it is necessary to do a detailed analysis of the conversations, transcripts must be produced. This is a time-consuming and painstaking process, so limit the transcription to situations or portions of the tapes that are really needed.

Analysis of recordings depends upon what the researchers are looking for. In some cases the teacher is aiming to reflect in general upon their own teaching. In other instances specific aspects of teaching, consistent with the original goals of the project, might be examined. In the latter case, more specific or systematic procedures can be useful. One example – the inter-action schedule – is described below.

Interaction schedules

Interaction schedules are methods for analysing and recording what takes place during a class. A common approach is to note down at regular intervals (say, every minute) who is talking, and to categorize what they were saying or doing. An alternative to time sampling is event sampling, in which behaviour is noted every time a particular event occurs. Examples of categories could be: tutor asking question, tutor giving explanation, tutor giving instruction, student answering question or student asking question. The analysis can be by an observer at the class or can be made subsequently from a tape or video recording.

Figure 3.4 shows two profiles, which compare the interactions during two tutorials. An observer noted, at one-minute intervals, who was talking and the type of communication. The plots can be used to compare the extent to which the tutor dominated the session and the students contributed. The example is adapted from Williams and Gillard (1986).

There are other approaches to recording and analysing happenings in a classroom situation. Hook (1981) provides a comprehensive guide to methods. McKernan (1991) discusses an extensive range of techniques, gives examples of each and considers how the data gathered should be analysed.

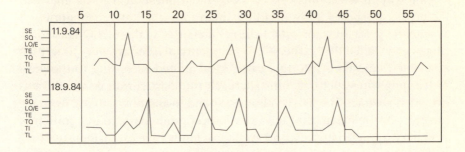

Nature of the transaction shown on the vertical axis (TL, tutor lecturing; TI, tutor giving instructions; TQ, tutor questioning; TE, tutor encouraging; LQ/E, local tutor questioning or explaining; SQ, student questioning; SE, student explaining). The horizontal axis shows the time sequence (in minutes).

Figure 3.4 Profiles of interaction during two tutorials
(Williams and Gillard, 1986)

STUDENT ASSESSMENT

Tests, examinations and continuous assessment can provide valuable data for action research. The goals of projects are normally related to learning outcomes, which is what assessment determines. Most courses have to be assessed, so it is efficient to make use of assessment data in projects.

There are two cautions, though. Firstly, care needs to be taken over interpreting examination results or assessment grades. Comparison of one set of results with another often has limited validity since assignments, examinations, markers and marking schemes are rarely held constant. In addition most assessment in universities is norm- rather than criterion-referenced. That is, students are compared with each other rather than examined to see whether they can meet pre-determined standards appropriate to the aims of the course.

It is also important to be very clear as to what is being assessed. Examination grades may bear little relationship to specific qualities that are being investigated. It is all too common for university courses to have fine-sounding high-level goals, but to have assessment that largely examines the acquisition of defined bodies of knowledge. In using assessment outcomes it is, therefore, important to think carefully about the qualities which need to be tested and whether the assessment is a true test of those qualities.

One way in which answers to assessment questions can be analysed for project purposes is by dividing them into qualitative categories. A systematic procedure for establishing categories is the SOLO taxonomy (Biggs and Collis, 1982). The SOLO taxonomy divides answers to written assessment questions into five categories, judged according to the level of learning: prestructural, unistructural, multistructural, relational and extended abstract. The five levels correspond to answers ranging from the incorrect or irrelevant, through use of appropriate data, to integration of data in an appropriate way, and ending in innovative extensions.

Answers to assessment questions may also be placed in qualitative categories based on the understanding of constructs. It is often possible to see that assignment or examination answers can be placed into a limited number of categories based upon the level of students' understanding of a concept. The types of categories that emerge will be similar to those from the research into conceptions of important constructs.

Diagnosis of student conceptions

It is often surprising how students can pass university examinations but still have fundamental misunderstandings of key concepts. The usual method of diagnosing student conceptions is to ask a question that applies the concept to an everyday situation: one which cannot be answered by reproduction or by substitution into formulae. Answers have been drawn from the students in interviews or in written form.

The students' answers can usually be classified into a small number (usually two to five) of conceptions or misconceptions about the phenomenon. As with the analysis of interview data, care needs to be taken when deriving classifications. These do not automatically emerge from the transcript but are subject to the experiences and knowledge of the researcher.

The most frequently cited example of this type of research comes from Dahlgren (1978, 1984) who asked university economics students the question:

Why does a bun cost about one [Swedish] crown?

Judges placed students' answers to this question into one of two categories:

A. The price is dependent on the relationship between the supply and demand for buns.
B. The price is equal to the true value of the bun.

(Dahlgren, 1984: 30)

Dahlgren went on to note that many students gave answers of the second type even though they had passed an examination on their first-year course, which taught the laws of supply and demand.

There is a great deal of research into students' conceptions and misconceptions of science concepts. The studies aim to categorize students' answers to applied questions into a limited number of categories, which reveal conceptions and misconceptions of the concepts that are fundamental to an understanding of the discipline. Again it is often revealed that many students construct their answers from a framework of naïve or outdated scientific theories, even though they have been taught more sophisticated or recent ones.

Bowden (1988) asserts that good teachers are able to draw upon their teaching experiences to formulate questions that will reveal student conceptions and misconceptions of fundamental concepts. They are also likely to be able to predict how the more common misconceptions will be revealed in answers to these questions, as it is a common practice for teachers to note mistaken ideas that arise in classroom discussion, or common mistakes in assignments.

SUPPORTING DOCUMENTS

Action learning is frequently associated with organizational change. Part of this process is likely to involve working through the formal decision-making and administrative processes of an organization. The documentation associated with these transactions should be seen as part of the data for projects. In a university context this documentation can include:

- documents for the course development and accreditation process;
- minutes of course committees;
- the course syllabus;
- memos between course team leaders and members;
- handouts to students;
- copies of tests and examinations;
- lists of test results and student grades.

Such documentation is particularly useful when reporting an action research study involving organizational change. It can provide evidence that the account of the author is an accurate report. The credibility of self-reported action research can be questioned if there is no substantiation. A good example is provided by the exchange between Busher (1989) and Williams (1991). The latter article provides sensible guidelines for establishing the authenticity of self-reported action research. It suggests citing documentation such as that listed above and asking appropriate people, within the department or faculty concerned, to read and verify draft versions of the reports.

TRIANGULATION

Triangulation is not a specific observation technique but, in the most widely used sense of the term, is the process of comparing and justifying data from one evaluation method against that from another. The most obvious return from triangulation is enhanced credibility. A conclusion reached by more than one method is more believable than that from a single one.

A further benefit can be greater depth of understanding. Evaluation methods yield different types of information. Examining an issue from different angles usually results in a better understanding than just using one perspective.

In action research the term triangulation has also been applied to the bringing together of data from multiple perspectives or voices (Elliott, 1991; McKernan, 1991). In the educational setting the obvious perspectives are the teacher and students, with additional possibilities being observers, fellow course team members or department heads.

There is a strong argument for a combination of multiple methods and multiple voices. The Action Learning Project itself was analysed using a multiple-level, multiple-method and multiple-perspective approach described in Chapter 8. Anyone intending to conduct an action research project is, therefore, strongly advised to make use of at least two, and preferably three or more, of the techniques described in this chapter. In choosing techniques it is sensible to try to ensure that as many perspectives as possible are incorporated. If this advice is followed the conclusions drawn from the evaluation are more likely to reach significant insights and be believable to outsiders.

PART B
CLUSTERS OF PROJECTS

David Kember

Part A introduced action learning and action research as a means of quality enhancement for teaching and learning. Chapters 2 and 3 have hopefully provided sufficient guidance to carry out an action learning project.

This part of the book moves on to wider initiatives of several projects. It is addressed more to the potential facilitator of projects or someone who might be in a position to form and organize a scheme for encouraging projects through the award of small teaching development grants.

There are benefits to having a wider aggregation of projects, particularly small clusters of projects dealing with similar topics or in related disciplines. In this part of the book the Action Learning Project is introduced and described. It is subsequently used as a case study for examining both mechanisms for organizing collective action research initiatives and as a large source of data to discuss the effectiveness of action learning as a mechanism for quality enhancement.

Chapter 4 discusses ways in which a facilitator can persuade teachers to participate in action research projects about some aspect of their teaching. The dilemma for the facilitator is to balance the wish to initiate projects with the participative nature of action research and the desire that the participants own their own projects.

Four strategies for initiating individual projects are described. Workshops about the action research approach are useful as potential activists may be unaware of this way of tackling issues concerned with teaching and learning. Projects may be associated with the development of new curricula or arise as the result of other educational development activities. Projects may also take the form of higher degree dissertations.

Involvement with a number of projects looking at a similar issue or in related disciplines started to reveal the benefits of relating several projects together. By forming a meta-project for five related sub-projects it was possible to use comparison and synthesis to draw conclusions that were more profound and more likely to be generalizable than would have been possible with individual projects.

These initial experiences provided the foundation for the bid for a grant for the Action Learning Project. This in turn led to initiating projects by providing grants, which led to the experience of supporting a large cluster of 50 projects.

The Action Learning Project in Chapter 5 was an inter-institutional project involving all seven universities in Hong Kong. This necessitated a management structure that involved representatives of the seven universities but at the same time provided a formal relationship to the coordinating institution. The relationship between the management committee, the coordinating team, the educational development-type units in the seven universities and the participants in the 50 projects is discussed.

In Chapter 6 the 50 projects are described by a number of different classification systems. This chapter also describes the process for awarding grants to 50 projects across the seven universities.

In Chapter 7 the Action Learning Project was committed to a programme of sharing insights between participants and of disseminating lessons to other academics not involved in the projects. An extensive range of seminars, workshops on evaluation and interest group meetings was held. A conference was held to present the final reports of the projects. The papers from the conference were collated into an edited set of final reports.

4

Initiating projects

Action research projects into teaching and learning issues started in the Hong Kong Polytechnic University by following up outstanding issues which were highlighted by a collaborative project into student approaches to learning within Hong Kong (see Biggs, 1992, for a review of the earlier work). A combination of deep approach scores that declined by year of study and interview data revealed that the types of learning taking place were frequently out of alignment with the expectations of lecturers or the course goals.

When the data were reported back to the collaborating departments they often seemed to confirm latent suspicions that the staff already had, that all was not as well as it might be. They were often concerned about some aspects of a course but uncertain how to make a start in dealing with it. The problems always seemed to concern issues, such as the syllabus, examination system, arrangements for classes or the attitude of colleagues, that were too difficult for an individual to contemplate dealing with. For anything to happen it was necessary to persuade some members of the department that there were issues which might be addressed over time and there were effective methods for doing so. Essentially it was necessary to persuade the staff that learning outcomes on their courses were within their locus of control and that problems could be addressed by them (Gow, Kember and Sivan, 1992).

This raises one of the paradoxes of action research if projects are to be initiated. For action research, the focus or topic of concern should be determined by the participants. Yet groups of teachers rarely rise as one, determined to tackle the same issue. Even if they do, they may be unsure how to proceed. This is the continual dilemma of a facilitator seeking to work within an action research framework.

The perceptive reader may well have observed that the action research approach can take place without any involvement of a facilitator or educational developer. Groups of committed teachers do at times gather together to change their teaching practices. Lecturers do publish papers about innovations and improvements to their own teaching independently of assistance or prompting by staff developers. Some of this work would satisfy the conditions for classification as action research.

The situation that prompted these initial action research projects suggested that there are more latent participants who can be catalysed into action, than there are self-starters. Other recent attempts to promote educational action research projects (Gibbs, 1992b; Kember and Gow, 1992; Kember and Kelly, 1993; Zuber-Skerritt, 1992b), also suggest that projects are more likely to be initiated within some framework for stimulation and organization.

The remainder of the chapter examines ways in which action research projects can be initiated by a facilitator. The ideas are organized by increasing scale. The following section starts at the individual project level. The chapter ends by looking at a large umbrella project, which supported 50 sub-projects.

As the scale becomes greater the level of resourcing needed obviously grows too. Many of the projects referred to in the initial section about individual projects started with no additional resources at all. This section is likely to appeal to staff of educational development units or similar units. Part of their role could well be, or become, that of initiating and supporting action research initiatives by teaching staff.

At the larger end of the scale, the material later in this chapter is more likely to be relevant to institutional managers or those who influence system-wide initiatives. Many universities now have schemes for awarding (often small) grants to academics for teaching development purposes. The example of the Action Learning Project given later in the chapter is probably larger than most of these schemes. As it was able to analyse thoroughly its operation, though, it may well have lessons as to how university level systems might operate.

STRATEGIES FOR INITIATING INDIVIDUAL PROJECTS

This section discusses four approaches that were explored for initiating individual projects:

- a workshop to advertise the concept of action research in education;
- projects taking as their theme the implementation of some aspect of a new or revised curriculum;
- projects arising as a result of other educational development activities;
- staff members enrolled for a higher degree selecting a topic concerned with their own teaching for their dissertation project.

Each of these approaches was utilized for getting projects started in the early stages of action research in the Polytechnic University before the Action Learning Project. The enlargements upon these approaches below are, therefore, all based upon practical experience. The amount of additional resources required for the projects was either nothing or a fairly small amount of the time of a research assistant. These approaches to initiating projects should, then, be feasible for staff of bodies like educational development or quality assurance units.

Workshop on action research

The first initiation strategy attempted was to advertise a workshop on small-scale action research projects in education, in the same way that lecturers were invited to participate in other educational development workshops in the institution. The advertising for the workshop suggested an expectation that participants would become involved in an action research project following the workshop. The expectation of some initial inquirers, however, seemed conditioned by previous workshops, which normally expect little commitment beyond the workshop session. There was a significant fall-off between responding to the advertisement and actually becoming involved in a project. As well as being offered to those responding to the advertisement, the workshop was put on for three departments that had expressed an interest as a result of other activities.

A booklet on action research for small-scale educational projects was developed to accompany the workshop. The booklet and workshop dealt briefly with the nature of action research and covered the phases of planning, action, observation and reflection. The cyclical nature of action research was stressed. An overview was given of a number of techniques for making observations and gathering data. A lecturer, who was already involved in action research, described her project. The workshop was deliberately kept short but provided ample opportunity for discussion and raising questions. It was not meant to be a comprehensive course in educational research; rather a brief introduction to the concept of action research and an invitation to participate in a supported project.

Following the workshop a number of projects were started. On-going support was offered to the groups by critical friends. Funding was eventually obtained for a research assistant to help with data-gathering and analysis, working across a number of projects. A number of these early projects are described in Kember and Kelly (1993).

Projects arising from curriculum development

Action research is a very widely accepted approach to curriculum development. Both Stenhouse (1975) and McKernan (1991) include the term 'curriculum' in the titles of their books about action research. It might, therefore, be expected that action research projects would fit naturally with new curriculum development, and that this would be a very common occurrence. However, in higher education the formal procedures for developing and approving new courses rarely have an action research character. In Chapter 1, programme accreditation was assigned to either positivist or interpretive paradigms. The official course planning procedures in most universities seem to imply a belief that, once planned and approved, the course will then operate according to the approved plans unless the approving authority agrees to change the plans.

Curriculum development through action research still involves detailed initial planning. There is a recognition, though, that however thorough the planning process, there will be a need for refinement and further development in the light of feedback obtained when the course is taught. The action research cycle is followed and the teachers modify and develop the course as it is taught and between offerings.

In practice many teachers ignore, to some extent at least, requirements to obtain formal approval to deviate from course planning documents. There is, then, leeway to utilize an action learning process during the introduction of new courses. Concerns over implementation can be turned into action research projects, particularly if facilitators are prepared to offer support during the implementation phase. Curriculum development, therefore, becomes an on-going activity involving full participation by those teaching the course.

An example was a project in optometry, which arose out of the need for accreditation of a course for part-time adult students. The department had only taught courses for full-time undergraduate students before, so recognized that the new course would need to employ more student-centred adult learning strategies. Members of the department prepared for the new course by starting a number of sub-projects to introduce various aspects of adult learning strategies into existing courses. This project is described further in Kember and Kelly (1993).

Projects arising from other educational development activities

Many of the potential facilitators for action learning projects will work in educational development units or similar bodies. For most of the staff of these units, everyday work involves discussion with academics about issues in their teaching. They might for example be asked for advice on problems revealed through course evaluation or other forms of feedback. Where the issues are not straightforward such consultations can be used to trigger projects.

Advice can be offered as provisional recommendation in need of testing through a project-type approach. It can be accompanied by an offer to assist as a facilitator should the teacher decide to try out the recommendation. An example of this happening in practice was a project on student workload (Kember and Kelly, 1993). A concern about increasing student workload was clearly not an issue with a simple solution. The problem was, therefore, addressed initially by gathering data about student workloads through diaries.

Action research as higher degree project

If there are academics interested in researching their own teaching they may wish to make this research the topic for a higher degree project. In this situation the facilitator takes on the rather more formal role of supervisor. An example of this happening was a project concerned with organizational change and the change of curricula and teaching practices in the researcher's own department (McKay, 1995).

MOVING TOWARDS CLUSTERS

These initial projects served well to show that action research was a viable approach to educational development (Kember and Gow, 1992; Kember and Kelly, 1993; Kember and McKay, 1996). They also gave me an opportunity to develop my abilities as a facilitator for projects. Initially the projects were quite discrete. They were from different discipline areas and addressed quite different topics (see Kember and Kelly, 1993). There appeared to be little chance of bringing together engineers looking at workload with radiographers examining clinical placements – and no obvious benefits even if there were a meeting.

This perspective changed as the writer became involved with several projects in the broad area of the health sciences, which were all concerned with some aspect of the development of reflective practitioners. Bringing the participants in these projects together resulted in some very fertile critical reflection as insights were shared, and comparison and synthesis across projects took place. Eventually this initiative grew into a large long-lasting meta-project with five action research sub-projects, each concerned with a different discipline within the health sciences (Kember, Jones, Loke, McKay, Sinclair, Tse, Webb, Wong, Wong, Yan and Yeung, 1996a, 1996b).

All of this was good preparation for the quantum leap that came next. In 1994 a large grant was obtained from the central allocation vote of the University Grants Committee (UGC) of Hong Kong for a project known as the 'Action Learning Project'. The stated aims were to encourage and support academics in all seven universities in Hong Kong to participate in action research projects concerned with aspects of their own teaching.

The project initiation method used by the Action Learning Project was to call for project proposals and make grants available to the best projects. The availability of grants can be the best spur for starting projects, though obtaining the funds to award the grants may not be an easy task; and it is likely to be particularly difficult to obtain the level of funding necessary to support the extensive range of projects funded by the Action Learning Project.

CALL FOR PROPOSALS

To initiate projects the Action Learning Project Fund called for proposals from academics in each of the (then) seven UGC institutions in Hong Kong. Submissions were invited from individuals or, preferably, teams of academics for action learning projects on some aspect of courses they were teaching. There were two rounds for applications with deadlines of July 1994 and January 1995.

The expected format for submissions was similar to that for normal research grants. The call for submissions made it clear that proposals should include the following information:

- The aims of the project had to be described. This section was expected to identify the issue or problem in the course that the project intended to address. There was the expectation of an explicit statement showing how the proposed project would contribute to improving the quality of teaching and learning.
- A description of the intended project was required.
- A timetable for the project was requested, which had to fit within a maximum period of two years. Applicants were advised that action learning projects normally proceed through at least two cycles in which any innovation is introduced and refined.
- Proposers were expected to describe a mechanism for the evaluation of the effect of the innovation.
- The expected outcomes of the project needed to be identified.

- The requested budget had to be placed under the headings of salaries, equipment and general expenses, and a justification given for main items.
- Applications had to be endorsed by the respective head of department so that there was evidence that the project would be allowed to proceed. Priority was given to applications that were shown to be part of wider departmental initiatives.

Workshops were held to give guidelines for making proposals and conducting projects. These also aimed to raise awareness of action research as a process for improving teaching quality. Contributions were made by academics who had been involved in earlier action research projects. Booklets were also prepared to explain the processes of action learning and to suggest types of projects which might be suitable.

Potential applicants were advised that they could seek advice on draft proposals before submission. For each institution, one adviser from the educational development unit was nominated. Advice was also available from myself, as by this time I had been appointed to the role of Coordinator of the Project in an acting capacity. Quite a high proportion of the eventual applicants for grants either attended the seminars or sought advice on draft proposals, or both.

SELECTION PROCESS

The selection committee which examined the proposals was a subcommittee of the management committee, containing a representative of each institution. The management committee adopted outline selection criteria, which were developed and refined by the selection committee. The criteria were as follows:

- The main objective was to fund as many worthy projects as possible.
- Strong priority was given to projects with smaller budgets.
- Priority was given to collaborative group proposals, especially those likely to have impact across a whole department.
- Potential benefits and outcomes of the projects and their potential for dissemination across institutions were taken into account.

The Action Learning Project, in its first round, supported 50 sub-projects within the overall project theme. Funds awarded were used for purposes such as:

- hiring support staff such as research assistants;
- hiring temporary teaching staff to relieve full-time academics from teaching commitments so that they could work on the project;
- obtaining equipment or materials.

Further information about the supported projects is given in Chapter 6.

PROVIDING THE CATALYST

When the call for proposals went out there was considerable uncertainty over both the number and quality of the proposals that might be received. One member of the management committee felt that there might be a reasonable number of proposals from the former polytechnics as there was some history of action research projects within them. However, he doubted whether there would be many proposals from his own university as there was no history of project work, it had no scheme for teaching-development grants and it had only recently set up an educational development unit. He turned out to be pleasantly surprised when his university produced the greatest number of applications.

That a university with little history of encouraging any form of teaching-development initiative could produce a substantial body of proposals suggests that there must have been a substantial body of academics with a strong interest in teaching. Their interest and concern about particular issues must have been lying dormant, needing some catalyst to develop activity.

The existence of the Action Learning Project was a catalyst to initiate a project. Without its existence the interest or concern about a problem could easily have remained latent. The framework and impetus of the Action Learning Project was the spark that brought most of the projects to life.

The applicants for grants can be characterized as academics who were interested in their own teaching and motivated to introduce change. They were all potential activists who saw a teaching and learning need in their own setting but had not found a mechanism for addressing it. The Action Learning Project provided the appropriate framework and methodology. Several commented that it also provided both grants and recognition for research into teaching.

TIMETABLE

The grant for the overall project came through in about the middle of the second semester in the 1993/94 academic year. A commitment was made to distribute the initial round of grants in time for projects to commence at the start of the 1994/95 academic year. As a result of this decision it was necessary to work rapidly to establish an infrastructure for managing the project, liaising between institutions, communicating the concept of action learning to academics in all seven institutions, offering grants, receiving proposals, determining awards, dispersing grants and establishing a support mechanism.

Table 4.1 shows the sequence of steps and the timeframe. The timetable shows the major steps that were necessary to organize and carry out the project. Hopefully it will provide insights into the nature of the project and its activities. It gives a framework for understanding the subsequent parts of this book, which expand upon each facet of the project.

Table 4.1 Action Learning Project: timetable

Date	Overall	First Call for Proposals	Second Call for Proposals
04/94	Formation of management committee		
	Appointment of Acting Coordinator		
	Development of outline material		
05/94	Workshop for educational development staff	Promotional work within each institution	
06/94	Initial workshops at each institution	Call for proposals	
07/94		Award of funds to fully formed proposals	
		Consultation for promising proposals	
09/94	Appointment of 3 Associate Coordinators		
10/94	Appointment of Coordinator	Initial cycle begins	
11/94	Appointment of remaining 3 Associate Coordinators		Promotional work within each institution. call for proposals
01/95			Award of funds to proposals
02/95	Workshops on evaluation		

Table 4.1 Action Learning Project: timetable *(continued)*

Date	Overall	First Call for Proposals	Second Call for Proposals
02/95 to 06/95		Initial cycle for projects	
Summer 95		Interim report	Interim report (optional)
09/95	Workshops on evaluation	Reports due	Reports due
10/95		Second cycle begins	
09/95 to 06/96		Interest group meetings by project teams	Interest group meetings by project teams
06/96		End of projects – preparation of final reports	End of projects – preparation of final reports
06/96	Workshop for educational development staff		
10/96		Final report	Final report
11/96	Conference for project teams to present findings		
12/96		Revisions to final reports	Revisions to final reports
07/97	Final evaluation report		
09/97	Completion of collated case-study reports		

CONCLUSION

For those concerned with bringing about educational change, launching initiatives is probably the most difficult part of the role. When starting with an action research perspective it is particularly difficult, as studies need to be concerned with topics chosen by participants and ones they wish to tackle. However, potential activists often lie dormant because they are unsure how to tackle the potential issue, particularly if it also concerns others and making changes would imply working within a wider organizational system.

This chapter has dealt with initiating projects on an increasing scale, from individual initiatives to large groupings of projects under an organizational umbrella. Accompanying the increase in size is an implied growth in the need for resources. The individual initiatives may be undertaken with no additional resources at all, while the large umbrella projects require substantial funding.

At the individual-project and low-resource end of the scale, four mechanisms are suggested for initiating projects. Workshops explaining the action learning approach to bringing about educational change are useful as they explain a mechanism of which many potential activists might be unaware. For those in an educational development role, teachers who take advantage of consultation services can sometimes be persuaded to pursue projects designed to tackle issues raised as problematic. A related initiation strategy is that of treating new curriculum developments as action research projects. This can be particularly effective when the introduced curriculum has to deal with issues that are new to the department concerned. A final strategy is that of supervising a higher degree student whose project has an action research orientation concerned with an aspect of the student's teaching.

Potential facilitators who are successful in utilizing these strategies to initiate a number of projects are eventually likely to see the benefits of clustering together related projects. If projects are addressing related issues, deeper conclusions can be drawn by comparison and synthesis across projects. Bringing together participants also provides a mutual supporting environment.

The final parts of the chapter moved on to the more substantial cluster under the Action Learning Project umbrella. This did require substantial funding to set up and operate so such a project may well be out of reach of most readers. Lessons drawn from the operation of the project, though, would be applicable for smaller schemes which award grants for teaching development initiatives. Many universities now have such schemes and the evaluation of the Action Learning Project did reveal lessons for the operation of such schemes, which will be discussed in detail in the remainder of the book.

5

Organization

The original proposal for the Action Learning Project promised that the project would be inter-institutional and would encompass the seven UGC institutions. The UGC nominated the Hong Kong Polytechnic University (PolyU) as the coordinating institution, which meant that funding for the project was deposited with the PolyU, which assumed financial responsibility for the project. It was, therefore, necessary to develop an infrastructure and management model that reflected the inter-institutional nature of the project, but acknowledged the role of the PolyU as the coordinating institution.

MANAGEMENT COMMITTEE

To ensure its inter-institutional nature, the project was governed by a management committee. The membership of the management committee was constituted in such a way as to include representatives from all seven UGC institutions. It also included those who submitted the proposal to the UGC so as to incorporate their expertise within the committee.

The Chair of the management committee was from the PolyU. The Chair acted as a constitutional and administrative interface between the project, and its management committee, and the PolyU as the coordinating institution. The project, as far as possible, adopted practices compatible with those of the PolyU, while at the same time seeking to achieve its inter-institutional mission.

Meetings of the management committee

The full management committee met eight times during the first phase of the project. Initial meetings were concerned with establishing an appropriate infrastructure for the project and with making plans for its operation. As the project progressed, the meetings introduced an element of reporting and discussing progress.

At times it proved difficult to find a time-slot when a quorum of the management committee were available to attend a meeting. One meeting had to be postponed owing to a typhoon on the day the original meeting was scheduled. The committee adopted the practice of dealing with routine business by e-mail.

Sub-committees of the management committee also met to decide on the allocation of funds to proposals put to the Action Learning Project Fund and as appointment committees for the staff of the project.

STAFFING

The project had a full-time staff of a coordinator and six associate coordinators. Two of the associate coordinators left towards the end of the project's duration and were not replaced. All staff were appointed as staff of the PolyU but could be based at, or spend a portion of their time in, one or more of the other universities.

The coordinating team organized and administered the project with guidance from the management committee, as shown in Figure 5.1. Relationships with project teams were, therefore, maintained by the coordinating team. The nature of the support provided for project teams by the coordinating team is the subject of Part D.

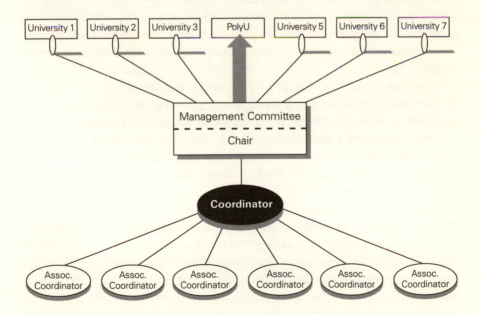

Figure 5.1 Action Learning Project: management and staffing

Information technology was used to reduce administrative overheads. One of the associate coordinators provided administrative support to the coordinator, but also operated a central service for the analysis of quantitative data. The project did not employ any secretarial or clerical assistance. Instead electronic mailing lists of project participants were built up and e-mail was used for all routine communications.

The project also made a conscious effort to reduce bureaucracy to a minimum, while still maintaining a necessary regulatory framework. The number of forms was kept to a minimum.

RELATIONSHIP WITH EDUCATIONAL DEVELOPMENT UNITS

Nearly all of the management committee were from units charged with improving the quality of teaching within institutions. These units had diverse titles, like their counterparts elsewhere. For convenience they will all be referred to as 'educational development units'.

Inviting senior members of these units to become members of the management committee was an attempt to ensure that the Action Learning Project would be able to work with and through such units. These units provided a channel through which the Action Learning Project was able to communicate with staff in the seven institutions.

In return the Action Learning Project resourced and supported projects within each institution. Its associate coordinators, who provided front-line support for projects, worked in conjunction with staff of educational development units and were, as far as possible, located within the respective unit.

The Action Learning Project also aimed to raise interest in initiatives to improve the quality of teaching and learning within each institution. If the ALP was to have any lasting impact it was desirable that these initiatives worked in concert with staff from these units. Accordingly the associate coordinators were, as far as possible, based within educational development units and worked with the staff of these units. Figure 5.2 shows the relationship in a stylized way.

The structure established for the organization of the Action Learning Project tried as far as possible to work within existing infrastructure. This was partly pragmatic, as building an entirely new structure would have been prohibitively expensive and time-consuming. More importantly, working through educational development units in each institution meant that the project developed a strong inter-institutional character.

There is also evidence in at least some of the universities that working through the educational development units built up relationships between

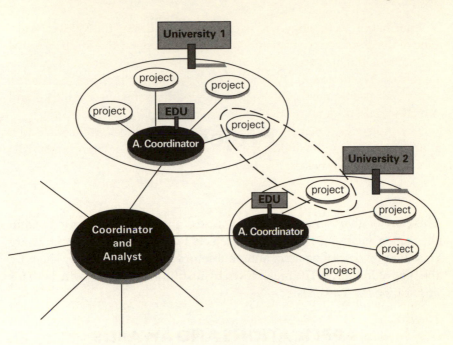

Figure 5.2 Coordinators and the educational development units

the staff of the units and those who participated in the projects. It seems likely that there will be an expectation of project-type activity in the future, which will be facilitated by staff from the educational development units. All of the universities now have some form of internal teaching-development grants. Some of the universities have drawn upon the experiences of the Action Learning Project to provide support to the project teams and to develop a mechanism for disseminating lessons from the projects.

6

Projects

This chapter gives some idea of the nature of the projects supported within the Action Learning Project. The projects that were awarded grants are classified by discipline area, and an attempt is made to classify them by the type of initiative. The breakdown by institution is also shown, both for applications and awards.

APPLICATIONS AND AWARDS

A total of 109 applications was received, 80 in response to the first call and 29 for the second. The much lower figure for the second round was because it was made clear that only a relatively small sum was still available, so both the number of grants awarded and the size of them would be lower than for the first call. Those who were awarded grants in the first round were also excluded from applying for a further grant.

Figure 6.1 shows the total number of applications received, by institution, in response to the two calls for proposals. The number of applications from the University of Hong Kong was well in excess of what would be expected, as it is only the fourth largest institution measured by student enrolment (Hong Kong Government Publications, 1996). Applications from the Polytechnic University were also somewhat on the high side, despite it being the largest institution. Applications from Lingnan College were on the low side, despite it having the lowest number of students.

Awards made

Altogether, 50 projects were awarded grants. After the first call for applications, 42 awards were made at the start of the 1994/95 academic year. Following the second call, six grants were awarded in February 1995 and a further two projects, having initially been placed on reserve, were awarded funds in late March 1995, when the availability of funding became clearer.

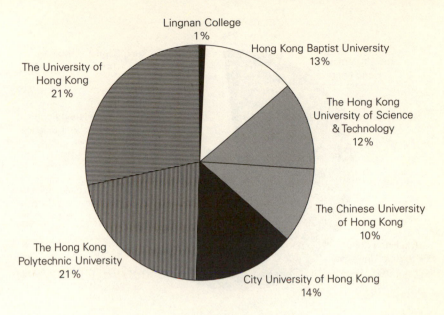

Figure 6.1 Action Learning Project: number of applications by institution

A number of applications, particularly in the first round, were designated for provisional acceptance. A grant was awarded conditional upon the applicant meeting specified conditions before agreed funds were released. The conditions were normally in the form of amendments to the proposal. Other applications were designated as being in reserve and proposers were requested to do a major revision of their proposal before it was further considered by the selection committee. Advice was available to applicants in each category as the management committee was committed to a formative development policy for proposals that showed promise but had some deficiencies.

Figure 6.2, which shows the proportion of the projects in each institution, can be contrasted with Figure 6.3, which shows the total value of the grants given to each institution.

While the PolyU received the greatest number of grants, three other institutions received larger sums. The largest grants tended to be awarded to multimedia development projects, since producing a worthwhile package of this kind needs a substantial investment. The PolyU had just one project in this category.

Distributing funds

Successful applicants were notified by letters containing a formal agreement, to be signed before funds were released. The agreement committed

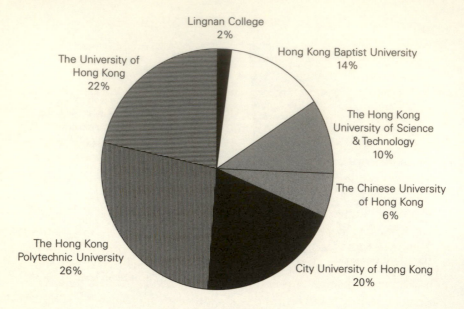

Figure 6.2 Action Learning Project: number of projects in each institution

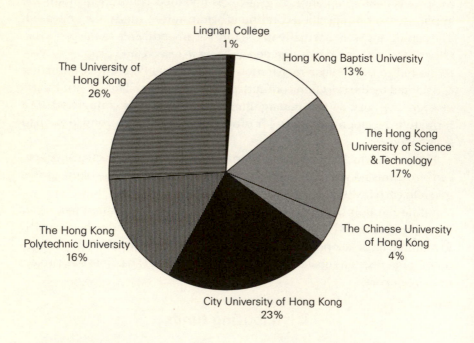

Figure 6.3 Action Learning Project: value of grants awarded to each institution

project teams to producing interim and final reports and participating in an interest group meeting and the final conference. There were other items concerning matters such as financial reporting.

Funds were distributed to project teams through the research offices in each institution. The Research and Postgraduate Study Office in the PolyU transferred the appropriate sum to each institution and requested their research or finance offices to open an account for each project. The institutions were informed, through a copy of the letter of offer, of the amounts to be allocated under appropriate budget headings for each project. The letter of offer prohibited transfer between budget headings without written permission from the coordinator.

Within institutions the procedures adopted for administering the grants were identical to those for external research grants. This procedure not only provided an efficient way for the Action Learning Project to administer projects across seven universities, but also contributed to the campaign to enhance the academic status of these teaching development activities. The mechanism for distributing funds meant that the projects were subject to the control mechanisms used by each institution for administering projects in receipt of internal or external research grants. It ensured that spending was within the specified limits and budget headings. The requirement to produce interim and final reports provided a formal check on progress.

A large proportion of the awarded grants was allocated for research assistants or student helpers. These were recruited through the normal procedures of the university to which the grant had been transferred. They were appointed as staff of that university, reporting to the project leader. In all other respects projects also followed the normal procedures and were subject to the same requirements as other research projects within the university. It was expected, though, that monitoring of progress would principally be the responsibility of the Action Learning Project rather than the university's research committee.

The procedure of transferring funds and hence grant administration to each of the participant universities enabled the ALP to administer each of its sub-projects in an efficient manner while ensuring accountability. Having the grants treated in the same way as external research grants helped in the quest for legitimizing teaching as a scholarly activity.

Figure 6.4 shows the division of projects by discipline area. English teaching and health sciences (including medicine) are well represented, while engineering and (even more so) science are somewhat under represented compared to their size in the universities.

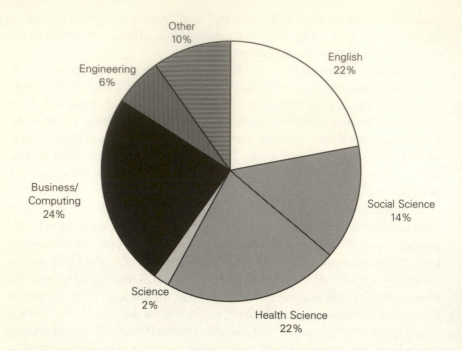

Figure 6.4 Action Learning Project: projects by discipline area

Type of initiative

The 50 projects were very diverse in respect of the nature of their innovation or initiative. Classification, therefore, was difficult, particularly as many of the projects had multiple aspects and so could be classified under a number of headings. Nevertheless a classification of the themes of the projects may be useful to the reader in identifying the range of topic areas covered, so one is attempted in Figure 6.5. For a more detailed view of individual projects, a list of titles is given in Appendix C.

The multimedia projects accounted for the largest single category. The proportion of such projects was, though, less than that in some comparable projects. The Australian Committee for the Advancement of University Teaching (CAUT) ran one of the largest schemes for awarding grants for teaching-development initiatives. In the 1996 academic year, for example, a pedagogical classification of their projects (CAUT, 1995: 65) put 73 in an 'information technology based' category, two were shown as 'internet applications' and seven as 'distance education'. Only 23 projects were in the remaining seven categories, so at least 78 per cent of the projects were information technology related. This is over three times the proportion of information technology based projects for the Action Learning Project.

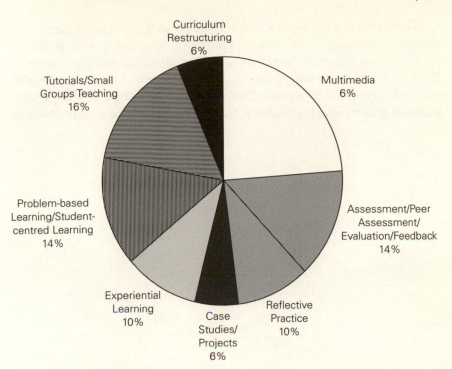

Figure 6.5 Action Learning Project: type of initiative

Some recent internal teaching development grant schemes in Hong Kong universities have also tended to be more technology based. This may be because of a developmental orientation to these projects, in contrast to the action learning orientation of the ALP.

CONCLUSION

For readers outside Hong Kong the most important implications of this chapter are the number and distribution of the applications, and the diversity of the nature of the projects. Applications came from all of the universities including those with no history whatsoever of engagement with action learning projects and at the time limited evidence of encouraging their academics to engage in teaching-development activities. Yet within a short period of time at the end of an academic year, a substantial number of applications were produced, with all universities well represented. This shows clearly that there were many academics who were strongly interested in their teaching and concerned about the learning of their students. It took the emergence of the Action Learning Project to catalyse the latent interest into direct action.

The diversity of the applications and the projects provides evidence that the action learning framework for enhancing teaching quality is widely applicable. Applications were received from all major discipline areas so there are no grounds for arguing that it is more suited to academics from particular types of discipline. The very diverse nature of the projects indicates that it provides a suitable framework for a wide variety of issues.

7

Dissemination of outcomes

The Action Learning Project made a significant commitment to the dissemination of lessons learnt from the projects it supported to a wider audience of academics in Hong Kong. The rationale was that others might modify their practices in the light of findings from the various projects. It was also hoped that this process would contribute to increasing interest in teaching and learning, and enhance the credibility of teaching as an academic activity.

SEMINAR SERIES ON RESEARCH INTO TEACHING AND LEARNING

A series of eight seminars on tertiary teaching and learning research in Hong Kong was held during the first year of the project. The aim was to acquaint those conducting projects, and others, with the extensive research into teaching and learning in Hong Kong. This was meant to provide attendees with a sound framework for conducting projects and interpreting data.

The series was open to all academics in Hong Kong and was widely advertised. Each seminar was held at two institutions so as to broaden the impact. Lunchtime was the chosen time-slot with the aim of minimizing conflicting commitments. The programme was quite well attended.

An annotated bibliography of research into tertiary teaching and learning in Hong Kong was produced to supplement the seminar series. A second edition and second print run proved necessary within a year, which gives some idea of both the level of research and the demand for the bibliography.

TRAINING PROGRAMME IN EVALUATION

The Action Learning Project, in conjunction with the EDU of the PolyU, mounted two series of workshops on the evaluation of teaching. These were open to both research assistants and academics. Participants could attend either individual modules or the whole series. The programme was changed slightly between the two series, but the modules for the latter series were:

- using closed questionnaires to evaluate teaching;
- classroom observation;
- using interviews as a qualitative evaluation method;
- skills in conducting interviews;
- assessing qualitative differences in student performance;
- analysis of qualitative data with computer software.

INTEREST GROUP MEETINGS

From the outset it was realized that some funded projects had common interests, by discipline area or type of project. During the initial round of meetings between the coordinating team and the project teams it became apparent that there was both interest and value in putting teams in touch with others with similar interests. This led to the 'matchmaking' facet of the coordinating role discussed in Chapter 14.

The most formal facet of this role was the interest group meetings. As part of the agreement for receiving a grant, project teams were asked to produce a short interim report after about one year of their project and to make a presentation of these findings. These presentations were organized along the lines of interest group meetings.

Interest groups were formed for the following topics:

- active learning;
- assessment;
- English-language teaching;
- multimedia projects;
- problem-based learning;
- reflective practice.

Relevant project teams were invited to present and discuss their interim findings at the meetings. Each session was held in conjunction with a relevant department or EDU-type unit to increase involvement. Each meeting was at a different university to increase impact. As with other dissemination activities, the meetings were open to those not participating in the Action Learning Project.

A list-serve mailing list was compiled for the multimedia group in an effort to promote discussion outside the formal meetings. The list was built up from those engaged in multimedia projects with the Action Learning Project, plus others who were on various university-specific lists. In total over 150 names were on the list. The list-serve was not monitored so all on the list were free to post messages and comments.

This was the one dissemination activity that was not successful. Initial seeding messages were placed on the list-serve by the coordinator and two multimedia specialists in EDU-type units. The response was a deadly electronic silence – not one other message was posted. Possibly there are now so many discussion networks that those on the list saw no need to become involved with yet another.

CONFERENCE

The main Action Learning Project conference was held on Saturday 30 November 1996 at the Polytechnic University, Hong Kong. The conference had two plenary sessions. There was an opening keynote address by Don Anderson, the inaugural Chair of the Australian Government Committee for the Advancement of University Teaching. The final plenary session consisted of a report on the project by the evaluation panel of John Biggs and Raymond Lam.

The remainder of the conference was devoted to the conference teams giving the final reports on their projects. To allow each team 40 minutes for presentation and discussion, there were eight parallel sessions. These were grouped along the lines of the interest group meetings discussed above.

The conference was open to all academics in Hong Kong and there was extensive advertising to try to attract a wide audience. There was no registration fee but intending participants were asked to register so that catering could be planned and adequate-size rooms arranged. A total of 343 participants registered for the conference. The breakdown by institution is shown in Figure 7.1.

By no means all of the registrants attended the entire day of the conference but, by monitoring the collection of name tags and observing the number in the various rooms, it was estimated that over 300 attended at least part of the conference. Overall the parallel sessions were better attended than the two plenary ones. No formal evaluation of the conference was performed as there was no certainty that another similar event would be held in the near future. Informal feedback from those attending, though, suggested that the conference had succeeded in generating considerable discussion about innovative approaches to teaching. The substantial attendance and the associated publicity suggest that the conference must have raised the consciousness of Hong Kong academics towards teaching as a legitimate scholarly activity.

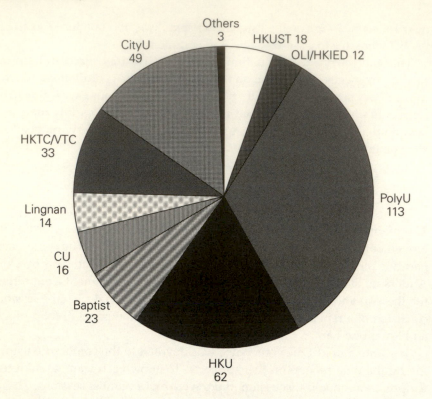

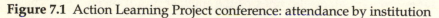

Figure 7.1 Action Learning Project conference: attendance by institution

PRINTED MATERIALS

A set of booklets was produced about action research and evaluation methods. These were mostly used to provide help in the initial formulation of proposals and in the early stages of projects.

The interim reports submitted by the teams were collated together in a booklet and distributed widely around the seven Hong Kong universities. Before producing the booklet all reports were refereed, revised if necessary and edited for style and consistency. The intention was to use the reports as exemplars of good practice, so it was seen as important that all the reports included were of high quality.

A similar process was used to prepare a collected volume of the final reports. These were based upon papers that were first presented at the conference. The authors were given a chance to revise their papers after the conference in the light of any discussion, though not many took advantage of the option. All reports were then refereed and edited. The collated volume was a very substantial collection, which was widely distributed within Hong Kong (Kember, Lam, Yan, Yum and Liu, 1997).

WEB SITE

Before the conference an Action Learning Project Web site was started. Information about the conference, abstracts and conference papers were placed on the site. The intention was to make this information available to participants prior to the conference without the logistical difficulties of producing, printing and distributing them on paper.

For the second phase of the project greater use was made of the site. The information in the booklets, mentioned above, was available there. The conference papers from the first round were a valuable resource for those drawing up proposals and eventually beginning projects, designing evaluation and writing up the outcomes.

Having the material available on the Web dispensed with the need to produce extensive print-runs of booklets and distribute them firstly to each participating university and then within each university. This removed the need for a lot of lifting and transportation of heavy boxes of booklets.

The intention is to continue to maintain the Web site as a resource for anyone wishing to initiate an action learning project. The address is http://alp.polyu.edu.hk.

IMPORTANCE

It would have been possible to operate the Action Learning Project without any of the dissemination activities. It is clear that had the project been run in this way that many of the most significant outcomes would have been sacrificed.

The interest group meetings and the less formal contact between those involved in similar projects often resulted in one project influencing another. These contacts could provide mutual support for what was a new venture for most of the participants.

Having the dissemination activities meant that the lessons learnt from the projects were not restricted to those participating in the projects. Passing on the lessons meant that other teachers could make similar changes to their own teaching. This dissemination process was conducted in a scholarly way, providing evidence that researching into one's own teaching is a legitimate scholarly activity.

PART C
PERCEPTIONS AND EXPERIENCES OF PARTICIPANTS

David Kember, Tak Shing Ha, Bick-har Lam, April Lee, Sandra Ng, Louisa Yan and Jessie C K Yum

This part of the book deals with the experiences of the participants in the projects supported by the Action Learning Project. It is both an account of what it was like to be involved in a project and an evaluation of the experience and the outcomes that resulted.

The Action Learning Project adopted a three-level evaluation design, as explained in Chapter 8. At the individual project level, teams were responsible for evaluating their own projects, consistent with an action research philosophy of encouraging participants to become self-reflective and empowered to take responsibility for monitoring and improving the quality of their own teaching. An external panel was appointed to provide a more objective evaluation of the overall project at the macro-level.

This book draws mainly on the third level of evaluation by the coordinating team. Through their active involvement from the conception of the project, they were best placed to give a reflective account of it. Again following an action research approach to evaluation, it was appropriate to draw from these experiences, and those of the participants, lessons for conducting educational development through action research in other contexts. Data were gathered through a questionnaire to all participants and interviews with eight teams. The reflections of the coordinating team and project participants were also an integral data source.

In Chapter 9 the overwhelming motive for becoming involved in the projects was a desire to improve the quality of their own teaching and their students' learning. The participants had had a latent interest in a topic or a concern about a particular problem. The Action Learning Project framework provided the catalyst for the latent concern to become action.

In Chapter 10 the participants recognized that developing effective teamwork was an important element in the success of the projects. The types of teams that evolved are examined, together with the mechanisms for developing effective collaboration and communication. Discovering a competent research assistant, who soon became a part of the team, was seen to be of importance to the projects.

In Chapter 11 the teams seemed to fit naturally into the action research cycle of planning, acting, observing and reflecting. The participants clearly came to recognize the importance and value of reflecting upon their practice. Project teams found that the action research cycle provided a suitable framework for introducing and evaluating educational innovations. The process of participation and what was learnt from that process were seen as one of the most important outcomes of the initiative.

Chapter 12 reports that, from the perception of the participants, the projects were highly successful in influencing teaching and student learning for the better. Most felt that there would be a lasting effect upon the courses they taught but they were less certain whether there would be an impact upon departmental colleagues. Many expressed the view that their efforts to improve teaching and learning were not given the recognition they deserved by their universities.

8

Evaluation design

This part of the book and the following two parts draw upon the evaluation data for the Action Learning Project. To make sense of the data and their interpretation, it is necessary to know how the data were gathered and analysed. The data-gathering processes followed from an evaluation design based upon an explicit philosophy developed from the commitment to action research. The design itself may be of interest to other substantial projects with sub-projects.

This chapter, then, outlines the design for the evaluation of the Action Learning Project. It explains the philosophy behind the evaluation and how data were collected. It should be noted that this book reports only a part of the evaluation of the project.

EVALUATION BY LEVELS OF PROJECT

Overall, the Action Learning Project encompassed 50 projects, each dealing with a range of issues, so altogether there were numerous questions to examine. There were over 100 academics actively involved and several thousand students directly affected. These individuals and their projects together constituted a complex loosely structured organization which itself needed to be evaluated. The evaluation design needed to deal with the magnitude and complexity of the project.

To make some sense of the whole it was necessary to see it as composed of a number of parts. The most appropriate division seemed to be by level within the structure of the overall project. At the base of the pyramid were the individual projects, which were the core of the whole enterprise. Each project was a distinct entity with its own focus, topic and issues to be addressed, so each project had to be evaluated individually.

With a substantial set of projects operating under an explicit methodological framework, it seemed reasonable to anticipate that it might be possible to draw more general conclusions across some or all of the projects. The original evaluation design, therefore, included two meta-project levels.

The first grouped projects by similar discipline areas or topics using the interest group categories outlined in Chapter 7. It was thought that there might be some differences perhaps in the way that those in different disciplines reacted to the reflective action research approach or in how applicable the action research methodology was to different types of initiative. It turned out that such effects within these groupings of projects were hard to detect. Any group effects by discipline that did exist were largely masked by the variations between individual projects. In drawing conclusions, therefore, little use was made of the interest-group level of analysis.

The aggregated level of all of the individual projects was important. It was possible to draw many valuable conclusions through comparison and synthesis across the projects. The material in this part of the book is largely from this level of the evaluation.

The final level of evaluation was that of the Action Learning Project as a whole. The evaluation at this level looked at the organization of the project and the method of providing support, with the aim of drawing conclusions about how project-type quality enhancement initiatives are best organized and run. This level of evaluation also considered questions about the viability of the action research approach to quality enhancement of learning and teaching.

Figure 8.1 shows these levels within the evaluation design for the project.

MULTIPLE VOICES

As well as reflecting the multiple levels of the project, the evaluation design needed to draw upon the multiple voices or perspectives of the many

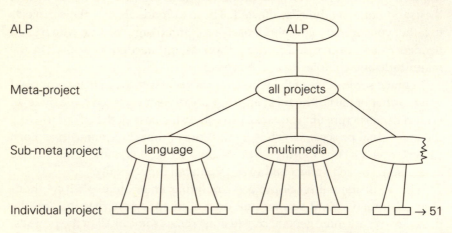

Figure 8.1 Action Learning Project: levels of evaluation

people involved. Directly involved were the students in the classes targeted by the initiatives, the members of the project teams, the coordinating team and the members of the management committee, most of whom were also affected through their position in an educational development unit. Less directly affected were those in the departments in which the projects were taking place.

Drawing upon these different perspectives introduced the element of multiple-voice triangulation, which was explained in Chapter 3. In action research projects it is seen as good practice to triangulate across both multiple methods and multiple perspectives.

MULTIPLE LEVELS BY MULTIPLE VOICES

In terms of the overall design, the various voices seemed to relate to particular levels of the project discussed above. The Action Learning Project, therefore, adopted a multiple-level by multiple-voice design. Each category of those involved was asked to play a part in evaluating the level of the project most pertinent to their involvement.

Project level

From the time of the original proposal for funding there was always a very clear commitment to requiring the project teams to take responsibility for evaluating their own individual projects. The commitment followed axiomatically from the framework of the initiative in action research. If the evaluation of the projects had been conducted by anyone other than the participants, the entire theoretical foundation of the method of quality enhancement would have been undermined.

Asking the project teams to take responsibility for evaluating their projects also implied a commitment to them acquiring the ability to do so. Advice and support were available from the coordinating team to enable them to conduct a proficient evaluation. This in turn was envisaged as an important outcome of the project. If the academics learnt how to evaluate and research their own teaching and recognized the value of doing so, there was the possibility that they would continue to take responsibility for monitoring the quality of their students' learning beyond the completion of the projects.

Involving the project teams in evaluating their own teaching also brought the student voice into the evaluation design. The evaluations of the individual projects all sought feedback from students through means such as interviews and questionnaires. The students may have been unaware of the Action Learning Project as a whole, but they were aware that something was happening in the target courses and it is hard to see how an evaluation design could have been seen as complete without their opinion.

Internal or external evaluation

Before considering the remaining levels of the project and evaluation design, it is first necessary to deal with the question of whether evaluation should be internal or external. Should it be conducted by those participating in it or should it be evaluated by some external agency?

At the individual project level, the action research nature of the individual initiatives dictated an internal approach of evaluation by the project teams. Further justification for this decision was the desire for the participants to become experienced in evaluating their own teaching.

At the overall level the decision was less straightforward. In evaluating a large project there is a tension between internal and external evaluation. Internal evaluators have the considerable advantage of being immersed in the project and, therefore, acquiring considerable insight and knowledge about it. However, internal evaluations can lack credibility because it might seem to be in the interests of those involved that the project is seen as successful.

External evaluators would find it hard to obtain a full and accurate picture of such a large and complex project unless they spent considerable time with those involved – in which case much of the external credibility disappears. Extensive evaluation by academics from outside the coordinating team would also be expensive and counter-productive as high levels of payments to evaluators would diminish their credibility, as they could be seen as having a stake in the project.

The Action Learning Project took the reasonable compromise of dividing the responsibility for the evaluation according to the levels within the project and the questions appropriate at each level. This decision added further weight to the multiple-level and multiple-voice triangulation.

Coordinating team

The case for making the project teams responsible for evaluating their own projects has been argued above. There was a similar logic to involving the coordinating team in evaluating the projects at the meta-project level and of addressing some issues at the overall project level. The Action Learning Project was itself an action research project. This book reports what was learnt from the action research project of establishing and running the Action Learning Project.

Each associate coordinator had responsibility for assisting a number of projects. The team as a whole was intimately involved with every facet of the project's operation. They, therefore, developed insights into questions such as which factors contribute to making projects successful and how support can most usefully be provided.

The involvement of the coordinating team ensured that the evaluation contained a reflective narrative of the project. In understanding such a large and complex initiative it was essential that the evaluation was accompanied by an account of what took place. This participative and reflective style of evaluation was consistent with the action research stance of the project.

The coordinating team were best placed to compile an account of the project. This description was compiled from sources such as reflective journals, experiential accounts, reports, discussion papers and agenda items for management committee meetings. The coordinating team were also well placed to gather accounts and opinions of the project from stakeholder groups, such as project participants, seminar attendees, staff in EDU-type units, senior administrators and academic staff. It was felt that an evaluation by the coordinating team, addressing these issues, should have credibility.

Evaluation panel

The evaluation panel consisted of John Biggs and Raymond Lam. At the time John Biggs had recently retired from the position of Professor of Education at the University of Hong Kong. He has an international reputation as one of the leading researchers into student learning. Raymond Lam is also from the University of Hong Kong and specializes in evaluation. Their brief was to address issues, such as the effectiveness and impact of the project, for which an evaluation by the coordinating team might lack credibility. The main audience for its report was seen as the UGC, which provided the funding for the project, and would wish to know that this funding had been well spent.

Interim and final case-study reports by the project teams were given to the evaluation panel as soon as they became available. Similarly the panel was given both data collected and reports prepared by the coordinating team.

The evaluation panel also collected its own data, primarily through interviews, with a sample of project leaders, members of the coordinating team and other relevant figures. John Biggs visited Hong Kong three times to gather and analyse data. Assistance to produce interview transcripts was provided.

The evaluation panel investigated, assessed and commented upon the calibre of the evaluations conducted at other levels by the project teams and the coordinating team. In particular the quality of the evaluations conducted by the project teams on their projects was examined through perusal of the submitted case studies and a limited number of interviews with project leaders.

The evaluation panel reported its initial conclusions in a keynote address by John Biggs and Raymond Lam at the Action Learning Project conference in November 1996. At that stage the report concentrated largely on 'process', making use of data gathered in the previous visit.

After the conference a set of final project reports was given to the evaluation panel, together with summaries of outcomes and the report by the coordinating team. The panel was then able to properly examine the project from a product perspective. Its report was included as an independent part of a report to the UGC on the overall project.

The division by level and voice

The division of responsibility for evaluation between the project teams, the coordinating team and the evaluation panel was a function of these levels of operation within the Action Learning Project. The divisions of responsibility are explained in Table 8.1. The table suggests a methodology and responsibility for each level.

The division by level and voice was then further elaborated by specifying evaluation questions or issues for each level by voice cell. These questions are shown in Table 8.1, which shows that different questions are applicable at each level.

APPROACHES TO EVALUATION DESIGN

The decision to structure the evaluation design by this multiple-level and multiple-voice design can be justified against prevailing evaluation theory in the literature. In considering evaluation design, it is important to appreciate that there are many different models of evaluation framed by differing perspectives and paradigms. The extent of these differing approaches to evaluation can be demonstrated by the existence of books and encyclopaedias which discuss a range of models (eg Walberg and Haertel, 1990; Worthen and Sanders, 1987). These compendiums typically report, within the space of a chapter, models of evaluation that were originally propounded at book length by their initial advocates.

Clearly, any discussion of how the evaluation design discussed in this chapter fits with the alternative approaches needs to take a condensed view of alternative approaches to evaluation. This seems to be worth attempting, though, in an effort to convince the reader that the evaluation method was

Table 8.1 Action Learning Project: responsibility for evaluation, by level and voice

Level	Questions	Who Asked?	Method	Responsibility
Individual project	Aims of project → evidence that aims were met? Evidence that quality of teaching and learning improved?	Students	Diverse: related to project aims	Project teams responsible for evaluating own projects
Sub-meta-project	Were there differences in project outcome by category of project? How effective were the differing dissemination strategies for each category?	Project leaders/ teams/ students (indirectly)	Perusal of project reports and case studies	Coordinating team
Meta-project	What does a successful action research project look like? How do variables impinge upon the success of projects? For example – experience/expertise of participants – support of colleagues/department/hd of dept/coordinating team/ administration – attitude of colleagues and students – initial experiences. Motivation for participating in project/applying for grant? Research ↔ teaching nexus? Did teaching improve? Did attitude to teaching change (self and/or colleagues)? What lessons can be passed on about organizing and supporting educational action research projects?	Project leaders/ teams/ students (indirectly)/ administrators	Questionnaires/ interview with sample of project leaders and team members/ perusal of project reports and case studies	Coordinating team
ALP	Is action research an appropriate concept for improving the quality of teaching and learning? Was the ALP an effective implementation of the concept? What lessons can be passed on about the use of educational action research as a quality enhancement mechanism? Does this method of educational development appear to offer reasonable returns compared to alternative measures for quality control or enhancement?	Project leaders/ coordinators/ administrators	Interviews/ perusal of project reports and reports of coordinating team	Evaluation panel

justifiable and that the conclusions drawn from the data are, therefore, reasonable and valid.

Perhaps the most succinct and most easily assimilated way to explain alternative approaches to evaluation is to equate them to paradigms for research methodology as outlined in Chapter 1. This should be a readily acceptable position since the research paradigms, evaluation methods and, indeed, curriculum development models were developed in parallel and drew upon a similar literature base.

The evaluation design for the Action Learning Project had aspects that should be attributed to both the critical paradigm and the interpretive one. This should be seen as perfectly logical as, in Chapter 1, the approach to quality enhancement had been attributed predominantly to the critical position, with some influence from the interpretive paradigm. An evaluation design could only be harmonious with the overall philosophy of the project if it was derived from the same paradigmatic position.

Critical influence

The most significant part of the design attributable to a critical position was the insistence that the participants took responsibility for evaluating their own projects. In terms of the characteristics of action research given in Chapter 2, the most pertinent one, in this respect, is the participative nature. The participants were encouraged to feel a sense of ownership of their projects and to take responsibility for all facets of them. The coordinating team made it clear that they were supporters and advisers rather than directors.

The Action Learning Project operated with an action research philosophy. It was consistent with an action research approach that individual projects were evaluated by those involved in the projects. Such responsibility helped participants develop their abilities to evaluate their own teaching. Hopefully, it also contributed to developing a climate in which academics saw it as their responsibility regularly to reflect upon and evaluate their own teaching. Imposing external evaluations upon projects was seen as contrary to these aims.

The involvement of the coordinating team in the evaluation of the overall project can also be seen as following a critical influence. The Action Learning Project can be seen as their action research project into how to organize and support action learning initiatives that aim to enhance the quality of teaching and student-learning outcomes. If a critical paradigm is accepted they should be the main actors in evaluating that project.

Naturalistic stance

Many of the evaluations of the individual projects also took on some aspects of a naturalistic approach. There are several variants of naturalistic evaluation but Worthen and Sanders (1987) believed that such evaluations generally include the following four characteristics:

1. They depend on inductive reasoning rather than sticking rigidly to a design drawn up at the outset.
2. They make use of a multiplicity of data from a number of sources.
3. They do not follow a standard plan.
4. They record multiple rather than single realities.

The first of these characteristics was not universally followed as most project teams did draw up an initial evaluation design. However, many found that both the plans for the project and the evaluation design needed modification as the project progressed in the light of what was learnt on the way.

All of the projects used more than one data-gathering technique and most made use of a number of sources. There was certainly no standard plan for the evaluation of the projects. The topics for the projects were so diverse that each needed an individually designed plan. It would also be reasonable to claim that all project teams recorded multiple realities. Most teams realized from the outset that they were dealing with complex ill-defined issues and so approached them with a wide-angled perspective. Those that did not soon came to recognize the multiple realities and adjusted their focus accordingly.

There was also a naturalistic character to the other levels of evaluation. Stake's (1976) countenance model was one of the first and most influential contributions to the theory of naturalistic evaluation. Stake argued that the two fundamental components of an evaluation should be description and judgement. The description of the project was seen as important and the participants and the coordinating team were in the best position to provide a good description. Complex projects, particularly those which break new ground, need a detailed and vivid portrayal of the project for the reader to make any sense of what it was all about. It makes no sense to judge whether something is successful if the reader has little understanding of what was being judged.

There is, though, a need for judgement so that the reader can come to some conclusion about the worth of the venture. Again, the way a judgement was approached needed to reflect the nature of the project as a substantial initiative with many actors, each with their own sets of goals. Measuring the attainment of these goals was neither feasible nor likely to be useful. A more feasible position was that of taking an illuminative approach (Parlett and Hamilton, 1976) in which the evaluation attempted to reach a broad understanding of the project as a whole. This would encompass the revealing of achievements and difficulties as well as providing a triangulated set of data to allow the reader to make sensible judgements as to the value of the initiative.

DATA COLLECTION

All known participants in projects were asked to complete a questionnaire in late April 1996. The questionnaire had both closed- and open-ended questions. Responses to closed-response items were completed on optical mark reader forms for ease of processing. The open-ended part asked for some demographic information. Questionnaires were distributed by mail. The questionnaire is included in Appendix A.

The questionnaire was distributed to 110 academics listed as participants in projects in the original grant applications. After an initial mailing and a reminder, usable responses were received from 72 participants. This represents a 65 per cent response rate, which would be considered reasonable for most surveys, but is particularly good for academics, who can be notoriously unwilling to return questionnaires. The return rate may even be somewhat higher than that indicated as some of those listed on grant applications appear to have played little or no active role in the projects.

At about the same time, eight project teams were randomly selected for an interview. All active members of the team were interviewed together as a group. Interviews were conducted by an associate coordinator who had not been involved with the project. The interview schedule is included in Appendix B. The interview questions on the schedule indicated broad areas of interest. They served as initial prompts for an open discussion. The interviews were tape-recorded and a full transcript produced.

The questionnaire and interview schedule were designed by the coordinating team. The evaluation panel were invited to comment upon and add questions to both the questionnaire and the interview schedule.

There was some potential for overlap between the evaluations of the coordinating team and the evaluation panel, as both had access to the questionnaire and interview data. However, the two approached the data from different perspectives and with different questions in mind. The evaluation panel approached the data with greater objectivity and could address issues of comparability, performance and impact.

The coordinating team had the experience of intensive participation in the project so they could triangulate the gathered data with their reflections upon these experiences. The outcome was a narrative of the project with reflective insights and conclusions for the practice of others. The concern was to adopt a naturalistic (Simon, 1987; Williams, 1988; Scriven, 1991), rather than an objective, approach to the design of our evaluation. The philosophy of action research recognizes that evaluation is process-orientated and itself enhances reflection. The holistic descriptions and the theories produced by this evaluation serve to illuminate understanding and also hopefully yield insights and learning that can be usefully applied in different circumstances by others.

ANALYSIS

Responses to the questionnaire were analysed by the simple technique of counting the frequency of responses in each category. These are presented in consistent graphical form. Figure 9.1 is typical and illustrates analysis of the responses to questions 2 to 7. Note that the caption alongside each bar chart is a shortened version of the item on the questionnaire. The full version of the relevant question is given in Appendix A, and was included in the accompanying text of the report if wording seemed important.

Responses to the open-ended questions on the questionnaire were typed into a computer. Verbatim transcripts of the interviews with the eight randomly selected project teams were produced and given to the teams for checking. Final transcripts were combined with the open-ended responses in a consolidated NUD•IST (QSR NUD•IST, 1997; Richards and Richards, 1991) database.

The qualitative dataset was then analysed by looking for the main themes that emerged. Categories within these were coded using the NUD•IST hierarchical coding structure.

Typical quotations were used within the text to illustrate themes that emerged from the analysis. Other quotations came from the journals or reflective writing of the coordinating team or other participants in the project.

SUMMARY

The evaluation design for the project had several features that might be incorporated within designs for other large projects. Responsibility, methods and questions were devised within a multiple-level by multiple-voice framework. The levels ranged from that of the individual projects to the Action Learning Project as a whole. The principal voices were the participants in the projects and their students, the coordinating team and the management committee. The framework aimed to ensure that appropriate voices responded to pertinent questions at each level within the project. The design also employed multiple methods to ask the questions so that triangulation was possible.

The approach used within the levels was consistent with the action research philosophy of the Action Learning Project. Those participating in the projects were expected to take responsibility for evaluating their own individual projects. At the overall project level the coordinating team played a part in evaluating their action research project into how best to organize and support schemes for clusters of action research initiatives. The design also encompassed an external evaluation panel to provide a perspective that might be seen as more objective for questions concerning the effectiveness of the venture.

9

Aims

This chapter looks at the aims that the participants set for participating in their projects. It, therefore, examines their reasons or motivations for becoming involved in this type of quality enhancement activity.

MOTIVATION

The approach to the project and the outcomes sought are likely to be governed by the reason for taking it on. The initial part of this chapter, therefore, deals with the motivations for participation. In questions 2 to 7, the questionnaire suggested six possible motives for becoming engaged in a project and asked respondents to agree or disagree with them. Figure 9.1 quantifies the responses to these questions.

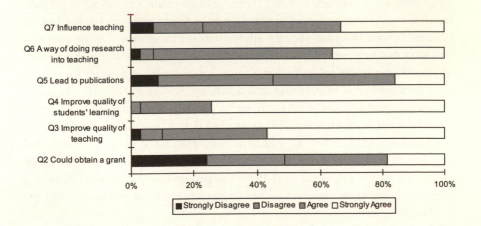

Figure 9.1 Action Learning Project: motivation for participation

The highest level of agreement, almost to the point of unanimity, was for the motivation to improve student learning. There were also very high levels of agreement that improving and influencing teaching were important. Presumably most respondents saw the two going together, judging by the similarly high ratings.

Slightly over half of the respondents saw publications and obtaining a grant as motivating factors. Interestingly, though, far more saw doing research into teaching as a motivation. This, presumably, implies that the participants recognized that researching their own teaching was an ideal way to improve the quality of their students' learning.

Concern for teaching

The responses to these particular questions are a rejoinder to those who have a vision of academics as interested only in research and seeing teaching largely as a distraction from their research. It is abundantly clear that this vision is far from true of the participants in the Action Learning Project.

They can obviously not be taken as a representative sample of Hong Kong academics as they had made an application to be involved. However, there were also a substantial number of applications that were not funded.

Internal teaching development grant schemes in Hong Kong now attract numerous applications. A recent call for proposals for internal teaching development grants within the Polytechnic University resulted in 85 proposals, seeking in total over four times the available sum. The institution has about 1,000 full-time academics so the proportion of staff involved in the submissions is quite significant, particularly since most of the proposals were from more than one person. There were also others involved in projects funded from money awarded directly to departments and a further 30 proposals were received shortly afterwards for funding of larger, external teaching development grants. The number of proposals suggesting ways of improving teaching indicates a substantial body of academics with a very strong interest in teaching and a concern for their students' learning.

They would appear to be far from alone in this position. The first two rounds of applications for grants from CAUT in Australia resulted in 1,062 proposals (CAUT, 1994: 8). There would also have been a substantial number that did not reach the committee since all proposals had to be subjected to an approval and ranking process within the originating university. Some universities would undoubtedly have not forwarded the weaker proposals.

Boyer (1990) reported a major survey of US academics conducted by the Carnegie Foundation for the Advancement of Teaching. Seventy per cent of all respondents indicated that their interest lay primarily in teaching rather than research (Boyer, 1990: 44). Four of the five categories of university showed a majority for teaching. Similarly, 62 per cent of all respondents agreed with the statement that teaching effectiveness should be the primary criterion for promotion of faculty (Boyer, 1990: 32). However, their universities appeared to take little notice of these opinions as the academics clearly perceived that the most important factors in granting tenure were publications, research grants and research reputations, particularly in the three more prestigious categories of university or college (Boyer, 1990: 30).

Ramsden and Martin (1996) reported the results from a large survey of academics in six typical Australian universities. The questionnaire asked respondents to indicate the extent to which they felt teaching and research should be valued and were valued in their university. The results may be interpreted as showing that the academics felt that both teaching and research were important, as 95 per cent felt that teaching should be highly valued and 90 per cent agreed that research should. However, there was a marked difference in how they felt their institution regarded the two activities, as 84 per cent thought that research was highly valued but only 37 per cent perceived teaching to be valued.

Taken together, this evidence suggests that if there is any tendency for academics to concentrate upon research at the expense of teaching, it does not in the main arise from the inclination of the academics themselves. To the contrary, the evidence suggests that many, and possibly most, academics view teaching as a highly important part of their role. That many academics apply to schemes such as the Action Learning Project and the CAUT scheme indicates that not only is teaching taken seriously but there is a widespread desire to engage in time-consuming activities to enhance the quality of the courses they teach and the learning outcomes of their students.

The evidence of this mismatch, between how academics feel teaching ought to be valued and how they perceive their universities do value it, suggests that any pressures to concentrate upon research rather than teaching emanate from either university management or at the system level. In many countries it would appear that the two are acting in concert and there is often a suspicion of either mismatches between espoused theory and theory in use or of unintentional outcomes resulting from lack of compatibility between quality assurance procedures for research and teaching.

The government-appointed bodies which administer university systems must be concerned with the quality of teaching, as most have introduced system-wide processes for reviewing or assuring the quality of teaching. Many, though, have undermined their own teaching review processes with the parallel research review procedures, which appear to be accorded greater weight because they have disproportionate influence upon funding.

In both Australia and the UK, for example, reviews of teaching quality are taken seriously because they can have an influence upon student intakes. They must have some impact upon reputations, as highly rated universities are always proud to publicize results that cast them in a good light. If a university or a department are highly rated for the quality of teaching, though, they receive little direct financial benefit from the rating.

By contrast, the research rankings in the two countries can make very substantial differences to the funding received by a university. Departments or universities judged to be in the lower ranking levels are awarded little or no research funding. Those in the top echelons receive the major portion of the available research funds, which amount to substantial sums of money. Those receiving the major part of the funding will inevitably be better placed for the next review exercise as they can use the extra funding to produce still more research output.

Clearly these distinctions must influence vice-chancellors and department heads. If high research ratings attract significant amounts of extra funding while high teaching ratings produce little direct benefit, there is little incentive to accord teaching the same priority as research. The funding distinction is magnified by the greater prestige normally accorded to the research rankings. The traditional ways of ranking or according status to universities are based upon indicators of research output and reputation. Boyer (1990), for example, classifies US colleges into five categories based upon research and higher-degree granting status, even though his book was a plea for a broader interpretation of scholarship. Many would interpret research rankings as being more important than those for teaching even for attracting student enrolments.

The prestige factor must further influence the actions of many vice-chancellors and department heads. The head of a university naturally wants their institution to be perceived as having a good reputation. As research status is the traditional measure of prestige and status there must be a temptation for many to see research as a priority. Such a position would be compatible with their earlier careers since there are few senior managers in universities who do not have good research records.

Evidence for the desire for higher status for institutions comes from the many cases of institutions elevating their status. Over the past few years many colleges or polytechnics have become universities. Institutions that offered the majority of programmes at sub-degree level now frequently offer mainly degrees and higher degrees. If there are institutions that have deliberately aimed for a lower market niche they are certainly hard to recall.

The conclusion of this section questions the view that academics tend to neglect their teaching because their principal interest lies in their research. If there is any tendency for teaching to take second place behind research, it is more likely to be because of pressure from department heads, vice-chancellors and university system administrators, rather than the preference of the individual academics. A fundamental cause of the pressure must be the funding associated with research review schemes.

Learning and teaching issues

The more detailed accounts given by the project teams in the interviews offer illumination of the quantitative results. When asked to describe what stimulated them to start their project, all teams within the interviewed sample reported some sort of teaching and learning problem they were facing in their own context. The issues mentioned can largely be divided into four categories.

The first one was student motivation. Several teams found their students lacked motivation to learn the subject the team taught because it was either a non-major requirement or a foreign language to which the students found difficulty relating:

> When you learn a language like German or French here in Hong Kong, it is something you really do not connect a real-world thing with. It is the subject matter. It takes a long time to understand and realize that this is a spoken language for the purpose of communication.

Another problem was a conceptual gap featured in the students' under-standing of the subject matter. Students studying information science didn't understand what their teachers were talking about during class because they didn't have relevant experience to help them imagine the application of database designs to solve practical office problems.

> Then we discovered one of the biggest problems in students' learning was that they had no working experience. Very often they didn't understand what we were talking about. For example, when we described the various offices and the order processing, they had absolutely no idea. They might just sit there and take a passive role. Thus, we had the idea to make an office interface. It will enable the student to 'walk' into an office and see how it looks. Then they needn't imagine the office by themselves. They can walk through the various departments and click the objects to see what information they contain. This will be more like a real office situation. So we do research along this line of thought and try to see how we can use such kind of metaphor to help students learn. And we took the Action Learning grant to try this out.

The third problem was related to teaching approaches. Two teams claimed that the conventional methods were obsolete and greatly in need of improvement. An example here had its focus on fieldwork training. The old way of training supervisors and then letting them instruct the students during their fieldwork was found inadequate in facilitating students' adjustment to the new learning environment:

> I notice there are some difficulties in students learning. For example, they have problems in adaptation at the beginning. This hinders their learning because they are not familiar with the environment and interpersonal communication. They need time to stabilize in the placement organization. They can only learn after they get used to the environment. Sometimes, there are problems in the cooperation between the supervisors, students and the organizations. At first, we thought these are only particular problems. But I can see that the action learning project may help us to collect some data to see whether there are some patterns existing.

The last problem concerned assessment issues. For example, one project team found that students in their department knew nothing about how their projects were assessed. This seriously curtailed their opportunities to learn about the criteria of a good product and develop their commitment to learning:

> We found out that assessment will have a major influence on students' approaches to learning and also their outcomes. Previously the assessment method was that the lecturer designed the assignment or the project and then students do it. The students knew nothing about how their project would be assessed. In this case, we think that's not good. Also, we should lead the students to become the professionals, in the sense that, if we want them to develop a good product in the future, certainly we should have more precise or explicit criteria.

The fact that all of the interviewed teams' first response was directed towards a learning and teaching issue confirms this as the predominant motivation, as suggested by the quantitative results.

RECOGNITION

Secondary motivations, besides the desire to improve teaching and learning, were identified from interviews as well as the questionnaire. Various participants mentioned opportunities to obtain a grant, achieve recognition in their university and extend the scope of research to areas other than the participants' discipline. One of the project teams made the value of such incentives particularly clear in their interview:

> What stimulated us to start the project? Okay, in fact you can look at this from several angles. First of all, when we do things, we want to get things recognized. Secondly, we want the work, I mean, the things to be done. In this case, the best way would be . . . if we could apply for some prestigious grants like Action Learning Grant, certainly it is good. It is also a kind of recognition in the university as well as for individuals. That may be the major motivation for us to apply for this grant and then start the project work.

> I think that there is a trend that [my head of dept] foresees. That means how to use the information technology to support learning. Actually, because this is the [department], we want to expand our domains on different areas. So actually we choose education. We are in a university, so it will give us a good environment for us to do the research.

It was clear that participants did expect their efforts and achievements to be recognized. Although the primary motivation may have been an interest in a student learning issue, there was an expectation that the work of tackling the issue should receive recognition. This, though, was often expressed as a recognition of the importance of teaching or the value of research into teaching rather than personal recognition:

> Overall I think this has been a very good approach to encourage faculty to improve teaching and learning. However, until faculty evaluations reflect the importance of high-quality teaching in academic life the impact will be limited. Perhaps the relatively formal nature of the ALP will help to improve the status of teaching research at [my institution].

SIGNIFICANCE

In response to these problems, the teaching staff concerned were highly motivated to study their nature and introduce change. They were all potential activists who saw a teaching and learning need in their own setting and were generally inclined to participate in projects like the ALP, which set out to improve teaching and learning. The ALP, according to these teams, was particularly relevant and useful as it provided the appropriate framework, methodology and recognition for research into teaching.

10

Teamwork

There were a small number of projects that were largely conducted by individuals. Even these, though, had some input from research assistants, an associate coordinator, other staff or students. For the rest of the projects, teamwork was a very important factor. It is teamwork that is examined in this chapter.

IMPORTANCE OF TEAMWORK

There has been some debate within the literature as to whether action research has to be a group activity or whether it can be conducted by an individual. Stenhouse (1975: 159) talks of 'mutually supportive co-operative research' while Carr and Kemmis (1986: 200) recognize the need for solitary reflection, but see it as a precursor to public discussion. They justify their position by quoting Habermas' (1974) warning that solitary self-reflection requires the subject to split one part of the self from the other in such a way that it can still render aid to itself. McTaggart and Garbutcheon-Singh (1987) are quite adamant that activities undertaken by an individual cannot be classified as action research.

Others, however, are more open to action research as an individual problem-solving activity. This is consistent with early formulations by Lewin (1946, 1952). Those who see a close affinity with reflective practice (Schön, 1983) also tend to be more open to individual activity.

Within the Action Learning Project, grants for projects were available to individuals and some were awarded to projects largely conducted by individuals. Some preference in their award was given to teams. This preference was governed more by a concern for impact and implementation than by a stance on action research as a group activity. If the benefits of participation are envisaged as an outcome, as suggested later in the chapter, it is desirable to have high levels of participation. It was also recognized that it is often difficult for an individual to effect change within a department. Effective implementation is more likely to occur if all members of a course team are initially committed.

Partly because of the selection process and partly because of the realized need to involve others, the project participants came to recognize the need for and the importance of teamwork. The questionnaire outcomes show that this recognition was almost unanimous (see Figure 10.1). Some participants considered teamwork difficult but the large majority appear to have found ways to make teams work effectively. The mechanisms for this are discussed in the remainder of this chapter.

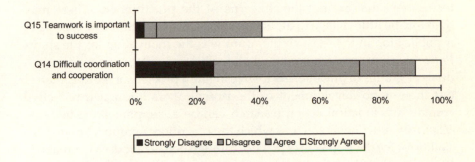

Figure 10.1 Action Learning Project: views on teamwork

TYPES OF TEAM

The study identified three types of teams, characterized initially by their size, but with considerable impact from the way they formed and their mode of operation. Each implied different forms of cooperation and different levels of involvement.

In the first category an active teacher or a relatively small number of active teachers in the department perceived the need for some change or the development of a package, either for their own teaching or for others in the same department. They either worked on their own in a detached manner or involved other teachers in different stages and different aspects. In the latter case, for example, they might have concentrated on the development side and involved their colleagues in the evaluation side by inviting them to evaluate the package and give comments for further improvement.

Secondly, members of a subject team perceived the need to improve the quality of their students' learning in the particular subject they were teaching. The resultant pattern of their project team was distinguished by a rather localized structure including all or almost all the teachers responsible for delivering the subject.

Thirdly, some active members in a department perceived the importance of improving major aspects of their department's teaching so sought to actively involve the whole department in the investigation of these aspects throughout the process. The aim was for the study to become a general concern of the staff and develop into a joint venture of the department. These were invariably the biggest projects.

There is an element of correspondence between this descriptive team category system and Carr and Kemmis' (1986: 202–05) classification system for action research, based upon Habermas' (1972) knowledge-constitutive interests. *Technical* action research investigates issues raised by external researchers that are not the concerns of the practitioners. There may therefore be little change to the action or beliefs of practitioners, especially if publication in the research literature was the motivation for the study. *Practical* action research occurs when facilitators collaborate with individuals or groups of practitioners to investigate a problem of mutual interest but there is no development of the practitioners into a self-reflective community. Practical action research can be a stepping-stone towards *emancipatory* action research, in which the practitioner group takes responsibility for the development of practice through democratic decision-making. It implies that the group becomes concerned with the social or power sphere, which influences the actions it desires to take.

Taking the definition of technical action research literally, none of the projects fell into this category as the participants defined the topics themselves. Some of the teams were content to work in comparative isolation, particularly some of the projects of a technical development nature, so their work remained within a technical/practical category. The others developed a self-reflective community at least among those involved in the project. Some projects, even at the beginning stage, followed various strategies to involve others in the department. They sought others' opinions or participation or actively introduced the ideas. These projects could be classified as emancipatory.

DEVELOPING THE TEAM

Effective teams do not just happen: they need development. It was clear that project teams recognized the need for effective teamwork and worked to achieve it.

Finding time

The majority of university academics are busy. Most of the teams commented that coordinating team members for meetings was difficult:

The most difficult is to accommodate different schedules of our colleagues. We are all busy . . . It is difficult for all of us to be present in the meeting. There is always someone absent.

We needed to sit together and share our different ideas and compromise but there wasn't much time for us to do so.

Communication

It was common that not all members could be present at meetings, so there had to be a mechanism for informing everyone of work that had to be done. The interviews provide evidence of team members trying to establish their own pattern of communication:

It has been difficult to meet each other to discuss, anyhow it is important to meet and talk, we have been trying to meet as often as we can and found our way of communication.

It was beneficial to be allocated within a physical network where most participants were working closely together. But the sense of cooperation could overcome the problem of distance:

It was important for us to talk among ourselves so that we can share our ideas in the project, since we are altogether five in the group, it was helpful to have discussion between us through telephone.

Actually, the formation is quite good . . . we chatted and we talked on the phone and e-mail, e-mail files . . . the e-mails fly back and forth.

It is interesting to note that the organizational structure of the Action Learning Project relied upon electronic communication. The evaluation of communication patterns within the project teams also revealed a high reliance upon electronic communication. It seems as though action research is taking advantage of the electronic era to explore new patterns of critical dialogue.

Leadership

Leadership, organizational skills, and the commitment of the project leader also contributed to good teamwork. More than half of the interviews showed the participants recognized the importance of cooperation and the development of teamwork spirit among them:

I think our project was successful. The important factors for its success are: good co-operation among team members, enthusiasm of members in this project and competency of the research assistant.

Yes, the project was successful. Co-operation and co-ordination of the team led to the success.

Yes. Most important is the co-operation of the team members in helping out with the massive amount of work in the entire project.

Considerable emphasis was attached to the importance of having persons in their team to coordinate, lead and enthuse people as the project was developed and implemented:

Yes, highly successful. [The important factor is] the excellent organizational skills of my colleague.

I think [*name*] has done a very good job, ie the coordination was well done. Although we encountered many problems when we first picked up the project, he helped us to solve them.

[The project is] successful to the extent that we met our initial objectives – mainly due to unity among the research group and help from project leaders.

Proactive individuals, not necessarily the project leader, were also important in creating a participative atmosphere so that participants could make full use of their creativity and incorporate their unique ideas in the work:

Success is attributed to focusing on one issue and having each teacher deal with it in his or her own way. Sharing our styles, beliefs and teaching experiences during the project was enriching for all.

In fact, we don't want to have too strict control over the student assistants. Multimedia is quite a creative kind of work. You have to allow them some freedom to develop their own ideas.

I think the animation is very well designed, which is better than I expected. If you asked me to design the animation, I think it would be very boring. But when you allow them [the student assistants] to design, they'd produce something which is very interesting and unexpected. Then you realise that they would think in such a way! [All laughed.] So it's better for you to allow the students to put in their own design, which is closer to their learning atmosphere, than we set everything for them.

Dividing responsibilities

Most of the project teams reflected on the necessity of organizing regular meetings among team members at every stage of action cycles, because it could facilitate and monitor the progress of projects. They described the importance of meeting and sharing:

> It was important for us to talk among ourselves so that we can share our ideas in the project.

Team members suggested that they also explored possible ways of sharing responsibilities and contributions, taking account of their own interests and expertise. The collaborative effort took advantage of complementary abilities:

> We have people with different backgrounds who come from different fields. For example, [name] has been the subject coordinator for the previous two years. We three are teaching this subject. [Name] is from the Centre for Educational Development. We need the centre's support for filming. On the one hand, we have people from the hardware aspect and on the other hand we have people from the software aspect. We gather together to work for this project.

> We wrote the proposal and essentially we tried to divide it evenly, [name] would take the conceptual part and I would take care of the guided tour to the software. But we did have to get together to try to resolve a common example [conceptual tutorial].

Developing a working relationship

The initial division of responsibilities then had to develop into an on-going pattern of work:

> From the very beginning, the procedure can be divided like this. The first one is that we have to decide in which aspect should we use the multi-media. . . . The second one is that we have to decide the direction when we discuss. Next, for each particular unit, how we can help the presentation of the subject matter.

Action research encouraged teamwork. Team members interacted, discussed problems and helped each other in their reflection. Some teams saw this as an important outcome of their effort.

This should be seen as a successful outcome because the teaching teams became more involved and had closer contact with each other at the times when new or revised teaching plans were formulated.

Collaboration

Many projects attributed their success to the existence among the participants of a willingness to put effort into their project and collaborate with others in a united front. This sense of ownership of some common goals led to the commitment to persevere towards the outcome:

> I think the most important factor [that makes our project so successful] is the commitment of people. Although there were problems in coordination at the beginning and technical difficulties, all of us are very committed. We are determined to complete the project. Otherwise, we could not have done the evaluation. So although there were some delays, it's because every one of us wanted to give our best. We all put in great effort to make it work.

> I agree with [name's] point of view. If there had not been such great commitment, it would have been difficult to complete this project. At first, we got many problems and quite often had to work overnight. Without that commitment, we just couldn't do it. Besides, the animation was very creative. I didn't expect it would be so interesting. I don't think I could make it myself.

With a shared understanding of why the project was necessary and a commitment to this mutual goal, participants tended to focus on their project instead of their self-interest. They were eager to imagine themselves to be the learner and find out the best way to facilitate their learning:

> Moreover, I think that we need to have great commitment and involvement in doing the project. In other words, we have to imagine that we were the users while doing it. We have to imagine we were the players, so asking ourselves what we would learn from it and then plan how to write the program or how to 'walk' or what animation would be included. So there must be good sense of involvement. This is important. We must be clear about what we want to bring to the users in every event, ie what they can learn from it.

Criticism was acceptable if it could help enhance the project's effectiveness. A problem-solving norm was upheld. People became out-spoken and open-minded, taking initiatives to evaluate their work for further improvement:

Here, the culture is, as it has been said earlier, more open. We can discuss our problems openly. We don't need to hide anything. That should be better. I have learnt how to cooperate with other people and give suggestions to one another for improvement. This is what I've gained apart from the technical side.

Besides, everyone is willing to speak out. If there's a problem, it would be known. Everyone is willing to make suggestions and accept the need for changes when necessary. All of us are willing to be open. So if there is any problem that needs to be solved, it will be solved first. We are not afraid of criticizing our own systems. This is also very important.

Moreover, working in groups for a common goal cultivated in participants a sense of belonging and motivated them to care about one another. They sought to help each other whenever such circumstances arose:

At the beginning, I didn't know of any ways to present those abstract ideas by animation. I found the work difficult. Also, technically I didn't know how to use the software and I had no experience with Mac computer. There were many things that I didn't know. I had to learn from scratch. So at that time I didn't have high expectations for this course project. However, it turned out we have learnt a lot because of the cooperation of other colleagues. They taught us many things. Also, [*name*] has helped us do a lot of work. Therefore the outcome is satisfactory. At least I think it is a complete project.

MEETING PATTERNS

Some projects took longer than others to develop a good pattern of communication. Some of the team members mentioned that effective team cooperation did take time to develop:

I think we have spent quite a long time to explore how we might work together.

So we need good sense of cooperation. But this can only be developed after a period of time. We have to work together and gradually develop that sense of cooperation. This takes time to build it up.

As discussed below, other factors may also affect the quality of teamwork. As projects progressed, project teams developed their own pattern of coordination. There were three major team coordination patterns among the projects under evaluation. These tended to follow fairly logically from the nature and size of the teams.

Meeting formally and regularly

The first type of cooperation involved team members meeting regularly, through weekly or monthly formal meetings. These projects usually contained members who were not working together in the same department or university. A fixed schedule of meeting was more suitable for these teams and it saved time in fixing appointments. The action focus or the discipline itself sometimes determined the regularity of meeting:

> We are all busy and some of us are also doing other research at the same time. Thus, we hold regular meetings every month.

Meeting informally and frequently in the research setting

Some projects were able to meet regularly in the research setting. They usually belonged to the same teaching team and were physically located in the same department, or even shared the same office. These teams were usually of a small size and favoured informal meetings. A team developing computer-learning materials for learning languages were working together in the same computer laboratory. Their offices were situated near the laboratory and they shared the same room:

> We work together on the day-to-day basis. [Name] and I have the same classes. Obviously there is a lot of exchange going on every day between us. [Name] is not actually teaching these classes but she is meeting the students practically every day in this centre. Since we also share the room here, every day one hundred and fifty times we talk about the subjects for the action learning project.

They said that the physical network helped them develop very close relationships between team members, and the Action Learning Project became their topic of day-to-day conversation.

Meeting dependent on need

The last type of group held meetings when needed. This was normally the preference of the sizeable projects with more participants. The frequency of meetings depended upon the cycle of the project. They could go a whole month without meeting each other during data-collecting phases. However, at times of data analysis, they sometimes met two to three times a month:

> It has been difficult for us to meet together since there are many in the group. We did not fix a regular meeting time since there are many in the group. Sometimes we will meet a couple of times in a month, but for certain periods, we were not meeting each other; so it all depends on the need of the project.

For large projects, a good e-mail communication network was usually developed for keeping each other informed about the progress of work. Sometimes teams discussed and exchanged written materials through the internet to save travelling time. For large groups, meetings were usually well prepared with a distributed agenda:

> I guess . . . to make this more efficient, you should really have focus in your meetings. If you have a well-prepared topic and then certainly you can invite people to make comments.

RESEARCH ASSISTANTS

The large majority of the funds allocated in grants was spent on full-time or part-time research assistants. The teams recognized that the availability of a capable, efficient and knowledgeable research assistant was an important factor contributing to the success of their projects:

> I must also say that the help of the research assistant who is competent to research is crucial.

> A highly skilled linguist as research assistant was one of the key factors.

The quantitative data confirmed these statements (see Figure 10.2). Over 80 per cent of respondents felt that employing a research assistant was essential to the success of their project. The majority of the teams had also found it difficult to find a suitable one, a factor in the projects' progress that is discussed further below.

Part of the team

The original plan for the book was to include this section with Chapter 15, so treating the research assistants as a form of support for the project teams.

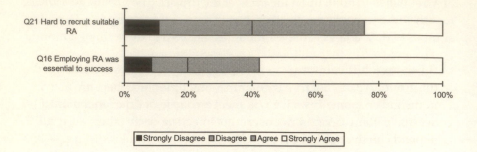

Figure 10.2 Action Learning Project: views on research assistants

It was realized, though, that this would be quite inappropriate as the lecturers regarded their research assistants as integral parts of the teams. The relationships between senior academics and research assistants seemed far more democratic than the marked differences in status and title:

This point was brought home to me in our early workshops on evaluation techniques. The participants usually ranged in status from full professor to research assistants. They seemed to be quite happy to be learning together. I remember one workshop on NUD•IST where the [full] professor was getting a lot of help in the exercises in using the program from his research assistant.

Interestingly, many project leaders involved their research assistants in the process of planning and decision-making, in addition to their technical routine and principal tasks, such as data transcribing and interviewing. Three multimedia teams had invited their research assistant to help with the design of methodology and development of the software. Another social work team reported that their research assistant was not only responsible for coordination among the student helpers, but also conducted tutorials for students in the shadow group. More than that, a research assistant can even 'maintain the dynamic of the research at times when the team are overwhelmed by other duties within their department'.

Finding research assistants

Some teams struggled to find a competent research assistant. Others were fortunate enough to have a good one initially but did not have the same person working for them all through the project:

> Our biggest problem has been finding and then training suitable research assistants.

> The possibility that you have someone who is capable and would finish the job is very low.

Finding and keeping research assistants seems to have been one of the chief concerns of the teams and considered by them an important factor in whether the project would succeed. The main concern in losing an assistant was that extra time and effort would be required for training the new research assistant, which could be a heavy workload for the team and subsequently delay the progress of the project.

Students as research assistants

Three of the eight interviewed teams employed their former students as research assistants. These students were either full-time helpers or Masters degree students working part-time for the teams. One of the advantages was that the students might have a better understanding of, and a stronger commitment to, the project.

> She was our student before and she understands better our research. She has the sense of belonging to the project. She does not treat it as a job only. Like some people do, who just come to work at nine in the morning and leave exactly at five in the evening.

Another advantage, reported by one team, was that the students could offer more practical and relevant suggestions and constructive feedback. With their valuable prior learning experience related to the projects, these students could help pinpoint the pitfalls that might not seem a problem to the project members and highlight the difficulties the new students might be facing in the implementation of initiatives.

TEAMWORK AS AN OUTCOME

Much was said by project teams on the difficulties they faced in coordination and cooperation. Yet every project seems to have developed a pattern of communication that suited themselves. The effort in reflection and evaluation, sharing and communicating among team members helped to shape an encouraging environment for exchanging experience and knowledge among academics, which is a facilitating environment for teaching.

This is an instance of the process being an outcome. The ability of the participants to forge themselves into effective teams should have an enduring impact. As many of the project teams were formed because of a common involvement in a particular course, there are likely to be some more effective course teams as a result of the projects. It is also possible that participation may have helped in the development of teamwork skills which are not always well developed in academia.

11

Action research framework

The interviews showed how the teams adopted the action research cycle of planning, acting, observing and reflecting, followed by a further cycle. It should be noted that there was no overt direction to the project teams to do this. They were given publications about action research methodology and a workshop was held to describe the cyclical action research method. Advice on the action research approach was available to those who sought it. However, there was no insistence that this approach was followed and it would have been impossible to monitor compliance even if there had been. It seems as though the teams found the stages of the action research cycle fitted to what they were trying to achieve and it became almost a natural process.

THE ACTION RESEARCH CYCLE

This first part of the chapter examines the ways in which teams formed their projects around the facets of the action research cycle. It shows that the steps in the cycle were appropriate for conducting the projects and that the teams did adopt an action research approach.

Planning

In the planning stage, the importance of team effort was seen in the design of a feasible plan. This was usually a time-consuming process including the negotiation of ideas among team members, and a thorough discussion of all practical considerations in the research context:

> Actually, before the concept of action learning is introduced, we have already hoped to find AV to supplement and support the teaching. But we find that there are some problems. It is because when we try showing the transparency, showing the slides and videos. The teachers

are just like performing a big show in the classroom. The setting up is also very difficult . . . At the beginning, we have also considered multimedia, but the technology is not mature. By the time the Action Learning Project was advertised, this technology is becoming more mature. So we decided to try it. We use the concept of multi-media and we hope to do the presentation project.

Projects do not come out of nowhere. The quotation above is typical of interest and concerns that developed over time. It took the Action Learning Project to galvanize the teams into action. The quotation below also shows the depth of the initial consideration and in this case the need for initial explorations before substantive work could commence:

At the very early stage, we have done some research on how to make the [. . .] course more interesting. It was because many students reflected that it was too dominated by lecturing. But the teaching of information systems involves very practical problems, so it's hard to teach this subject by simply talking. Later on we've tried using audio-visual presentations to attract students to attend the lectures. That would make the students feel less bored. That was very early stage. After that, we have also carried out an experimental CD-ROM case study and piloted it on some students. The results of the pilot study were very interesting. Students found the presentations in CD-ROM more interesting than reading textbooks. Nevertheless, it didn't mean they got better academic results using such method of teaching. That means the method didn't result in effective learning. Moreover, we found that the high achievers had no difference in their scores, whether we used audio-visual presentations or ordinary textbooks. But for those low achievers, the score they got when using audio-visual presentations, ie multimedia reading, was significantly higher than their counterparts who learned by reading texts. This gave us some insights into the way that we should use multimedia in our teaching to produce effective learning. We shouldn't just get the students to go through the multimedia reading by themselves. That's why we applied for this learning project.

Reflection on action

Reflecting on one's practice is the hallmark of an action researcher. Many teams talked about their experience of self-reflection:

It has helped me to reflect on my own teaching as well as trying to understand how the students learn.

There was individual self-reflection but there was greater emphasis in the interviews upon reflection as a group activity. The majority of the teams noted the importance of reflection-in-action in fine-tuning their teaching practices. They expressed the need to discuss and listen to others' experiences in the action process, because this has helped them in stepping back from the action and gaining perspectives:

> The most useful was the team meeting in reflecting the results and the experience.

> That is important because we would like to know how to adjust our own teaching by knowing the effect of other classes.

Very often, research begets more research questions and these projects were no exception. The teams obviously realized the effectiveness of determining future actions through the outcomes of their reflections. This led to fine-tuning of their initiative as the outcomes were implemented:

> By involving a group of colleagues in active regular discussions of teaching styles and learning needs, it has raised questions about what we are trying to do and how best we should go about this.

> To implement action research in teaching and learning, we need to change to adjust our method of teaching to accommodate the need of students.

This is another example of the process being an outcome. Firstly the process of reflection led to insights into better approaches to teaching and a greater understanding of student learning. Secondly, and perhaps more importantly, by engaging in this collective reflection the participants realized the importance of reflecting on their teaching and hopefully should adopt a reflective stance in the future:

> Data collected enabled reflective on teaching styles and obstacles to learning.

> It [the Action Learning Project] gives me a better insight to reflection.

Changing the plan

In the action research cycle, reflection leads to revised plans and a further action step. In this way the process results in iterative improvement:

You know that we have to redesign the cycle as the research goes along. That is the characteristic of action learning. It is required to redesign and make amendment to the action, when you have new data and you need to decide how to use the data. These are important and we need to discuss together.

The realization that plans had to be modified was often mentioned in meetings between the participants and the coordinating team members. Often the issue was raised in the form of the team checking to see if it was permissible to deviate from their proposal. In the words of one coordinator:

I soon realized that many of the participants found the opportunity to change and adapt their project as they went along was quite different to their experience of other types of research. A large proportion of the teams asked whether it was all right to deviate from their original proposal. They seemed encouraged when told it was almost a requirement that they did not stick rigidly to their original plan. They were used to conventional research plans and having to account for even minor deviations to research committees. One of the universities' research offices used to write to me requesting permission each time a team wanted to modify the original timetable. I never managed to convince them to treat these as rough guidelines rather than legalistic commitments.

As a result of numerous conversations about the processes of adapting the initial plans, three questions were included in the questionnaire on this topic. The questions asked: whether too much data was collected, whether the original design was adhered to, and whether the project stuck to its original schedule. The results, shown in Figure 11.1, are indicative of the impressions we had built up during the project.

The question of sticking to plans is largely one of degree – which is perhaps not reflected in the item statement used in the questionnaire. Most project teams stuck to their original aims, but a large majority of teams did seem to modify their plans through a process of positive adaptation and fine-tuning. The failure to stick to the original schedule by a significant proportion of teams usually indicated some slippage due to unforeseen problems, such as the inability to recruit a suitable research assistant. This should not be seen as an inherent part of action research as it is not uncommon for other types of project or initiative to experience similar delays.

It was also of interest to see the questionnaire results confirming our suspicion that many teams spent too much time and effort gathering data that were not subsequently used. There was a tendency to get stuck into

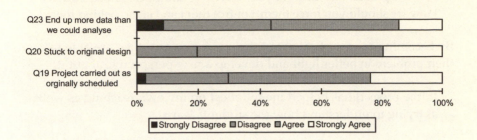

Figure 11.1 Action Learning Project: changing the plan

conducting a set of interviews or observations. Only after the set had been collected did examination and analysis start. At this point it could become apparent that not all of the data were useful or that the volume was too great for it all to be analysed. As this happened with nearly half the projects it would certainly be worth encouraging participants in educational action research to make a preliminary examination of their data early in the gathering process. This early analysis should at least reveal whether continued collection will be fruitful or whether some modification to the interview schedule or observation process is necessary.

It also shows that it is better if the cyclical action research process is not envisaged as a series of discrete steps which take place one after the other. The aspects of planning, action, observation and reflection all need to be present but good projects often have a considerable overlap among the four facets. It can be quite a messy process in practice but it is hard to capture this in diagrammatic representations.

Changing their perspective

By acting on their project plan, assessing the effects of their action and reflecting with other team members, many participants come to realize the inadequacy of their original interpretation of what was causing the problem defined at the beginning of their project. Many were surprised by their findings, which alerted them to question the validity of their previous assumptions about teaching and learning:

> In our forum, we found that the students had great anxiety. This really surprised us. We found out about their responses to the fieldwork. They become sick and cannot sleep.

> And the problem is of course you want to create autonomous learners.
> How far should you force them, control them and stand behind them?

By becoming more critical about their assumptions, they are able to cast their problem in better light and develop a new perspective about it:

> It [the project] has helped me to reflect on my own teaching as well as trying to understand how the students learn.

> The most useful was the team meeting in reflecting the results and the experience.

Changing others' perspectives

Some projects further sought to influence and transform the perspectives of their colleagues and people in their discipline or profession. They were aware that their project could only have a wider impact if all the stakeholders within their field attended to the problem they perceived, got together to share their perspectives and provided their support for new ideas. So, they incorporated strategies to encourage participation and had dissemination practice built into their project design. The following quotation illustrates how such strategies, adopted by one project team, were successful in helping their part-time colleagues and people in their field to understand more about their students' expectations:

> Yes. That is exactly the response of the students. If there is no such evidence, the supervisors would think there is nothing wrong with their teaching methodology. They would supervise the students in a way as what their former supervisor did in the past. Also they would tell the students that they were like that before. The students would be very annoyed whenever they heard their supervisors say things like that. The students would argue that they don't necessarily have to follow the footsteps of their supervisors as times have changed. Actually there is really a conflict here between the supervisors and students. Frankly, the supervisors are getting older and older. The more experienced the supervisors are, the larger the gap is between the supervisors and the freshmen. And this is a problem of generation gap. Yet it cannot be denied that the teaching methods, the community and expectations of the students have been changing, moving forward. This research really helps us to get more insight on these aspects.

> The response of the [social work] agencies to the research forum is very good. They also want to know about the students . . . – students'

feedback on the agencies' – the organization of practice. This is because they have offered our students a placement. The agencies are required to apply for the placement. We invited them to come to the seminar. There are many agencies. Are there five to six agencies? Some of them are participants but some are not.

Having an opportunity to come into contact with others' perspectives and directly confront alternative views proved to be an indispensable step towards critical reflection. This held true for the students too:

Actually on some occasions such as the seminar and the research forum, the students had a chance to listen to others like the [social work] agencies, the teachers and other classmates. Then they know the problems they have are not uncommon. As we also distributed the research findings to the students, they know the responses and viewpoints of other students. That helped them to understand that the problems they have encountered are not unique. Really, their expectations on the agencies are very interesting.

It should be pointed out that the number of projects seeking to influence a wide group of people was quite small. Most were content to operate within the project or course team or perhaps also influence a few of the most pertinent departmental colleagues.

REACTIONS OF PARTICIPANTS TO THE ACTION RESEARCH FRAMEWORK

In the survey, participants were asked about their experience of action research. A substantial majority of respondents admitted to having had no previous experience of action research. Of these, most came from disciplines in which the scientific research paradigm would have been predominant and quantitative methods dominant, and often exclusively so.

In fact, there was a considerable range in the level of experience of project team members. Some projects were lucky enough to have people with relevant expertise to contribute to the different aspects of the project. Some of the project leaders openly acknowledged the relevance of their members' prior experience.

However, it should be noted that project teams with such a strong background only accounted for a small number in our sample. Others might have just started to look at the problems in their teaching and had little idea of working with others to improve their courses. These teams had to build up their teaching, technical, research and teamwork skills during the course of their project. The commitment and support to do so proved important and essential to the success of their projects.

In spite of this background and lack of experience, virtually all of the participants found that action research provided a suitable framework for their study. The quantitative data, shown in Figure 11.2, showed this to be an almost unanimous response.

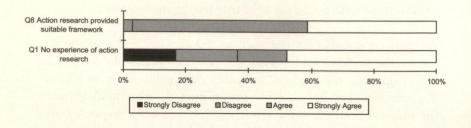

Figure 11.2 Action Learning Project: reactions of participants

In the qualitative data, also, a number of project teams attributed their success to application of an appropriate framework for their study. Half of the teams interviewed mentioned that the paradigm of action research benefited their project. The continuous cycles of action and reflection, and the reciprocal process of change and evaluation were relevant and useful to the teams. Obviously the case for action research providing a suitable framework for educational development meshed with the participants' practical experiences:

> Learning by action, that means we have to make our own evaluation . . . I think our students really need to learn by action. If you haven't tried it out, it is indeed difficult for you to understand what you do. Such idea [action learning] is particularly appropriate to our subject.

> The focus of action learning is to search for something and make changes . . . The method is very suitable for us to improve our teaching.

This chapter has given an account of teams adapting to an action research approach. They were not pushed towards this but seem to have fitted into the approach well. Action research seems to provide a natural framework for work of this type:

Q: Is this your first time doing action research using this kind of research paradigm?

A: Yeah.

Q: How did you find it?

A: I didn't feel very much pressured into the action learning approach. The whole paradigm seems to me quite common sense … it simply means you get the opportunity to apply your common sense.

THE PROCESS AS AN OUTCOME

The conclusion of the previous chapter argued that the development of teamwork skills was a valuable outcome of the project. Evidence given in this chapter presents a compelling case for the conclusion that the process of engaging in action research was a similarly beneficial outcome of the project.

Firstly the participants learnt, from practical experience, how to conduct an educational action research project. Those who, in the future, face some other problem or issue in their own teaching should feel confident of tackling the issue and should possess the necessary expertise to do so.

Secondly, many of the projects acted as a spur to cause the participants to critically reflect upon their own teaching practices and their students' learning. That the process of engaging in action research can cause a re-examination of practice and beliefs must be seen as a valuable outcome. What is more, such re-appraisal could occur even if the project did not proceed particularly smoothly towards its original goals. Indeed, there was some evidence that more radical retrospection was perhaps likely to occur in projects that encountered difficulties or the unexpected. When the original plans could not be implemented as anticipated, the participants could be forced to re-examine their assumptions and beliefs.

The act of striving and reflecting together in action research projects should, therefore, be recorded as an achievement regardless of the outcomes of more objective measures of student learning outcomes. With the bonus of learning, through experience, how to conduct action research, the process of engagement might well be seen as one of the most important outcomes.

12

Participants' perceptions of outcomes

The interviews and questionnaires solicited the views of participants about the impact of the projects. Essentially this is seeking the participants' perceptions as to whether their projects met their aims.

PERCEPTIONS OF SUCCESS

From both the questionnaire and interview data, it was found that most participants did consider their projects successful. Most also felt that their expectations had been met (see Figure 12.1).

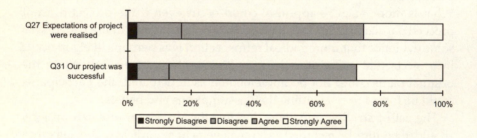

Figure 12.1 Action Learning Project: perceptions of success

The remainder of the chapter looks at the aspects of the projects mentioned by the teams as reasons for their involvement and considers the participants' perceptions of their achievements in meeting their aims. The outcomes will be considered from four different aspects, namely the teachers, teacher/student relationships, the impact on students and the impact on other members of the department.

TEACHERS

The quantitative data clearly indicate that the respondents felt that participating in the projects had influenced their teaching for the better (see Figure 12.2). Their teaching had improved, they became more aware of important factors in teaching and more reflective on their teaching. They also saw themselves as turning into educational researchers. Each of these aspects will be explored in more detail below through the qualitative data.

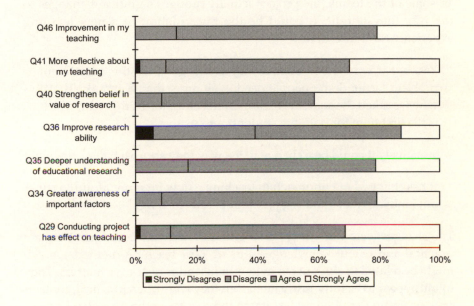

Figure 12.2 Action Learning Project: effects on teaching

Understanding of teaching

Many participants said they had acquired a deeper understanding of innovative teaching, or had changed the way they conceptualized teaching:

> I am more aware of my teaching effectiveness and teaching style through students' feedback and regular recordings of students' discourse.

However, it did not mean that they always had the solution to problems they were facing:

The project succeeded in making the team more aware of our teaching programme and our students' likes and dislikes. The most useful was the team meeting in reflecting the results and the experience. The project failed to achieve the objective of identifying actions for improvement. We were going around in circles as we did not know what we were measuring.

Change in teaching practice

To some of the teams, the project actually brought significant changes to the way they taught. It could be the introduction of a new learning experience for the students:

Yes, but it would be better if they could get over the adjustment problem faster. Some people need even more than a month. That's why we asked the students to do summer assignment this year, which is the first time for both the students and us.

Alternatively it could be a change in the way they approach their teaching:

It has changed my approach in teaching – now I am not afraid to try out innovative methods eg problem-based learning.

The changes were not always on a grand scale. They could just be some practical and useful knowledge in using new teaching methods, which might be related to student behaviour or just administrative matters. They might appear to be nitty-gritty items, but they were often practical, context-specific findings and could be vital to the success of the project at times:

But there are many local factors. At the beginning of every lecture, there is always a piece of loud music. Because the students are very noisy.

Learning about educational research

For some, it was their first attempt at action research, or any type of educational research for that matter:

It helped me to learn research methodology and [that] benefited both teaching and learning in this course.

You know, because there is a set of the educational papers that I read through. Definitely it allowed me to read through them and to get a much better idea of what other people are doing.

Again some of the discoveries are very practical applications, such as how to record the process of a student working with a computer:

> When you transcribe only what you hear on the tape, it is very difficult to relate it afterwards to what the students had actually done on the computer. So what [name] did on top of transcribing it, was when she went through the whole exercise again she identified and printed out the screens at each point when students were working. So then we could sort of verify what was actually going on.

The emphasis is on the teacher, who is also the researcher, developing theory through the authentic teaching context. The research teams were encouraged to be reflective on their experiences in innovative teaching.

The action research approach to educational development assumes that the teachers involved have an appropriate attitude and will be able to develop necessary abilities to carry out their project. Indeed, the act of participation is itself an outcome. The journey could be seen as more important than the destination. By being engaged the participants are learning to become self-sufficient and underlying attitudes can change through critical reflection and discourse. Empowering participants to take responsibility for their own quality monitoring is seen as a key outcome.

TEACHER AND STUDENT RELATIONSHIPS

The large majority of the participants felt that the projects had led to an improvement in the relationship between teacher and student (see Figure 12.3). This is an interesting finding as there are two potential reasons why the projects could have worsened relationships. Firstly, there is a wide perception that students, particularly in the Asian region, are resistant to change and prefer passive forms of learning. Innovative forms of teaching might upset them, if this belief were true. Secondly, the innovations could involve students in more work and would certainly have led to interviews, classroom observations, and questionnaires to be completed. Yet, in spite of this potential for worsening relationships, they improved.

Understanding student learning

The project experience enabled some teams to acquire a new conception of student learning:

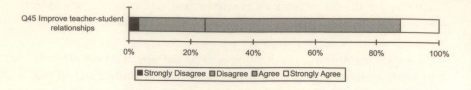

Figure 12.3 Action Learning Project: teacher–student relationships

It was also successful in that it provided the team with a much richer understanding of the approach to study and the 'consumer' characteristics of study of students.

Our project has so far investigated the factors which encourage students to use spoken English.

Some discovered what they felt were significant research findings about student learning:

> We thought probably there could be a correlation between individual students' profiles and the way they go about learning with computer. Now, the data we have, do not show any implication of that.

Understanding student attitudes

A few teams focused their attention on students' attitude towards their study, their expectation of the course, their anxiety and their needs:

> We have some idea on that before the research . . . Yet from the in-depth interviews with the students, we found that our ideas on students' anxiety are very different from the real situation.

> Teachers are more aware of the needs of students, as well as the students' feelings.

Building relationships

A number of projects worked with the students rather closely. Friendship between teacher and student grew as a result:

> At the end of this term one of the classes invited me to be in their class photo; it did not happen before, and I was delighted.

STUDENTS

A large majority of the respondents felt that there had been improvements in their students' attitude, performance and learning (see Figure 12.4). As most of the participants would have seen a substantial amount of evaluation data, these perceptions are considered significant.

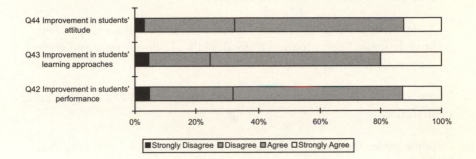

Figure 12.4 Action Learning Project: effect on students

Learning experience

In conducting their own evaluation, the learning experience of the students was constantly a focus of the teams. Some said the students found their new teaching method exciting or interesting:

[It] makes students have more interest. They won't feel bored when attending lessons.

My own experience and informal responses from the students indicate that the multimedia software has made teaching and learning in my course more enjoyable.

Students reportedly had much deeper learning experiences than before:

The project was really quite successful in giving students an alternative learning experience.

The problem-based learning approach engaged students far more actively and sustained their involvement far more than any other courses within the department.

Learning behaviour

The project seemed to have changed the learning behaviours of students in some cases:

Students were more active in learning.

Students contribute more in discussion.

As far as learning is concerned, I feel that students are gaining – their attendance and participation is good, skills are developing and their performance is improving.

There were also negative comments, but largely limited to a small number of students:

Some prefer the traditional one more . . . For example, some say that 'I am conservative in thinking, so I like the traditional one'.

Learning outcomes

Learning outcomes were more appropriately evaluated through a macro-analysis of the reports of the projects where data on the learning outcomes of each project were reported. However, the perception of some project teams was that the project reports did demonstrate improvements in learning outcomes:

The student results from the second cycle show a marked improvement on last year. A preliminary view of the data from the second cycle suggests that important life learning as well as leadership learning has taken place . . . For instance, students on interview and in questionnaires expressed [the view] that they have not only learnt about such things as group process, negotiation and conflict management but have learnt to use them within the context of learning activities. Learning to relate as peers with more senior group members has been for most a revealing and positive experience.

But some were not so sure:

I cannot really tell you the [bold] assumption how much, with the three extra hours per week we put in the curriculum for self-access study, [that would] raise the level of German they achieve after a year or after two years. I wouldn't dare answer at the moment. I cannot really tell you. It is a very difficult question to answer.

OTHER STAFF

The participants were more confident that they had had an impact on the course they taught than they were of having influenced the teaching of colleagues in their department (see Figure 12.5). The large majority felt they had passed on something worthwhile to other teams, in sessions such as the interest group meetings. However, their colleagues in their own departments were obviously less interested in what they had discovered and it was even harder to have an impact on their teaching.

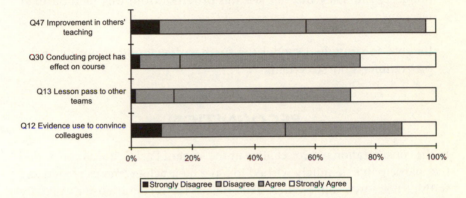

Figure 12.5 Action Learning Project: effect on other staff

The qualitative data give a similar picture. At least some of the projects felt that they had had an impact upon course design and the way teaching took place within their departments:

> My department head has expressed interest in developing similar tools for other courses in the department.

> It will inevitably affect the ways in which other courses are taught in the future.

> Yes, a more problem-based approach in teaching and learning has been considered by many departments in the [. . .] faculty.

When asked if the project had had any effect on other members of the department not involved in the project, many said it raised their awareness of innovative teaching methods:

> Yes, it has challenged staff to a 'new' form of teaching and learning.

> I think definitely it enhanced the awareness that such a programme exists. As any influence on their behaviour, I really don't know.

But not all of them were so positive about having an impact on departmental colleagues. Educational developers always hope that their initiatives will have a wider impact through a knock-on or trickle-down effect to those not immediately involved. This was clearly happening to some extent, and probably more than in most educational development programmes. The projects were not, though, acting as emancipatory agents across whole departments in line with some action research rhetoric:

> Actually the department is resistant to this style of teaching; they did not accept it. They did not see the progress from this method of teaching.

> Its goal to provide a model for further development within the programme is not so certain.

RECOGNITION

In the consideration of project aims at the start of Part C, it was concluded that participants definitely wished to have their achievements recognized within their own universities. This desire for recognition was usually couched in terms of a feeling that universities should place a greater value on teaching or research into teaching. The participants in projects were clearly those who had always seen the importance of teaching and in some cases felt frustrated that others did not. Both the quantitative results and a number of comments suggest that this position persisted:

> Despite UGC and [other] funding and rhetoric to the contrary, we feel that that academic work involved in providing supporting materials for students' use does not carry the same respect and value for staff development as other types of research and publication. This means that staff participating in such projects do so as a result of personal commitments to what they believe to be worthwhile, and at a cost in terms of their career development.

There was a surprising degree of loyalty to the Action Learning Project as a whole, which developed among a significant proportion of the participants. They seemed to see it as an expression of their feeling that teaching should be taken more seriously and a hope that a large-scale teaching research initiative might eventually change the attitude of policy makers who did not share this view:

I think this was a far-sighted initiative. It was able to support such a variety of different projects generated bottom-up, from the delivery point of instruction. It had more impact on the quality of learning than any of the top-down quality initiatives I've encountered!

I appreciate this opportunity to conduct research on teaching and learning. I would like to thank the coordinators of the Action Learning Project for their insights into the value of improving the quality of tertiary education. They have provided us a supportive environment to improve teaching and learning in the tertiary level, which has often been given lower priority to research.

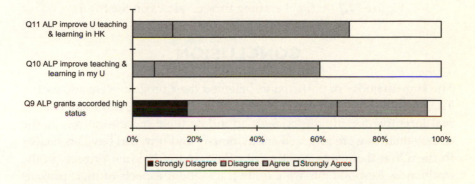

Figure 12.6 Action Learning Project: achieving recognition

The participants obviously felt that the Action Learning Project was an appropriate medium for educational development and quality enhancement but did not feel that others appreciated it to the same extent, as shown in Figure 12.6.

Desire to continue

Educational development initiatives always hope for a lasting impact. It is, therefore, pleasing that participants in these projects felt that they would continue this type of work (see Figure 12.7). There was a strong majority in favour of continuing it through the project framework:

I believe that the whole Action Learning Project was a success. However, it was only the first step. Results of the various teams should be formally published, and another round of action learning projects solicited to further the impact on teaching and learning.

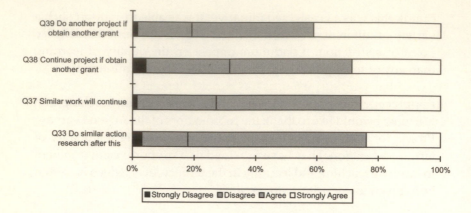

Figure 12.7 Action Learning Project: views on the future

CONCLUSION

The large majority of participants believed their projects were successful. The reliability of these perceptions may be questioned, but there was no real incentive for the respondents to inflate their success ratings as the questionnaires were returned anonymously and it would have been clear to them that there was no element of judging individual projects in the evaluation. Respondents were quite frank about aspects of their projects which had not progressed as well as they might. More fundamentally, the interviewees were able to cite evidence for their perceptions from the detailed evaluation they had conducted. Their evaluations had examined the impact of the projects upon student learning, so these results informed the perceptions.

The participants were, in the main, convinced by their evaluation data that their projects had had a beneficial impact upon student learning outcomes. The majority felt that the students had developed a better attitude, were more motivated and more inclined to adopt a deep approach to learning. The respondents also felt that their relationship with their students had often improved. This is an interesting finding as it calls into question the widely held opinion that students prefer passive forms of learning and are resistant to change.

It is likely that the projects will have some lasting impact because many of the participants felt that participating in the projects had influenced their teaching for the better. They had developed a better understanding of teaching and of the factors that influenced student learning. Most felt that they had become more proficient at conducting educational research and evaluation, which means that they should be able to monitor their own teaching in the future.

They were more hesitant to claim that the projects had affected others. Many felt that there had been an influence upon courses and curriculum design. However, they were less inclined to believe that the teaching practices or beliefs of their departmental colleagues had been influenced. This is perhaps not surprising as it is hard to alter deep-seated beliefs, but it does suggest that few of the projects reached out to involve a wider circle, so taking on an emancipatory character.

PART D
PROVIDING SUPPORT

David Kember, Tak Shing Ha, Bick-har Lam, April Lee, Sandra Ng, Louisa Yan and Jessie C K Yum

The Action Learning Project provided support to projects by a small team of facilitators. This part argues that such support is necessary and discusses the role of the facilitators. The level of support from students, staff and those in other project teams is also considered.

Chapter 13 considers the question whether projects should take place within an organizing framework with the assistance of supporting staff. The large majority of the participants in the 50 projects expressed the view that advice and support were necessary for several facets of the projects, particularly evaluation strategies. The organization of contact between groups with similar interests was valued. Further evidence for the need for support came from comparison with a scheme that did not provide it.

Chapter 14 explains that support for the 50 projects was provided by a small coordinating team dispersed across the seven universities. This chapter discusses the relationship between the participants and the support team using the 'critical friend' as an analogy. The support team negotiated their level and type of involvement with each of the project teams. They evolved towards a multi-faceted role encompassing financier, project design consultant, rapport builder, coffee maker, mirror, teaching consultant, evaluation adviser, research adviser, resource provider, writing consultant, matchmaker and deadline enforcer.

Chapter 15 argues that another factor in the success of the projects was the level of support from students and colleagues in the department. Respondents to the evaluation questionnaire felt that the majority of their students had willingly become involved in the innovations. This finding calls into question the impression that students are resistant to change and prefer passive learning methods.

The majority of the teams felt that they did receive support from their department heads for their initiatives, though there were some notable exceptions. There was a lower level of support from departmental colleagues, but this seemed to be non-involvement rather than obstruction.

Support also came from participants in other projects, through interest group meetings and less formal contact. Some participants with similar interests developed quite strong collaborative relationships.

13

Is support necessary?

The Action Learning Project drew upon the initial experiences with educational action research to work on the assumption that projects were more likely to proceed to successful outcomes if provided with advice and support from a facilitator. It has to be admitted that the evidence to back this conclusion was not strong. What evidence was available could only be described as experiential insights. By making the assumption that support was necessary, it was possible to provide a much better test of the assumption. Evidence that it was a correct assumption comes from comparison with an unsupported scheme and from the perceptions of participants.

THE EDG EXPERIENCE

A useful comparison was provided by an internal grant scheme operated within the Polytechnic University known as the Educational Development Grant (EDG) scheme. It operated for about four years prior to the start of the Action Learning Project and for about one year in parallel with it. Essentially the EDG offered, usually fairly small, grants to staff within the university, on a competitive basis, for a variety of initiatives and developmental projects concerned with teaching and learning. There were no formal requirements of grant recipients and no support was provided, except in the case of a small number of projects which involved EDU staff as part of the team requesting the grant.

The institutional records show that 231 proposals were funded. Grant recipients were eventually contacted by the EDU for a report, product or evidence of outcomes from their project. Only 44 (19 per cent) of the recipients produced any sort of report or other response. As there was no formal requirement to do so, this cannot be taken as conclusive evidence that the remaining 81 per cent of projects produced nothing reportable. That such a high proportion of projects did not choose to report or have anything to show does certainly call into question the ability of unsupported projects to proceed to satisfactory outcomes. It definitely shows that this unsupported scheme was not effective in disseminating conclusions from projects to a wider audience.

The contrast with the Action Learning Project is marked. In this supported scheme all but three of the 50 funded projects proceeded to produce reports, and following sections here argue that there was considerable evidence of beneficial influences upon teaching and learning. The reason for two projects not being completed was that participants resigned to take up positions elsewhere.

The contrast between these outcomes has persuaded the Polytechnic University to replace the EDG initiative with a grant-awarding scheme, which incorporates a more formal structure for reporting and on-going support from the EDU. The Polytechnic University should be commended for having the vision to initiate the EDG scheme in the first place and for modifying its practices in the light of a better model.

PERCEPTIONS OF THE PROJECT TEAMS

Further evidence of the need for support comes from the results from the questionnaire completed by participants in the Action Learning Project. A series of questions asked participants to rate their need for nine types of support using a four-point scale: very necessary, necessary, not very necessary, or definitely not necessary. Figure 13.1 shows the frequencies of responses for 'necessary' and 'very necessary' to these items.

Perceived need for support

Clearly, from the questionnaire responses, the project teams felt the need for support to carry out their project. The majority of respondents felt that support was either necessary or very necessary for each of the cited support facets except training a research assistant.

The facet rated with the highest need was that of arranging contact with others doing similar projects. The next highest ratings were for a group of three items (evaluating project, research method and data analysis), which could reasonably be grouped as help with the evaluation of the project. This would encompass evaluation design, advice on evaluation methods and help with data analysis.

The findings here are similar to those of the CAUT evaluation report (Hayden and Speedy, 1995) which found that 'many project leaders found that they did not have adequate skills or experience to undertake all aspects of their projects competently by themselves' (p 35). Again it was in the area of evaluation where there was the greatest need.

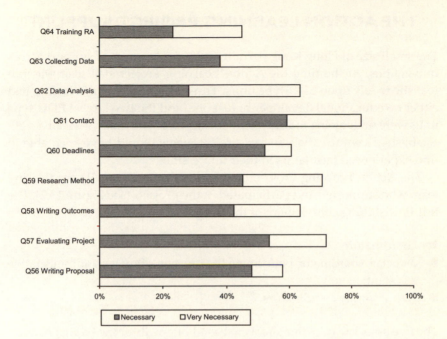

Figure 13.1 Action Learning Project: perceived need for support

PROVIDING THE SUPPORT

The above sections have established the case that project teams felt that there was a need for support. Further, there is evidence that projects are more likely to start if a supporting infrastructure is present. A supporting environment also seems to be a factor in projects resulting in tangible outcomes.

Having established the need for a supporting infrastructure, the next decision is how to provide it. There are two available options. The first is relying on existing staff, mainly those in educational development-type units, to provide assistance. The second is to use part of the resources of the grant scheme for providing the infrastructure. Intermediate positions are also possible.

CAUT in Australia adopted the former position. Given the distances between universities in Australia this was probably the only realistic option, as it could never be economically realistic to base a support person at each university. It was also reasonable in view of the fact that most Australian universities have EDU-type units, and many have reasonable levels of staffing. In the UK the population is concentrated in a much smaller area and EDU-type units are possibly less well staffed. There have, therefore, been a number of centralized staff development initiatives.

THE ACTION LEARNING PROJECT SUPPORT

The small size of Hong Kong permitted the deployment of support across universities. At the time the Action Learning Project started it was not realistic to rely upon EDU-type units. Three or four of the universities had either no educational developer or just one, and the two largest EDU-type units were undergoing radical restructuring. Action research was not a well-established venture at all, so few project teams would have been able to find experienced facilitators in their universities.

The Action Learning Project, therefore, recruited a small coordinating team who supported and participated in the projects (see Figure 13.2). The full-time staffing complement of the project was:

- coordinator;
- associate coordinator, performing the function of analyst/administrative assistant;
- five associate coordinators.

The five associate coordinators were based primarily at the Baptist University, CityU, HKU, PolyU and UST. Each, though, was also allocated to projects in other institutions.

In addition a part-time editor was employed, at certain times, to edit the case studies of the projects and other publications. Part-time staff were also employed to help organize and run the conference.

Supporting projects

The main function of the coordinating team was to support and participate in the sub-projects supported by the ALP. The involvement of the coordinating team varied from project to project and defining the role was an evolving process.

As far as possible the associate coordinators worked in conjunction with members of the respective EDU-type unit. The aim here was two-fold. Firstly, it provided a supporting framework to both the associate coordinator and the project team. Secondly, it provided openings for staff of EDU-type units to build relationships with departments active in teaching initiatives and established the unit as a focal point for such activities.

The associate coordinators were, as far as possible, housed within EDU-type units. Inadequate space provision prevented this in one case, and the associate coordinator was found accommodation by the English Centre at HKU, which had four projects.

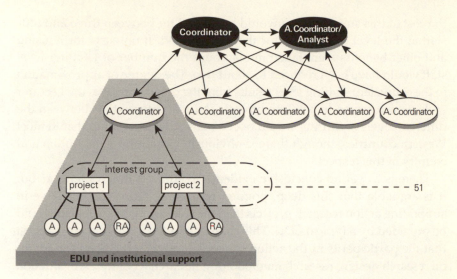

Figure 13.2 Action Learning Project: the coordinating team

LEVEL OF SUPPORT STAFF

An issue with respect to support staff is the level at which they are appointed. For any given sum, at a reasonable level, various different distributions of staff will be available. The level at which staff are appointed is an issue which is worth considering in respect to this project as the distribution was so different to the normal distribution within an academic department or more pertinently an educational development unit.

A typical academic unit or EDU has an even, triangular distribution of staff. Typically, a well-appointed EDU will have a head at the level of Professor or Associate Professor, a Senior Lecturer, several Lecturers, perhaps a Tutor and, if they are successful in obtaining grants, possibly a research assistant or two. This means that, if EDU-type units are to support action research projects, the support will to a large extent come from staff at the Lecturer level. The head and deputy will be principally occupied with organizational duties, the representative role and committee duties. Any research assistants will be assigned to the specific projects that fund their position. If support were plotted against cost, support to any action research projects would, therefore, come from a very shallow fat triangle.

By contrast the Action Learning Project had a support staffing structure of a triangle that was far more pointed, and had a significantly lower but perhaps broader base. In conventional academic terms the staffing was equivalent to a Reader or Associate Professor plus six staff at the level of Research Associate or Research Fellow. In Hong Kong, ignoring on-costs, the cost of this support team would have paid for between three and four staff at the level of Lecturer for the same period. If on-costs for housing and other benefits were taken into account the number of Lecturer-level staff would have been reduced to about two. The degree of approximation in the equivalent staffing level results from the broad spread in the Lecturer scale, which seems to be quite typical. The cost differentials between the different levels of staffing would not be markedly different to that in most Western countries, though there is obviously variation by institution and country in this respect.

There is as yet no conclusive evidence to support this contention, but it is arguable that this deep, pointed triangle is more cost-effective in supporting action research projects than the shallow fat triangle that would be provided by a typical EDU. This chapter and the following one suggest that the participants in the action research projects felt a need for advice on research design, research methodology, research techniques, evaluation strategies and the way of writing up their project to ensure publication in a recognized journal.

It might be felt that those appointed at the level of Lecturer in an EDU would have sufficient expertise in educational research to provide good quality advice on these issues. However, EDU staff are rarely appointed because of their ability to support projects, as this is a new type of venture. In many appointments teaching ability would be seen as more important than research productivity.

The literature on the research productivity of typical academics at the lecturer level suggests also that few would be prolific researchers. Boyes, Happel and Hogan (1984) suggested that on average as few as three refereed publications were required for promotion from assistant to associate professor and only five to become a full professor. There is also evidence of high proportions of academics producing no publications over survey periods of several years (eg Halsey, 1980). Evidence of low output, generally, comes from a wide range of studies (see O'Neill, 1990; Ramsden, 1994 for reviews).

There is no reason to question the assumption that this literature can be extrapolated to the typical EDU staff member who might be called upon to support action research projects. Therefore, this typical EDU staff member is likely to have few publications, may not have a great deal of research experience, and will possibly have no experience of supervising higher-degree students. One must, therefore, question the credibility of such staff in advising academics on how to conduct research.

This consideration is particularly pertinent when the level of both status and expertise of the participants in these projects is taken into account. The Action Learning Project participants included significant numbers of Deans and full Professors at the elite universities in Hong Kong. Clearly these were people with well-established research records in their own discipline, expertise in teaching and learning and the ability to determine whether offered expertise and advice was credible or not.

Having the temerity to offer advice to such people demands a modicum of self-confidence. Gaining the respect of these high-flyers through being able to offer worthwhile advice, which was beyond their self-recognized expertise, would seem to demand considerable aptitude. It must be questionable whether EDU staff, with a limited research track record, would seem credible to these well-qualified academics involved in action research projects.

This does not in any way question the ability of such staff to fulfil the other aspects of the 'critical friend' role. It then comes down to what is perceived as the most important aspect of the role. It is pertinent here that the aspects of support rated second, third and fourth most necessary by the project teams were advice on evaluating the project, research method and data analysis. These outcomes suggest that advice on research and evaluation is important.

Returning to the Action Learning Project support team, it might be expected that a coordinator appointed because of previous experience with action research projects might be able to pass on competent advice about research and evaluation. However, one might suppose that those Action Learning Project staff at the base of the narrow pyramid would find it even harder than Lecturers to attain credibility.

The Action Learning Project support team tried to overcome this issue by acting as a team. The initial meeting with project teams was with a duo, the coordinator and the respective associate coordinator. Broad research and evaluation design issues could be, and frequently were, tackled at this initial meeting. The associate coordinators then dealt with most on-going issues but could, and did, consult with the coordinator, who had some degree of familiarity with the project as a result of the initial meeting at least.

The level of appointment of the associate coordinators did mean that they were easily able to establish a rapport with research assistants appointed by the projects. As there were six of them they did have time to work with them on skills such as interview techniques and qualitative data analysis. It was also economical to provide the quantitative data analysis service.

The staffing structure of the Action Learning Project was arrived at almost by default as being what could be reasonably afforded with the grant and the type of staff who could be recruited. As it turned out, the combination of one high-level researcher with several research associate/ fellow-level staff does seem to have much to commend it. The above discussion has suggested that it may well be more appropriate for project support than the staffing structure that would typically be available in an EDU. If this is the case then EDUs might need to re-examine their staffing structure if they wish to make a significant shift towards project-based activities.

CONCLUSION

The conclusion was reached that support should be provided for initiatives involving multiple action learning projects. Evidence for this inference came from comparison with an unsupported set of projects, which had little evidence of reaching successful outcomes. Those involved in the projects funded by the Action Learning Project also felt that they had needed the support that was provided.

In terms of the types of support that were felt necessary, the highest rating was given to the networking and dissemination activities organized by the coordinating team. This provides a compelling argument for incorporating opportunities for sharing and dissemination activities within the programme for any similar ventures. The original rationale for having such activities was to pass on lessons learnt from the projects to non-participants. That the participants themselves found them so valuable provides an even more convincing argument for their value.

The other types of support which were most needed were related to the evaluation of the projects. This included producing a suitable evaluation design, devising appropriate evaluation methods and analysing the data which resulted. In providing support, this information should be borne in mind so that the support is provided by a facilitator with expertise in these areas.

14

The critical friend

The dilemmas felt in supporting action research project teams have been discussed in the literature (Elliott, 1985; Kemmis, 1988). In operation, many potential problems have arisen in the kind of cooperation possible between the teacher–researcher and the research facilitator (adviser or consultant). Some problems are caused by the power and authority in this relationship, which impedes the development of the teacher–researcher's reflective and learning capacity (Stenhouse, 1975). Other problems stem from uncertainty on the part of the facilitator over the extent to which direction and help should be given (Elliott, 1985). The dilemmas of these issues arise from the potential for undermining the logic of action research, in which practitioners employ strategies of their own for a practical problem they experience, and this whole process demands reflective capacity in order to foster meaningful outcomes.

Stenhouse (1975) suggested a solution to this paradox by advising action researchers or facilitators to act as 'critical friends'. The facilitator can encourage and prompt academics to start projects, leaving the choice of subject to the lecturers. Once projects start, the facilitator becomes a supportive collaborator. Any advice as to the conduct of the project or inputs from the educational literature can be advanced following Stenhouse's recommendations (1975: 142) as provisional specifications to be tested rather than unqualified recommendations. The relationship between facilitator and lecturer, therefore, moves away from an adviser/client one towards a more equal relationship with each respecting the expertise of the other.

METAPHORS FOR THE ROLE OF THE CRITICAL FRIEND

The involvement of the coordinating team varied from project to project and defining their role was an evolving process. There was an initial meeting with virtually every project team at which the level and type of involvement were negotiated. The role was multi-faceted and the various aspects of the role are discussed in the remainder of this chapter.

The project teams were not required to meet with, let alone use the available support of, the coordinating group. Those who felt confident about conducting their own projects were free to proceed on their own. All but two or three groups, though, did wish to have an initial meeting and most chose to maintain at least some relationship thereafter. The level and nature of involvement of the coordinating team varied considerably from project to project.

All of us were to a greater or lesser extent new to our roles – indeed the roles themselves were new and we had to define them ourselves. In our own initial team meetings the major topic was that of developing and working out our own roles. In this chapter we present our reflections on the role of the coordinators as critical friends. We came to see this as a multi-faceted role. The various aspects are discussed below, with a metaphor for each facet as the heading.

The information given is essentially a reflective account of how the roles developed. At appropriate points there are personal reflections on aspects of the role of coordinator, which are formatted as quotations from reflective writing. Each, therefore, identifies the writer.

The value of this chapter is that it advises potential facilitators on how the role might be conducted. The orientation with which the facilitator/ practitioner relationship is approached is shown to be important. Experience suggests that the facilitator should adopt a flexible approach determined by the needs of the client. There are multiple facets to the role of the facilitator, but the degree of application of each varies from project to project.

Critical friend as financier

Educational action research projects can be conducted with little or no additional resources, but they then require additional work from the participants. Academics are invariably busy people, so they can be reluctant to take on an extra load. Some of the work can be performed by research assistants or student helpers – most typically assistance with the collection and analysis of evaluation data. Assistants can conduct interviews, produce transcripts, analyse qualitative data, conduct classroom observations and analyse questionnaires.

Some potential participants might be able to obtain grants to fund research assistants themselves. Having funds available to support projects, though, proved to be a significant incentive in initiating projects.

In the initial stages, when projects were from the one university, several grants were obtained from the research committee and the educational development fund. The grants were used to fund two research assistants who worked for several projects. When lecturers came along with an idea for a new project it proved useful to have staff on hand so that the project could start right away while the enthusiasm was there. As new projects started, some of the original ones died away for various reasons, so the research assistants worked on a number of projects over a period of about four years.

The experience and expertise acquired through running these projects proved invaluable in writing the grant application to fund the Action Learning Project. Obtaining this grant took the role of financier on to a different plane – the critical friend became a grant-awarding body.

Critical friend as project design consultant

When applying for grants, applicants were informed that they could seek advice on their proposals. The grant-awarding committee also took a constructive approach with proposals. Any that seemed to be based on a good idea but had some deficiencies were either given conditional funding or recommended for resubmission. Advice was available from the coordinating team in either case.

Critical friend as rapport builder

Rapport, according to Goldhammer *et al* (1980), means the harmonious and mutual trusting relationship between people. The development of such a relationship, comments Robinson (1989), is essential to any kind of collaborative work. Krajewski (1993) further argues that rapport is a pre-requisite to the achievement of collegial effort and that the issue of how to encourage and nurture rapport should not be neglected.

All teams were invited to have an initial meeting with the coordinator and their designated associate coordinator. All but two or three wanted this initial meeting. The agenda was largely left to the teams to raise whatever they felt they needed help with, or information on.

Three of the six associate coordinators were not appointed until after the teams started their projects, in two cases by as much as four months. The intention of having the liaison associate coordinator present at the initial meeting was not always met. Either the coordinator was alone, one of the others filled in, or the meeting was delayed until the projects had progressed. This situation did seem to have had an impact on the rapport-building process with some of the teams.

The first meeting served partly as a warm-up visit where relationships could be developed, and it was an opportunity to communicate our interest in the team's work. It was a face-to-face chance for both parties to observe and learn to understand each other. We could clarify what the team needed while they were able to get a better idea of what we could offer. In this way it was possible to reach a mutual accommodation of expectations and working styles for successful cooperation in the later stages:

> It is our supposition that most teams will only vent their feelings, discuss their problems and seek help when they feel secure. Thus in initial contact and meetings, we were cautious to reduce any potential threats. We followed the teams' agenda instead of imposing our own. This helped develop a sense of safety and openness. *(Louisa)*

> Before becoming someone's 'critical friend', one has to be his/her friend first. When I went to the first meeting, I was just someone from the Action Learning Project. Like all friendships, it took time to grow. After a few meetings, we got to know each other better and became friends. My experience was that to build a strong relationship, it is important that we showed strong interest in the work of the project team and tried to be as helpful as possible. But it must be said that that was the ideal situation and did not always happen. I had better and closer working relationships with some project teams than others for various reasons. But then I suppose it is only natural that it turns out that way. *(Tak)*

The main function of the coordinating team was to support each project team in relation to its specific priorities, whilst at the same time providing all of them with information about, and perspectives on, action research methodology and educational evaluation strategies. To serve these greatly varied teams and participate in their work, establishing a method of working with each of them became a key concern for all of us at the outset of the project:

> Basically the projects I have coordinated can be classified into three categories according to the level of my involvement: open, cautious and distant. Working with the 'open' type of projects, I was seen as one of their group members. For instance, I was once invited by a team to sit on the panel to interview the research assistant applicants. Their reason was that I might be working closely with the research assistant, hence I should have the right to make the decision. It appeared that the more involved I became with the teams, the better I understood the projects, and subsequently the more I could con-tribute to the teams. The opposite was also true.
> As to the 'cautious' group of projects, my involvement was apparently less active. My role seemed to be confined to supplying information

such as the date of submitting the report, the possible ways of handling leftover funds, etc. I called these projects 'cautious' because they were very conscious of my presence in their team meetings and of the way they communicated with me. I felt very much the intruder in someone's place. I might be wrong but I sensed that they perceived me as an invigilator who evaluated, inspected and prescribed the work of their team. Inadequate understanding of the projects and limited communication with the project members, combined with the personal frustration caused by a sense of ineptitude to improve the situation were probably responsible for my 'peripheral' involvement.

As the name implies, the 'distant' projects are those with which I had the least involvement. Ironically, the initial meeting with the teams would sometimes become the last meeting. Our communication was almost silent after that. Yet I was not as frustrated as when I confronted the previous type of projects. Throughout the process, the teams were very independent and had shown little or no intention to get support from our coordinating team.

Reflecting on the valuable experience of working with different types of project at the same time, I have found that building a rapport with the teams is not an easy art at all, but involves motivation and effort of both parties. The relations I had with both the 'cautious' and the 'distant' projects were not healthy ones. As Goldhammer *et al* (1980) suggest, a good rapport should be one that can improve the professional self-image of the related parties. *(April)*

Critical friend as coffee maker

To enable the project teams to come to us for information and advice when they felt it necessary, it was desirable to meet them regularly. However, each associate coordinator had responsibility for 10 to 12 project teams, so it was difficult to fix a schedule for meeting regularly with all project teams. A flexible schedule was more suitable and proved to be more efficient:

By making use of geographical proximity, informal meetings of about twenty minutes during coffee breaks are a good idea. It allows me to meet team members face-to-face and for a much longer time than on the phone. In the coffee break, team members can talk about their ideas and reflect upon their actions freshly in a casual manner. In this way I will be well informed about the progress of their projects. Since the time spent is perceived as 'talking over a cup of coffee', the project teams become more ready to talk. We are able to discuss possible issues, seek possible solutions and remedies to particular problems, in a more comfortable manner. This is also a good way to start our working relationship as partners. Once confidence is developed, collaboration will become easier to handle.

Coffee meetings are not only a time for developing connoisseurship in drinking coffee, but also a chance to develop insight in teaching for both parties. In a non-threatening environment, we are more ready to exchange intellectual ideas and experiences in education. Only if academics share insight in real life, do they realize they are not living in an ivory tower. Our professional knowledge and judgement can be fine-tuned by the coffee conversation. *(Bick-har)*

Critical friend as mirror

As participant researchers, the project teams needed someone objective to advise them on the reflection process. Having established a long-term collaborative relationship with teams, it was appropriate for us to challenge them in a positive way. In this way we were seeking to push their thinking forward.

The roles vary from time to time and from place to place. On some occasions it involved questioning project teams in order to encourage them to 'think aloud' about their work. Often they told us that having an outsider who poses questions in a supportive way was in itself very helpful.

More than once, teams were witnessed having trouble in reaching an agreement on the meaning and implications of their data. The situation was worsened when some of the members tended to focus on the students' negative comment or the department's unfriendly environment and became rather upset. Such an uncomfortable atmosphere could be relaxed if the coordinator involved could step in and resolve the conflict. For example, the research assistant responsible for interviewing the students and reporting their feedback could be invited to participate in the discussion to clarify the students' responses, and give a more balanced picture and thus enabled the team to gain more insight into the strengths and weaknesses of their teaching programmes.

The team could be reminded that lessons learnt from what appeared to be failed work could be as valuable as those gained from what turned out successfully. It would be extremely helpful if such potential problems and unforeseen hazards could be disseminated to others interested in similar ideas and methods. Moreover, it was only the first cycle and the students should be given more exposure and feedback before they could fully benefit from an innovation. As to the department, it was the team's responsibility to demonstrate the effectiveness of their initiatives, ally with sympathetic colleagues and gradually gain the confidence and involvement of others.

However, these strategies could not be successful had rapport not already existed between the coordinator and the team. A sense of mutual trust was thus indispensable to our gaining the capacity to mediate and probe deeply.

Critical friend as teaching consultant

There were ways in which support was provided for the teaching of the project teams. One was by providing ideas and advice for their practice:

> One of the projects I am supporting uses a lot of group learning in their course. In the second year of the project, the team decided to use group presentations as the basis for assessment to replace one of the individual assignments. They needed some good tools for marking the presentations. Noticing their need, I sent them a paper recommending some criteria for grading presentations. They found it helpful and then quickly developed an assessment guide from it.
>
> In another case, I have tried developing a group project analysis form for a team, to help the teachers observe how well the students are working in the group projects. The form also provides a checklist for the students to evaluate their own group functioning and identify areas that call for improvement. *(Jessie)*

Another way of enhancing teaching was by helping the project teams to make use of their research findings to inform their teaching in the next step of the action research cycle:

> I remember once I had a meeting with a project team member before the start of his second action cycle. The teacher discussed with me what he would do in the coming semester and I noticed that the data collected in the first cycle had not been well utilized in the planning of the second cycle. I suggested he look at the interview data again and identify issues that needed to be attended to. Then we discussed the data together. I helped him to note what he had achieved in the previous year and what needed to be improved in the coming semester. The critical review and reflection was fruitful. The teacher had a clearer idea of the effects of his first action cycle. He then incorporated improvements in his second cycle of teaching. *(Jessie)*

It is important to add that at times more proactive roles were adopted. Upon the teams' request, we could act as an observer and offer ideas in the process of planning and implementing of teaching initiatives:

Here, a good example is the project with an aim to integrate theory and practice, and develop partnership between teachers and students in the education of registered nurses. I was invited to observe their lecture and tutorial classes to see if the methods adopted were effective in achieving the aims stated in their project. After classes, I usually joined their coffee break and made use of the chance to express my appreciation of their enthusiasm and effort invested in teaching.

Regarding their teaching programmes, both the strength of more intensive and meaningful teacher/student interaction and the benefit of providing additional teaching input to the students were immediately recognized. At the same time, problems were highlighted. For instance, the discussion in the tutorials, which was supposed to be incorporated in the lecture material, was not fully made use of. I made the suggestion that any questions or issues arising from the tutorial were collected on sheets of paper prior to the lecture. The team was really open. They welcomed the idea I recommended and made arrangements accordingly. The incident itself was so rewarding that it has also become an important validating experience in my career. *(Louisa)*

Critical friend as evaluation adviser

Action research has a strong emphasis on reflection and inquiry. Reflection is the essential building block of professional competence and confidence. It has to be grounded on systematic observation and reliable evaluation. So, besides offering advice on teaching, the facilitators contributed to the evaluation design. Here, process was given as much emphasis as content in the work.

Discussion of the evaluation design for the project often took up a major part of the time of the initial meeting. The participants clearly recognized how important evaluation was. Some were concerned to establish a design that would provide proof that their project had succeeded in its aims. However, there was not always a recognition of the importance of obtaining feedback for refining the initiative in second or subsequent cycles:

Incorporating procedures to evaluate the project is something that was suggested to all project teams at the planning stage. Some of the teams thought only of summative evaluation. We suggested to them that, since action research goes in cycles, it is especially important to have formative evaluation. Some teams were more familiar with quantitative methods: we introduced to them qualitative methods as a useful option. Teams that built educational software found that computers could be most useful in tracking learners' behaviours, thus providing valuable information for evaluation purposes. *(Tak)*

Many of the teams were willing to admit to a lack of expertise in evaluation. Attention was then drawn to some important factors when planning evaluation. These included the methods available, the importance of triangulation and developing a plan with a realistic timeframe that was consistent with the teaching timetable. Working in partnership with the teams, an action plan could be drawn up with the evaluation methods scheduled to be implemented in the action research cycle.

Advice alone was sometimes not enough. There was a growing demand for some form of training programme where the project teams and their research assistants could gain practical knowledge and experience on how to carry out their evaluation scheme. To meet this need, evaluation workshops were run to demonstrate skills involved in designing and conducting particular evaluation methods, offer practice to the participants and provide feedback related to particular techniques.

Many teams wished to use questionnaires. Many were given advice and help with the design of these. They were normally able to identify the main areas to be asked about, but appreciated advice on the development of appropriate items. They also needed to be shown how to design a questionnaire to be used with the standard optical mark reader forms we provided.

It proved to be more efficient to provide a service for analysing questionnaire data than to teach participants how to do it themselves. The teams were told that as long as they used standard optical mark reader forms, which were provided, the data would be processed for them. This data processing was not a time-consuming exercise and results were normally returned within a day or two:

> In my position, I need to provide a central service for processing and analysing quantitative evaluation data and providing advice on the interpretation of results. However, these depend on the needs of project teams and they vary from project to project.
>
> Besides working with the project teams, I also act in conjunction with the other associate coordinators assigned to the project. Advice is provided, where necessary, on the design of questionnaires and the type of analysis. The teams can choose to do the data entry by themselves but most use standard optical mark reader forms we provide, because of their reliability and efficiency. On return, these forms are fed through the optical mark reader. It only takes one day to get the data. The resulting data file is analysed with SPSS [Statistical Package for the Social Sciences] to give standard statistical output or specific tests requested by the teams. Advice on the interpretation of

results is provided if necessary. Sometimes we meet again if the teams want additional assistance or further refinement in the analysis. Often it is necessary to examine the data in conjunction with the qualitative analysis.

Some of the teams are more experienced and know what they wish to do beforehand. They tell me all the details including their question-naire design, methods of collecting data, analysis techniques and what they want to do with the results. Some teams may need more help in the whole process, from designing of questionnaires, collecting and analysing of data to interpreting the output. Since they are not familiar with evaluation, they almost completely rely on me. *(Sandra)*

Critical friend as research adviser

It was clear that the possibility of publications provided a rationale for many to participate in their projects. This is one form of teaching enhancement initiative which can result in rewards to participants under the traditional reward structure of universities. Before the advent of action research, taking part in educational development activities usually penalized participants as it resulted in less time for research, which is rewarded.

As stated above, the topic that took up the most time, overall, in the initial meetings was developing an evaluation design for projects. In most cases this was also a research design, which was commonly expressed as a need to find some form of proof that the initiative had been successful. The participants realized that if they were to publish a paper about the outcomes of their project, acceptance would be much more likely if they could provide evidence for the effectiveness of what had been undertaken.

More exploratory approaches, though, were often discovered to be necessary. As the teams were from most major disciplines, many par-ticipants faced the need for different paradigms or methods to those traditionally used in their discipline. It was perhaps surprising how ready many of the participants were to attempt qualitative research or to abandon experiment/control designs in favour of more naturalistic approaches. Some participants from the newer universities had limited research exper-ience so the issue was more that of developing a paradigm than shifting:

I was expected to dispense instant advice on research design, data collection and analysis to a whole range of projects. The aims of the projects were very diverse and their nature varied. A standard approach was not possible so advice had to be individually form-ulated and tailored for projects. I was aware that I was putting myself on the line each time one of these meetings was held. An inability to suggest anything that seemed sensible and practicable would have seriously impaired the process of developing relationships with the teams. Dispensing poor advice could have resulted in a recurring future nightmare if things did not work out or papers were consistently rejected on methodological grounds. *(David)*

There was also need for on-going help with research methods. Much of this was provided by the associate coordinators as they interacted with their assigned teams. As the amount of experience in educational research varied from team to team, the extent to which they needed our support varied accordingly:

> For example, a team invited me to help with the design of their questionnaire. For another team on problem-based learning, I not only helped with the literature search, but also the front-line area of work such as classroom observation and student interviews. It appeared that the more experienced teams were more confident as to how the data should be collected and analysed while the less experienced teams were a bit more cautious in every step they took, which meant more time could be spent on decision-making.
>
> It is worth noting that though the teams consult us for our advice, there is no obligation for them to follow what has been suggested; it is their project after all. Here is one example. To back up the data collected through videotaping of the class, I suggested that the team audiotaped the lesson as well. The idea was rejected and they insisted that videotaping was enough. Yet when they came to the point where detailed transcription was needed, they found that it was very troublesome to do the transcription with the VCR. Also the soundtrack on the videotapes was not clear. They then decided to use both audio and videotaping in the next phase. That is the spirit of our Action Learning Project – learning through experience, learning through action. *(April)*

Critical friend as resource provider

In order to encourage and prompt academics to start educational action research projects, information booklets were produced, at the very early stages of the project, for the reference of whoever might have been latent participants. One of these publications explained what action research was about and demonstrated to academics how the ideas could be applied to improving teaching practice. It included examples of some educational action research projects that had already taken place in Hong Kong.

Another booklet described and gave examples of the use of a method for establishing the effectiveness of educational innovations. There was also a booklet which contains an annotated bibliography of research into teaching and learning in the universities in Hong Kong. All these were available free to academics. Experience showed that these booklets were not only useful as catalysts, but also provided useful help to those project team members who had insufficient knowledge of educational research and teaching evaluation.

A further aspect of the resource-centre role was keeping a pool of general equipment items such as tape recorders and transcribers, which were made available to project teams on request. It was decided that this library-style lending arrangement would be more cost-effective than providing dedicated equipment to each of the projects that requested the items in the original grant applications. Also supplied were the standard optical mark reader forms for teams to use with questionnaires:

> The coordinating team provides equipment that can be borrowed by the project teams. It is available on a library-type system and there is no loan period. Most of the teams are cooperative and will return it when they have finished using it. However, problems over equipment availability do happen once in a while. Then I need to have a discussion with the users and find a 'suitable' time for each of them to use it. *(Sandra)*

Things did not always turn out as the team planned. Projects could get stuck for many different reasons. When this happened there was often a call for help, which often involved locating information or resources needed to fix the problem. We often used our own networks to get teams supplied with things ranging from a couple of references, widely used questionnaires, mini-cassettes, transcribing machines, data analysis software, multimedia packages for high-quality presentations in conferences, and even space for meetings and seminars.

A common problem was finding a suitable research assistant. This was most likely to occur to those with limited funds who could only make short-term part-time offers. There were several remedies that could be suggested. At times we acted as an employment agency by referring teams to research assistants already serving on other projects which were drawing to a close. If there were two or more projects on a similar topic in a university, the teams were advised to pool their funds and employ a shared research assistant, who could then be offered a longer contract. Others might be advised to look for part-time helpers in potential pools like students in their department.

Critical friend as writing consultant

Many of the participants saw publications as an important outcome of their projects. When it came to the writing-up stage, help was often called upon. The nature of the help requested could be placed on a spectrum depending on the degree of involvement required.

At the lowest level of involvement, advice could be sought on whether particular conferences might be suitable for presenting papers or on lists of journals that include articles about teaching innovations. Moving up a step came advice on the length, format, tone or style of educational articles. It should be borne in mind that most of those involved felt they were venturing outside their normal discipline in writing a paper for an educational journal or even one of the discipline-specific educational journals:

> Stepping up the level of involvement considerably we come to the requests to read and comment upon draft papers. The nature of the advice here could be quite varied. Commonly the papers could be improved by reference to some theoretical framework so the authors could be helped by providing appropriate references. Suggestions on presenting the analysis of data were probably the most common form of advice. Many of our prospective authors were writing in a second language and a fair proportion lacked confidence in their ability to write fluently to the standard expected by journals. Reassuring them that their English was really quite good, while correcting the odd error was fine. However, I tried to avoid the role of copy-editor, when this was needed, if at all possible.
>
> The final step up moved the role more towards writer than writing consultant. This only arose in the projects, started prior to the Action Learning Project, in which I was a full participant. Somehow when it came to writing up the projects I usually seemed to be the most involved. This seemed perfectly reasonable, though, as in other aspects of the project, such as the teaching initiatives themselves, I had normally been the least involved. *(David)*

Critical friend as matchmaker

From the outset it was noticed that some projects had common interests by discipline area or type of initiative. However, the teams themselves were less aware of the overlaps than we were. Therefore, in various ways, we tried to put teams with similar interests in contact with each other. In the initial stages the arrangements were informal:

The old Chinese saying 'Not to be a matchmaker and you will be prosperous for at least three generations' denotes the unpopularity of a matchmaker in Chinese society. While many Chinese see matchmaking as a job, which will bring the matchmaker bad luck, I have found the experience of 'matchmaking' enjoyable and rewarding. One of the most common concerns of the project teams I have worked with was their uncertainty about the direction of their projects. They questioned if they were on the 'right' track. One team has constantly reflected on the appropriateness of the research methodology used in their study and was anxious to know if there were other teams doing something similar to theirs. Another team worried that with twenty subjects, the results of the study, though apparently encouraging, might not be representative and persuasive enough. To lessen their worry and anxiety, we introduced related teams to them and at their request, arranged meetings with them. *(April)*

Matchmaking could be really useful. One of the team told us that they were trying to build a multimedia laboratory; we told them there was one in the same building now being used by another team. One team said they wanted to do 3-D simulation but lacked experience. We told them there was a team in another university using the same technology to build state-of-the-art learning tools. *(Tak)*

Positive feedback and positive outcomes from these informal meetings encouraged the development of the more formal meeting and dissemination activities described in Chapter 7. The principal avenues for sharing insights were the interest group meetings. Meetings were held which focused around the following common themes: English-language teaching, multimedia, problem-based learning, reflective practice, active learning, and assessment.

Critical friend as deadline enforcer

One of the guidelines set for administering the overall project was the reduction of bureaucracy to the absolute minimum. This helped maintain good relationships with participants and also made it easier to run the project. E-mail was used for virtually all communications. E-mail mailing lists were built up at the start, so it took only a matter of minutes to send a message to all 250 or so participants:

As an associate coordinator, I have to look after the ten teams I am responsible for, including following up why some of the teams do not respond to certain messages. That is why sometimes we need to perform the duty of 'deadline enforcer'. At first I was quite optimistic about this job. I thought that both technology and people can be trusted, so I did not bother to contact the team when messages were sent out. As time ran, I was surprised that there were so many signals telling me that my teams were not responding to e-mail messages. I had to make phone calls and send memos out to remind them about what was happening in the Action Learning Project communication network. I was surprised but dubious to discover so many problems in the delivery of e-mail messages! I become more conscious about time and watched the 'deadlines' more closely because of those teams. *(Bick-har)*

In spite of conscious efforts to reduce bureaucracy and build a rapport with teams, there was still a need at times to act as policeman and act to enforce deadlines. The overall project was accountable and did have to deliver. Furthermore the project was committed to disseminating outcomes. You cannot disseminate what you do not have!

The directive given to us was to use whatever means one considered to be within the rules of the law to ensure that deadlines were to be met. Fortunately we did not have to resort to drastic measures. Our experience was to give the teams ample notice and to set the deadline at some appropriate time in the academic year when the teams are not too preoccupied with other important duties. If one of the teams had difficulty meeting the deadline, it would be useful to meet with them and to lend our support. *(Tak)*

INFORMING TEAMS OF AVAILABLE SUPPORT

The Action Learning Project was itself an action research project looking at how to organize and provide support for large clusters of action learning projects. One lesson that was learnt was that it was important to be clear at the outset about the type of support available from the coordinating team. It is not surprising that some participants were not clear as to what support was available, as three members of the coordinating team were not appointed when the projects commenced and the supporting role was being developed as the projects proceeded.

The role is now more clearly defined to the extent of being able to write a chapter describing it. Potential facilitators now have this experience to draw upon, so should have a better idea of what might be expected and the most fruitful orientation in relating with participants. It should also be possible to explain both of these to participants at the outset.

Before an initial meeting it would be worthwhile providing an introduction to the supporting team with contact information. The relationship between the project teams and the coordinating team could be explained. The types of support available might be discussed. These will be along the lines of the facets of the critical-friend role described in this chapter. Teams would be told how to take advantage of each of the available services if they needed them. Resources available would also be listed.

CONCLUSION

The experience of working within the Action Learning Project was a learning experience for the coordinating team and our own action research project into how to be a critical friend:

> Having been an associate coordinator for more than a year, I am now fully aware of the importance and difficulties of building a non-threatening and mutual-respect relationship with the teams. Yet I have to admit that I was a bit naive when I first took up the job, which was in part due to the unfamiliar working environment and in part the ambiguity of my role.
>
> My experience is that displaying an interest in working with the team is only the beginning. Displaying the professional knowledge and competency and the use of interpersonal skills throughout is a crucial step. Had I the chance to start the job over again, I would definitely make every effort to develop the rapport with the teams as early as possible. *(April)*

We feel that we have all learnt about and developed into the role. Hopefully passing on what we have discovered about the role will be of value to other existing or potential critical friends.

We have described a variety of facets of the role of the critical friend that we have adopted in support of educational action research projects. We have come to recognize that the manner in which any of these aspects of the role is conducted depends upon our relationship with the team. Indeed, as the teams are not obliged to work with a critical friend, establishing a rapport with a team is a prerequisite for any of the roles to begin to function.

In this chapter we have described various facets of our role as critical friends in support of educational action research projects. Those facilitating action research in other contexts may find that some facets are not applicable to their situation. Nevertheless, consideration of the potential benefits from adopting such a facet should at least be examined. Similarly, in other contexts and other levels and types of education, the particular strategies or tactics we have adopted may not be the most successful. But again we feel that our experiences should at least provide some insights in devising alternative approaches.

Support from colleagues and students

As well as needing and receiving support from facilitators, there is a reasonable expectation that some level of support would be needed from fellow teachers, department heads, the department or course team as a whole and the students in the classes involved. This chapter looks at each of these constituencies to see whether there was a perceived need for their support and whether that support was forthcoming.

SUPPORT FROM THE DEPARTMENT

As well as valuing support from facilitators, it was reasonable to assume that participants would appreciate encouragement and support from heads and colleagues in their departments. One aspect of this support was the establishment of an encouraging environment, which helped provide the momentum to complete the project. The interest and respect of heads and colleagues could also be of importance where the impact of teaching initiatives and curriculum developments has some dependence upon others in the department, as they often do. If there is to be any wider impact within a department upon those not formally involved in a project team, there needs to be at least some level of interest from colleagues and the head.

The questionnaire to participants asked them to agree or disagree with statements that they had received support from their departmental head, colleagues and students in participating in the project. The results from these questions are shown in Figure 15.1.

Heads of department and colleagues

Just over a quarter of the respondents felt that they did not receive support from their department head. All submissions for grants had to be endorsed by the department head, to show that the participants would be able to

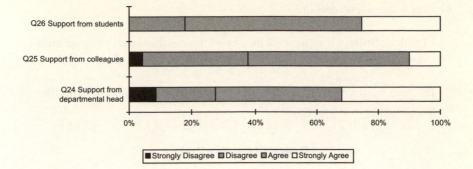

Figure 15.1 Support from students, colleagues and department heads

conduct their project. In view of the campaigns to have teaching accepted as a valued scholarly activity, it is disappointing that any participants felt their head failed to provide support beyond the initial endorsement:

> Actually the department is resistant to this style of teaching; they did not accept it. They did not see the progress from this method of teaching.

However, the responses indicate that the large majority of heads were supportive and the proportion of respondents indicating strong agreement suggests that a reasonable proportion of heads provided good support:

> My department head has expressed interest in developing similar tools for other courses in the department.

Indeed the heads or deans actively participated in some projects and in these cases the projects would be envisaged as a vehicle for making changes within departments:

> Yes, a more problem-based approach in teaching and learning has been considered by many departments in the [. . .] Faculty.

The level of perceived support from colleagues was lower. A reasonable interpretation of the overall response was that colleagues were neither openly enthusiastic nor unhelpful. Some participants felt they had had an impact upon their colleagues:

> Yes, it has challenged staff to a 'new' form of teaching and learning.

> It will inevitably affect the ways in which other courses are taught in the future.

Others were not so certain:

> I think definitely it enhanced their awareness that such programmes exist. As for any influence on their behaviour, I really don't know.

> Its goal to provide a model for further development within the programme is not so certain.

Providing facilities

Provision of adequate equipment and resources within the department facilitated the running of the projects, particularly those multimedia ones whose aims in most cases were to produce a learning package with computers:

> At least we got our workstations' software free of charge from the department.

> I think facilities are also very important. If there was no recording room, we could not make the sound effect. If we couldn't find disks containing good background music, there would be big problems for us.

Besides, the availability of appropriate technical assistance within the department was another favourable condition for the projects to achieve their aims:

> Our department is also very helpful. There is an assistant responsible for display. For example, if the teacher in last lesson connected the computer to world wide web, the mode would be different from the usual and we could not use it. It would be very troublesome. But now, there is a person to reset it at once.

Apart from tangible technical support, having a conducive climate within the department with the positive attitude of the department head towards the projects undertaken was also important:

> The department head is very sympathetic.

> Also the kind of supporting environment, the environment around you, allows you to practise and you have the freedom to do things.

Student support

It is of interest to note that the highest level of perceived support was from students. Conservatism and negative reactions from students to educational innovation are common items of anecdotal wisdom. It has perhaps been particularly prevalent with respect to Asian students, especially if the innovation involves a shift from didactic teaching to more interactive forms.

Responses to further questions about student involvement backed the conclusion drawn from the previous figure. The results in Figure 15.2 show that students played an active role in the projects and the large majority were happy to do so, even if some were not aware of what was happening.

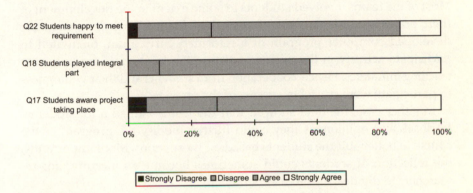

Figure 15.2 Support from students

The written comments substantiated this point by showing that the Asian students, who are often described as passive, were perfectly able to participate actively if the teaching encouraged active learning:

> The problem-based learning approach engaged students far more actively and sustained their involvement far more than any other courses within the Department.

> The project was really quite successful in giving students an alternative learning experience.

The large majority of participants felt that students supported their initiatives rather than resisting them. Comments of students preferring more active participation strongly out-weighed the remainder, which were limited to a small number of students.

The participants were also pleased with the impact of the projects on the students' attitudes towards teaching and learning, and on teacher/ student relationships:

As far as learning is concerned, I feel that students are gaining – their attendance and participation is good, skills are developing and their performance is improving.

The results of the survey show clearly that the attitude that students resist academic innovation is a myth, which needs debunking. If Asian students are truly more conservative, their Western counterparts must positively relish innovation.

Student participation

Most of the teams involved students to some extent in the development of their projects. Students were either asked for feedback on some new developed computer program or a reformed curriculum, or invited to participate actively in the project, assisting the teachers to try out some teaching initiatives. Hence, cooperation from students and their willingness to participate were crucial to success of the projects.

In either case, the data showed that the teams valued a lot students' feedback and opinion, as they could further modify the program or the course to better suit the students based on those input. More importantly, the reflection of students could sometimes become an incentive for researchers to dig deeper into their study:

In the evaluation, students reflected that the idea of providing feedback was good but they hoped the answers could stay longer on the screen. This proved that they had reflection. They noticed what could really help them to learn. This is very important for our future design. How can we structure the information in a way that we can ask students questions right after they've learnt it?

From the answers given by the students in the questionnaire, I am now very interested in finding out why there are students still preferring the traditional way of learning.

It is of interest that a team had involved in their study almost all the students in the department, which was uncommon:

As the students knew that almost all the staff in the department have participated in the project, they were quite willing to join us . . . Our department is not a big one, which has its own advantages.

Moreover some students were mature enough to 'realize that their participation would help the forthcoming students' and they were considered as partners rather than some kind of subjects for the study. This kind of relationship might have had an effect on the extent to which students committed themselves to the projects:

> They are quite clear of their role . . . Almost all of them have participated in the study. Because it is part of their job . . . They don't feel they are forced to do it.

SUPPORT FROM COLLEAGUES IN OTHER PROJECTS

The plans for the Action Learning Project included a range of dissemination activities. The original rationale for these events was so that lessons learnt from the projects could be passed on to non-participants who might incorporate some of the ideas into their own teaching. What was not foreseen was the extent to which the dissemination activities would be valued by the participants themselves.

The questionnaire to participants asked them to evaluate the dissemination activities by responding to statements about the seminars, workshops, interest group meetings and conference. Note that the data were collected before the conference. The results illustrated in Figure 15.3 show that the substantial majority of respondents felt these activities were a necessary part of the project.

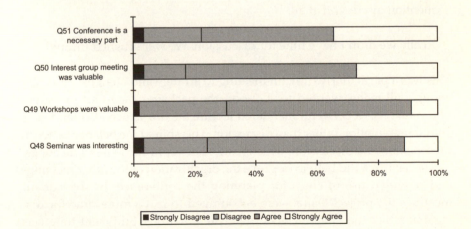

Figure 15.3 Reactions to dissemination activities

Interest group meetings

Qualitative data collected from the open-ended part of the questionnaires, and interviews with project teams, also contained feedback and comments on the various dissemination activities. These confirmed that the perceived value of the interest group meetings considerably exceeded our original expectations. It was clear that the meetings succeeded in developing high levels of collegiality among participants from different universities, who normally did not know each other prior to the meetings:

> We think the interest group is beneficial to us. We've learnt about different cases that broaden our knowledge in action research.

> Wonderful . . . [It] let researchers of different institutions meet and exchange ideas. It is a wonderful means to facilitate professional development!

> [It is] a valuable experience for teams to develop skills and learn through each other's cases. And it's good to know of people working together to improve teaching in different fields.

The format for meetings was informed by comments on one of the earliest meetings of the multimedia interest group, which suggested that insufficient time was allocated for discussion:

> There were too many presentations. We did not really have time to really get to know some of the reports and their products, not to mention discussion at all.

> Really we didn't have time for discussion. We were rushed through.

This was a particularly difficult meeting to arrange and chair as, naturally enough, all teams wanted to show off the packages they had prepared. The venue was a conventional tiered lecture theatre which also tended to favour presentation rather than discussion. This shifted the balance between presentation and discussion, which worked better in subsequent meetings.

The feedback did help to improve the organization of the other meetings and provided useful clues for planning the conference. In subsequent meetings the project teams were encouraged to leave more time for discussion rather than just focus on their presentations. Sufficient time was allocated to each project to allow for interaction, though there are always limits here, as meetings have to last a finite time. For the conference, papers were made available in advance from the Action Learning Project Web site.

These measures together led to more interaction and sharing among the participants and the effect seemed to be satisfactory to all.

Level of meetings

The response to the interest group meetings, in the evaluation and additional positive feedback received during and after the meetings, did lead to consideration of how frequent should be the organized sessions for cross-fertilization of ideas among project teams. The meetings did seem to be a very successful medium for critical reflection, which is an important part of action research. There were comments that suggested that more frequent meetings might have been appreciated:

> More problem-based sessions about research design and implementation would have been helpful.

However, even with the existing level of sessions, not all interested project members could attend these meetings:

> Workshops of interest were usually oversubscribed or at impossible times.

> Often difficult to attend the many and interesting workshops because of teaching commitments and distance.

Some of the seminars were offered twice in different locations in order that more participants could attend them; yet it was not easy, or in fact possible, to find a time which was convenient for all. There was a particular difficulty in Hong Kong of finding suitable time-slots as, at the time, the seven universities did not have common academic calendars – the start of the academic years, for example, differed by more than a month. In the two common holidays of the summer and Chinese New Year, many academics leave Hong Kong.

Increasing the level of meetings would, no doubt, have increased the tension between participants valuing the discussion and dealing with conflicting commitments. A similar tension arose with the duration of meetings. The views of some of the participants cited above suggest that one meeting was too rushed; yet increasing the duration would inevitably have meant that fewer would have attended the whole session. On balance we suspect that it would have been valuable to arrange more inter-group discussion along the lines of the interest group meetings – however, not too much more. The remark of one project member is particularly apt, at this point:

> More opportunity to meet with like groups could be useful but I am
> not sure how realistic given that we could have done this ourselves
> but didn't!

To conclude, the dissemination activities were valued by the participants at large and provided considerable mutual support. In particular, it proved helpful to provide opportunities for project teams to meet and exchange experiences with other research groups during the progress of their projects.

Although it was unrealistic to collect data from academics at large, it seems likely that the dissemination activities had a reasonable impact on those not involved with projects. The attendance at the various activities was always reasonable, culminating in over 300 coming to the conference. Beyond the beneficial lessons learnt from the sessions, the publicity for the events must have raised consciousness that teaching and learning are legitimate fields for academic endeavour.

SUMMARY

It seems reasonable to assume that action learning projects are more likely to be successful if they take place in an environment of appreciation and support. In the main the projects supported by the Action Learning Project did take place in a conducive atmosphere.

The teams reported that their students generally participated actively in the initiatives and were pleased to do so. This is a significant finding as it is common to hear that students, and particularly those from the Asian region, are resistant to changes away from traditional, didactic forms of teaching. The experiences of the participants in these projects suggest that this is an anecdotal impression, which has little truth.

Support from heads of department varied along a spectrum. At one extreme were those who saw the projects as important initiatives for improving the quality of learning and teaching within their departments. At the other extreme were heads who discouraged participants by under-valuing research into teaching and learning by a preference for research into the discipline itself. Fortunately the majority of the participants placed their head towards the supporting end of the spectrum, though the minority that did not was a significant one.

Colleagues in the same department were commonly seen as neutral in their support of the projects. There was generally neither hostility nor overt help. Colleagues who were very supportive were the participants in other similar projects. One surprising feature was the extent to which there was cross-fertilization and the development of collegial networks across the projects.

PART E
CONCLUSION

David Kember

The final part of the book draws overall lessons about action learning as a mechanism for enhancement of the quality of learning and teaching. It also examines its position and effectiveness alongside other types of measure for quality assurance and enhancement.

Chapter 16 points out that there are costs associated with schemes for ensuring quality in higher education, and naturally enough the more elaborate the scheme the higher the cost. Further, the marginal quality-returns decrease as the measures become more involved and more expensive. There are also differing relationships between cost and quality-return for quality-control and quality-enhancement schemes. In the former, improvement in quality tends towards a plateau as teaching and courses reach some minimum acceptable standard. There may even be a decrease in quality if schemes become excessively time-consuming or inquisitorial. Quality-enhancement schemes show smaller reductions in marginal quality-returns as investment increases. Workshop-type schemes tend to peter out as the level of offering increases but project-type approaches continue to show returns unless the investment becomes very high.

The relative cost structures are used as an argument for evaluating quality measures themselves, for simplifying quality-assurance measures where necessary and for a shift towards quality enhancement. It is suggested that institutions need a balanced portfolio of quality measures, with basic quality-assurance schemes to ensure minimum standards, workshops up to the level of market demand, and remaining resources allocated to support for quality-enhancement initiatives through schemes such as grants for educational development projects similar to the Action Learning Project.

The final chapter, Chapter 17, draws together conclusions from strands that have been developing through the book. It summarizes the case for utilizing action learning as an effective means of enhancing the quality of teaching and learning.

Arguments are presented that the action research framework is viable as a method for quality enhancement. Diverting resources from quality assurance to project-type measures would be accompanied by a shift from control to empowerment, which should have a beneficial effect upon morale and motivation.

The process of engaging in action learning projects is itself seen as a positive outcome as it encourages the development of attitudes and skills for the on-going self-monitoring and development of teaching. An essential point is treating teaching quality enhancement as an academic activity. It is argued that project-type activities proceed more effectively with an appropriate supporting infrastructure and that an integral part of that should be dissemination activities which can develop supporting networks and pass on lessons to others not involved in the projects.

Appendix A is a copy of the questionnaire sent to all participants in the Action Learning Project. Results derived from the questionnaire have referred to the question number so the appendix clarifies the nature of information provided by giving the item in full.

Appendix B gives the interview schedule, which was used as a guide in interviewing a random selection of teams.

Appendix C lists the titles of the projects, which gives more insight into the nature of the diverse range of supported projects.

16

Conclusions on effectiveness

The Action Learning Project is one of innumerable initiatives taken in recent years with the aim of verifying or improving the quality of teaching and learning in universities. In considering the value and accomplishments of the Action Learning Project, it therefore makes sense to assess its achievements in the light of those of other types of scheme with similar ends in mind. A venture can be successful, but it makes no sense to invest heavily in schemes of that type if other ventures, with similar destinations in mind, yield greater returns.

To do this with any degree of precision is extremely hard, as it requires some measure of cost-effectiveness, or quality improvement as a function of cost. There is an extensive literature on defining and assessing quality in higher education (eg, Barnett, 1992; Craft, 1992; Elton and Partington, 1991; Loder, 1990; Polytechnics and Colleges Funding Council, 1990). Given the extensiveness of the debate and the tentative nature of many of the conclusions, it is reasonable to deduce that it is hard even to define quality in teaching and learning. There are some performance indicators that have been used but, given the complex nature of quality in education, these can only be interpreted as indicators and not as absolute measures. Determining quality requires a judgement based upon a range of evidence related to the context and mission of the institution or course.

Costs ought to be easier to determine, though they are often not examined. When accounts are produced, many hidden costs are often ignored – most notably the time of those involved. It clearly makes little sense to produce accounts that do not include the most significant cost, though producing reasonable estimates of staff time may not be easy. There is an argument for making the effort to cost staff time to show how expensive some quality schemes have become. These days most academics are working to capacity so the time taken up by complying with quality measures is time that cannot be devoted to teaching or research.

Despite being a hard task, it seems worthwhile to attempt some analysis of the cost-effectiveness of quality schemes, since the accountability of higher education is important and the real costs of quality schemes have reached significant proportions of many universities' budgets. The reader must accept, though, that as neither quality nor cost have been or can be determined with precision the following analysis has to deal in qualitative arguments rather than measured comparisons.

COMPARISON OF TYPES OF SCHEMES

As there are so many individual schemes for assuring or enhancing teaching quality, any comparison must examine broad types of measure. Chapter 1 introduced a schema for categorizing quality initiatives into generic classes. Initially the schema contrasted quality-assurance and quality-enhancement measures. These were distinguished by Elton's (1992) grouping of the four quality 'A's (quality assurance, accountability, audit and assessment), defined as concerned with control of both quality and the people who control quality. Quality enhancement, on the other hand, was defined to encompass the four 'E's; empowerment, enthusiasm, expertise and excellence.

This chapter will also make use of the sub-division of quality-enhancement schemes into two categories of project-type initiatives and workshop-type activities. The project category is taken as encompassing a range of initiatives with similar underpinning to the projects supported by the Action Learning Project, but not identical in all respects. The category includes all project-type initiatives in which academics, often in groups, examine and tackle some aspect of their course with an apparent problem or needing a different approach. Inevitably these projects will last for some time. The projects may be supported by a facilitator acting in an advisory capacity. The initiatives may be isolated, or there may be a broader scheme of grants in place to encourage or initiate such projects.

The other quality-enhancement category encompasses workshop-type activities. 'Workshop-type' includes workshops themselves, courses for new staff, mini-courses, newsletters, individual counselling or other forms of advice-giving or teaching-how-to-teach that are essentially instructive in nature. The duration of the sessions is normally considerably shorter than the projects included in the previous category. These workshop-type activities are probably the most common form of quality-enhancement measures offered by educational development units (Moses, 1985).

This chapter will present an argument that the two types of quality-enhancement measures – the projects and workshops – have differing cost structures, and these both differ from that for quality-assurance measures. Each of the three categories is examined in turn. For each category, costs (including staff time) are considered and then anticipated quality enhancement is examined. The two are then related in a graph of teaching-quality improvement against cost, which is a measure of cost-effectiveness.

The graph is used because it is argued that marginal returns will vary with the level of effort and expenditure. More expensive and elaborate quality schemes may have quite different rates of return to simple inexpensive ones.

QUALITY ASSURANCE

It is hard to find data on the cost-effectiveness of quality-assurance measures because very few quality-assurance schemes are themselves properly evaluated. It seems quite hypocritical that this is the case since the schemes mostly exhort or require academics to have their teaching evaluated. When evaluation does take place it tends to be at a superficial level. Reactions are sought to the mechanics of the scheme with a view to making improvements within its existing operating framework. Such an evaluation fails to deal with the purpose of quality-control schemes, which is improving the quality of teaching and learning. A valid evaluation method should, then, examine whether the schemes do indeed impact upon teaching and learning and whether they do so in an efficient manner.

Nevertheless, an attempt is made to examine the cost-effectiveness of quality-control schemes. Firstly, the typical cost structures of quality-control schemes are examined. Secondly, some available evaluation data are examined. Thirdly, the constraints upon such schemes are examined to assess the limits of their impact. Finally, potential quality returns are related to costs.

The fact that we have limited data on both the effect and the cost of quality-assurance measures means that it is hard to draw conclusions about cost-effectiveness. As it turns out, though, overall cost-effectiveness is not necessarily the most important issue. Anticipating one of the conclusions of this chapter, for most institutions and national schemes it is more important to look at marginal effects than absolute comparisons.

The question of whether there should be quality-assurance, workshop-type schemes, or project-type schemes is not a useful one. Firstly, there is usually little or no choice about whether or not institutions have some form of quality assurance. Either they have to participate in a national scheme, or they may have to participate in a review process to demonstrate that the institution has effective quality-assurance processes in place.

Secondly, most institutions have some form of quality assurance and many have a degree of quality enhancement too. Few would be starting with nothing. It is, therefore, more relevant and useful to examine marginal effects and the balance between types of schemes. More useful questions are whether the level of quality assurance or enhancement is appropriate, or whether more or less resources applied to a particular type of scheme would produce a more effective outcome. If a finite level of resources is assumed, the intelligent question then becomes that of determining the most effective balance between the types of quality scheme.

Costs of quality assurance

Quality-assurance measures normally require academic staff to prepare submissions and produce records to justify the quality of their teaching and courses. As these activities would not be undertaken in the normal course of academic work, they reduce time for productive teaching and research, and so are a cost. The submissions are then discussed, in a process normally called peer review, which is again a cost in the form of the time of all involved. However, the 'peers' – who normally constitute the quality control review panels – tend to be drawn from the more senior university staff, often together with external experts, so their time is expensive. Submissions too are in most cases prepared by more senior staff within a department. The quality-control processes are normally run by a secretariat, or part of the registrar's unit, which constitutes a further cost.

The costs of quality-control measures rise with the intensity, frequency and complexity of the schemes, since the necessary time input rises. The relationship with these closely related variables presumably approximates to a linear one.

Evaluation of outcomes

The difficulty of determining the effectiveness of quality-assurance schemes is that so few of them have been evaluated at all, let alone evaluated to see whether any improvement in teaching quality is achieved at a reasonable cost. An illustration of this point is provided by edited collections of selected papers from two international conferences on quality assurance in higher education (Craft, 1992, 1994). The authors were mostly respected academics and/or senior figures in national accreditation bodies. A careful search of both books failed to locate any evidence presented to show that the quality-assurance schemes were having any impact upon the quality of teaching and learning, let alone doing so in an effective way. Some papers did show critical self-reflection upon aspects of the quality schemes, but many simply consisted of pure description.

The irony of this situation is shown by the editor's introduction to the second of these books. Craft (1994: xi) believed that:

The developments reported in this book document the birth of a new quality assurance 'profession' ... It will be important for this new profession to be seen to practice the self-evaluation and self-assessment it preaches.

That the authors of the various papers have taken little note of this injunction is hard to interpret. Possibly quality assurance has become accepted as an act of faith among its adherents, so they see no need to justify its value. It is also possible that, particularly for schemes at the national level, evaluation has not been conducted because the magnitude of the schemes is such that evaluation would be both difficult and costly. This is hardly an acceptable argument, though, because the cost and impact of the scheme itself must be of a far greater magnitude still. It might appear sensible to ensure that the largest schemes with the greatest impact are those that are more likely to be evaluated. In practice there appears to be a tendency for the opposite to occur.

The fact that quality-assurance schemes are so rarely evaluated could in itself be taken as a subject of concern. For the purpose of this book it is a side issue, which complicates the aim of comparing quality measures. Given the intention of concentrating upon marginal effects and the acceptance of broad qualitative effects, it should still be possible to draw some conclusions from the evidence that is available.

The first conclusion that might be drawn is that quality-assurance measures tend to have a limited effect upon teaching and learning quality. There is some evidence that the level of returns from quality-control measures can be quite low. For a given level of resource devoted to quality assurance, the effect on the quality of teaching may be limited and possibly less than that for other types of quality measure.

Returns from programme-approval mechanisms can be examined by comparing systems in operation when universities in the UK and Australia were divided into two distinct categories. These countries formerly had a two-tier system of traditional research universities and colleges (colleges of advanced education or CAEs in Australia, and polytechnics in the UK), which had more vocationally-orientated courses and did less research. The traditional universities had mostly relied upon internal procedures, which required little documentation and limited review processes. The non-university tertiary institutions in both countries, though, were required to submit proposals to external regulatory bodies. The procedures required extensive documentation, were subject to peer review by panels including external members and the processes could be quite lengthy. It might be expected that the extensive processes employed by the CAEs and poly-technics would leave them with better-designed courses and a more developed quality-assurance culture. Frazer (1992), for example, believed that 'often the better developed approaches to quality assurance are to be found in the non-university sectors' (p 10).

Following the unification of the tertiary sector in both countries, the universities have been appraised by a common system. One might expect that the former CAEs and polytechnics would fare very well in this review process when teaching was appraised. However, this has not been the case at all. In Australia the former CAEs were ranked in the lower bands for teaching and research in the original assessment. In subsequent reviews of teaching they did not stand out as a group ahead of the traditional universities. In the UK it is less clear-cut because teaching is appraised by department. The ex-polytechnics, though, certainly do not do noticeably better in obtaining excellent teaching ratings because of their history of more rigorous quality assurance. If anything, it is again the traditional universities that have better records in the teaching ratings.

Bryman *et al* (1994) examined the performance-appraisal scheme imposed upon UK universities. Their evaluation suggested that the response of most appraisees and appraisers could best be characterized as 'procedural compliance'. Their conclusion suggested that the schemes are widely disliked and there was scant evidence of the expected benefits. Further, similar conclusions have been reached when appraisal has been introduced in industry.

Student feedback questionnaires are one form of quality assurance that has been well researched. However, the very large majority of the work has concentrated upon establishing that student feedback is a valid and reliable measure of teaching ability. Marsh (1987) has written what is usually regarded as the definitive review of this work.

There is some work on the effects of feedback on teaching. Firstly, there is evidence of the stability of instructor ratings over time. Marsh (1981) showed that there were high correlations between the same instructor teaching the same courses on different occasions and different courses. Such findings are normally used as an argument for the reliability of student ratings. Stability over time, though, also indicates the difficulty of altering teaching behaviour in the light of feedback. Approaches to teaching are dependent upon beliefs and habitual practices, which are not easy to change.

There have been a number of studies that have looked at the effect of feedback on teaching behaviour in the short term. Marsh concluded (1987: 339) that 'the studies demonstrate that feedback without consultation is only modestly effective'. In a study of the longer-term effects of feedback (Marsh and Roche, 1993), only the group that received a consultation intervention at the end of term showed an improvement in teaching significantly higher than the control group. Overall, the use of student feedback questionnaires may result in some improvement in teaching quality, but it is likely to be only moderate. Improvement is more likely to occur if accompanied by counselling, though Brinko (1993) showed that the consultation needed to be client-centred and the process democratic for the intervention to be effective.

Using an investment analogy, which is further developed in this chapter, the evidence of this section would suggest that quality assurance is a reasonably low-return investment. Quality assurance might be seen as a staple part of a quality-investment portfolio producing predictable but unspectacular returns on investment. A portfolio should invest in quality assurance, as it is the only form of quality measure that encompasses all teachers and courses. Its function is to ensure that all teaching reaches an acceptable standard. Over-investment in quality assurance cannot be recommended, though, as higher returns might be expected from diversifying resources towards other forms of quality measure.

Potential limit on outcomes

The other characteristic of the effectiveness of quality-assurance measures that might be deduced concerns the nature of marginal returns as the level of resources put into schemes is increased. This section examines a number of arguments that suggest that as the level of resourcing increases the marginal quality return will decrease significantly and can even become negative.

Quality control seeks to ensure that courses and teaching reach some minimum acceptable level. As the quality starts to reach this level, the increase in the return on investment will level off to reach a plateau. When all courses and teaching reach the acceptable level little further return for effort invested can be expected. In most universities the threshold level tends to be set quite low. Few programmes fail to be approved, few academics are ever sanctioned for teaching poorly and it is almost unheard-of for an external examiner to refuse to authorize degree awards.

It is questionable whether quality-control measures themselves have much impact beyond some minimum required standard. Once a programme is passed it can then usually proceed for a few years at least until it is reviewed – and the review process is again one requiring minimum standards to be met. Peer review panels may make recommendations for the way a programme is taught or require modifications to proposals. Input of this type can lead to some improvements, but there is no guarantee that the recommendations of the panel will be put into practice in the form envisaged and normally no mechanism for monitoring compliance.

As extra effort goes into developing more elaborate and more expensive schemes the marginal quality return on extra effort and expenditure will undoubtedly decrease and eventually will probably produce negative returns. The decrease in marginal returns on investment is clearly shown in the quality-versus-cost graph in Figure 16.1. There are several mechanisms at work that tend to reduce the impact of more exhaustive quality-control measures.

Quality-assurance procedures can easily become a game played to a set of formal and informal rules. As the systems become more developed the informal rules become more extensive, better established and more widely known. Essentially, academics learn how to play the system and pass the test rather than aim to improve teaching. It becomes possible to anticipate the expectations and requirements of a review panel (Kember, 1991).

This issue is compounded by the fact that documentation about teaching is examined rather than teaching itself. If the expectations of panels become well known, documentation can be tailored to fit. Departments build up files of suitable material on their word-processing systems and crank it out with a few updates and modifications to suit the course in question. In the case of programme approval, the documentation may bear little relationship to what is taught and how it is taught.

Quality-control processes tend to operate on a pass/fail basis, so they may be able to identify courses and teaching which are below the acceptable standard or would benefit from improvement, but there may be no appropriate mechanism for remediation. Even if requirements are made for revisions to proposals, the alterations may be incorporated into a revised proposal but not put into effect. Peer panels are often transient bodies formed specifically for a particular review. Once that is over they cease to exist and have neither responsibility nor any mechanism for ensuring that changes or improvements they suggested are implemented. Even if course leaders or department heads embrace any recommendations, they too may find them difficult to implement. The practice of what happens in the privacy of the classroom may be quite different to the rhetoric of the accepted proposal (Bowden, 1988).

Quality-control measures frequently have negative impacts on morale by taking responsibility for quality out of the hands of the teacher. Even with peer review processes within an institution, the panel is usually made up of those not teaching the course and normally from outside the responsible department. More inquisitive or adversarial regulatory systems create an atmosphere of distrust, which results in conservatism and saps enthusiasm for innovation (Ramsden, 1992).

Whatever the quality of the control system itself, compliance with monitoring procedures takes time, which otherwise could have been spent on teaching or research. The imposition of the quality-control measures, therefore, diverts effort and energy away from the very acts that the procedures are supposed to encourage (Woodhouse, 1995).

A good example to demonstrate the effect of the costs of quality-assurance procedures is provided by the OFSTED inspections of teacher-training agencies in the UK. Several universities have decided that they no longer wish to comply with the intensive OFSTED quality-assurance procedures so have decided to opt out of initial teacher training. In terms of the analysis of this section, they decided that the costs of complying with the quality-assurance procedures exceeded the funding and other benefits from enrolling students in the initial teacher-training programmes. Clearly these universities decided that the costs of the inspections and other requirements were very high. Others no doubt also see them as very high, but have little choice over compliance because they are unable to attract sufficient students to other programmes not under OFSTED control.

The decreasing marginal returns from quality-assurance procedures provide a rationale for ensuring that the level of resources devoted to them is at an appropriate level. There is no doubt that quality-assurance procedures can be of benefit. Barnett (1992) articulates clearly the improvements that can result from the process of self-reflection upon practices, coupled with constructive input from sympathetic peer review. The requirement to take time to reflect upon actions can result in valuable re-appraisal of practices. Peer review conducted with a facilitative orientation can help the reflective process to consider alternatives, which might not have been apparent to those involved.

The more frequent or lengthy the reviews, the less likely is extra benefit to accrue. Also, if the tone shifts from facilitative peer review to inquisitorial inspection, those being reviewed are likely to perceive the process as a demotivating ordeal rather than a constructive renewal. The key to obtaining value from quality assurance is, therefore, to ensure that the orientation is appropriate and the investment is at a level at which returns are worthwhile.

Quality versus cost

The above argument suggests that, for quality-control schemes, the relationship between teaching-quality improvement and cost shows decreasing marginal returns. As the intensity of the programme increases the costs will increase but the incremental return will tail away to nothing. Once the majority of courses and teachers reach the minimum acceptable level, little further increase in quality can be anticipated so the curve levels off.

Still further increases in the level of operation are likely to show negative returns. Extra effort and more rigorous systems involve more costs, but little extra return and eventually over-intrusive systems result in disillusionment and resistance.

The level of quality return on effort and expenditure is shown as somewhat lower than the other two curves, which will be introduced in the following sections. The justification for the lower level of the curve is the argument above that quality-assurance measures tend to produce relatively low returns on invested resources and are expensive to run because of the extensive levels of involvement of senior staff.

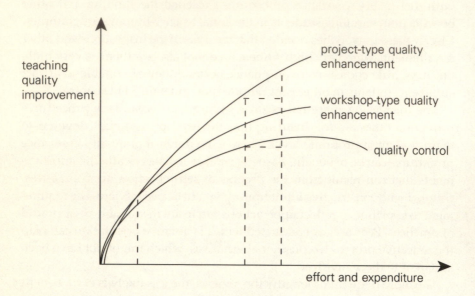

Figure 16.1 Teaching quality improvement versus cost for quality measures

The graph in Figure 16.1 shows the anticipated relationship between effort and cost in quality measures and the return indicated by the quality of teaching. The graph is at this point in time hypothetical, with the units on both axes arbitrary. It is the shape of the graph, though, which is important to the thesis of the chapter.

WORKSHOP-TYPE ACTIVITIES

Workshop-type initiatives by educational development units are commonly evaluated as a routine practice. However, the normal level of evaluation is for the workshop organizers to seek feedback from participants, often along similar lines to the information obtained from student feedback questionnaires. The information obtained is valuable for improving other similar workshops and the perceptions of those attending are of some value in determining the impact of the workshop. A workshop that is rated highly by the participants is more likely to have some impact upon teaching than one that was rated poorly.

Quality return

As to whether there has been any research or evaluation which goes beyond obtaining feedback, there have been a series of reviews which have concurred that there is remarkably little evidence that this widely used method of educational development is in any way effective (Eison and Stevens, 1995; Levinson-Rose and Menges, 1981; Rust, 1998; Weimer and Lenze, 1991; Wright and O'Neil, 1995). Many of these articles come to a similar conclusion to that of Weimer and Lenze (1991) who noted 'considerable concern . . . about the extensive use of a method to improve instruction with so little corroboration of its effectiveness'.

Feedback from participants on their perceptions of a workshop says little about whether the workshop experience impacted upon the attendees' teaching and even less about the effect upon learning outcomes for the participants' students. This type of evaluation, therefore, does not give insights into the effectiveness of the activities for improving the quality of teaching and learning.

Of the few studies that have tried to go beyond participant feedback, Rust (1998) asked a sample of workshop attenders, four months after the event, whether the workshop had changed their practice. Twenty-five per cent of attenders thought there had been a fair or great change, while 64 per cent thought there had been a little change. Questionnaires completed at the workshops revealed that they had generally been highly rated and that 69 per cent anticipated a change in practice resulting from the workshop as very likely and a further 21 per cent thought it possible. The results might be summed up as indicating that those attending them thought these workshops had had some impact upon their practice, but in most cases it was fairly small and the impact was not as great as they had anticipated at the end of the workshop.

Ho (1998a, 1998b) described a conceptual-change staff development programme of four half-day sessions, which aimed to change teachers' conceptions of teaching. Twelve participants were interviewed before and after the programme to monitor conceptions. Six were judged to have moved to more desirable conceptions of teaching. All of these six received better ratings for their teaching from student feedback and four of them were able to demonstrate more meaningful learning approaches by their students.

The overall conclusion must be that there is at present little evidence of the effectiveness of workshops in improving the quality of teaching and learning. The few studies that have examined impact do seem to show that the workshops studied have had a reasonable level of effect. It would not be sensible to extrapolate from such a small number of studies to workshops in general. The workshops reported by Rust (1998) were highly rated workshops organized by a well-established consortium. The programme reported by Ho (1998a, 1998b) was an extensive programme with a clear conceptual underpinning. Many other workshops would lack these qualities.

Given the level of evaluation of workshop-type activities, mentioned above, the notion that workshop-type schemes do improve the quality of teaching seems to be largely an act of faith. This really should be an issue of concern to those in educational development units, since the units are often under threat in times of cost cutting. Having no firm evidence that their major type of activity does lead to better teaching and learning must make it more difficult to justify their existence.

For the purposes of drawing the relationship between quality and cost, it is assumed that workshop-type activities are effective in promoting better teaching and learning. The assumption must become more questionable, though, as the level of investment increases and if the programmes aim to deal with more experienced staff.

Cost

The costs of workshops are largely time costs. The organization, advertising and enrolment process incurs some cost. There is a time cost of the facilitators organizing and running the workshop, which could be calculated reasonably accurately. Assuming that the workshops are run by an educational development-type unit, the involvement in workshop-type activities could also be seen as an opportunity cost, as it takes time away from other initiatives they might have been involved in.

For the teachers attending the workshop-type activities, the time of their involvement must also be seen as a cost. Indeed, the fact that time is taken away from available research time – and research is the activity universities have traditionally rewarded – has been seen as the major disincentive for participation in educational development activities (Moses, 1985). It should also be appreciated that time spent in workshops is time which is not available for teaching. It is only if the workshop equips the academic to be a better teacher that there will be a return on the investment of the time of the academic and the resources needed to mount the workshop programme.

Quality/cost relationship

In the graph, workshops are shown as initially producing a return of quality improvement, which rises with the level of investment. The return for workshops may be slightly higher than quality-control measures as staff costs which do accrue are likely to be below an average salary rate, since workshop attendees are more often those appointed at lower levels, and those who run workshops are rarely as highly paid as the senior staff engaged in quality assurance.

Once the measures move away from initial investments in founding schemes there will be some tendency towards decreasing marginal rates of return – there is only so much extra wisdom that is useful or can be absorbed. What is more likely, though, is that the curve peters out. As the level of workshop provision increases it will become harder and harder to attract an audience. Even the most enthusiastic start to find the time demands excessive or realize that they are learning little that is new. There may be some useful advice which can be gleaned from teacher counselling sessions, but eventually even the most perspicacious counsellor will be exhausted of productive advice.

Although it is not well documented, for obvious reasons, many educational development units have low levels of attendance at workshop-type activities. This is particularly true where programmes are extensive and have been in operation for a number of years. The low attendance is often put down to a lack of incentive, as teaching quality is inadequately rewarded. However, it is also possible that even enthusiastic teachers have discovered diminishing returns from course and workshop attendance.

The other manifestation of the petering-out effect is that attendance tends to decrease as the level of experience rises. New staff may feel a need for a body of knowledge about teaching and learning and a repertoire of skills, but more experienced ones probably feel they already have them. Many institutions have accepted this position by devoting the bulk of their quality-enhancement resources to programmes for new staff. Courses or short programmes for new academics and teaching assistants have become common. In the UK, the Dearing report (National Committee of Inquiry into Higher Education, 1997) has proposed accrediting the teaching competence of academics, but it was significant that the proposals were to be applicable only to new staff.

It is probable that more experienced staff who attend workshop-type activities soon discover that they are often unproductive because they fail to address the issues of either implementation (Kember and Gow, 1992) or the lack of homogeneity of either students or the teaching context. As Gibbs (1995: 15) so aptly puts it:

> Those who do attend courses . . . even when the topic is the right one and even when the training session is run superbly, often report being unable to introduce change because the generic solutions on offer do not fit the culture or practices their colleagues are engaged with, or because the structural changes which would be necessary are controlled by others who were not present.

Confirmation of this conclusion comes from a study by Rust (1998). He found that the number of workshop attendees who thought four months after the event that the experience had had an impact upon their teaching was markedly less than those who felt there would be an impact at the end of the workshop. It is common for a workshop to inspire those attending to feel that an idea is worthwhile. However, putting the idea into practice can be more difficult than initially envisaged.

The petering-out effect is perhaps further evidenced by the value placed upon workshops by those who organize them. A wide survey of senior figures in educational development units in four countries asked respondents to rate a number of potential teaching improvement practices in terms of their confidence in their potential to improve teaching practice. Workshops ranked only seventh in spite of their being probably the most common form of educational development activity (Moses, 1985). It seems that even those who run workshops recognize their limitations.

In summing up the quality-versus-cost return for workshop-type activities, it is again necessary to make assumptions because of a lack of evidence for effectiveness. That workshops are effective can only be taken as an act of faith as so little evaluation or research has been conducted on how they impact upon teaching and learning. It seems reasonable to accept this act of faith as long as it is restricted to those who volunteer to attend in viable numbers, so expressing a perception that the workshops are beneficial.

New staff tend to be those most likely to volunteer to attend workshops, which makes a great deal of sense because they are the ones most likely to lack confidence in their teaching. Once the concerns of novice teachers are dealt with, however, workshops tend to be less popular and offering them becomes less cost-effective. Experienced staff feel less need for advice on teaching and may well have realized the limitations of generic workshops in dealing with particular contexts and implementation issues.

PROJECT-TYPE ACTIVITIES

The other category of quality-enhancement measures is that of project-type activities, with the Action Learning Project as a specific example. Other project-type schemes are also examined, as are more individual initiatives not acting under a grant-awarding umbrella.

Costs

The costs of the Action Learning Project were determined in detail since it was funded by a grant. There seems little point in providing a detailed costing, though. The point of this chapter is comparison, and other quality measures have only been costed in a very approximate way. There is little value in comparing a detailed costing for one initiative of a particular category with general approximations for the other categories. In addition, the cost structures in Hong Kong are different in many respects from those in many other countries and so would be hard to interpret for many readers.

The largest cost was that of the grants. The second highest cost came from providing support to the projects by the coordinating team. Not all project-type schemes provide support, but it was argued in Chapter 11 that the support provided was essential to the success of the Action Learning Project. Administrative overheads were consciously kept as low as possible. One member of the coordinating team was allocated half-time to an organizational role. The other administrative time cost was that of the management committee and its sub-committee, which adjudicated the award of grants.

There was definitely extra effort by the staff involved in the projects, but much of this was directed towards the aspect of their teaching which was the focus of the project. There is no doubt that the staff involved did find that participation in the projects did involve them in extra work. It is hard, though, to allocate this extra effort as a cost to the quality of teaching unless the initiative actually makes the teaching worse, and the evidence on the outcomes of the projects reported in Part C suggests that the opposite was the case. There was also a research benefit for many of the participants as most of the projects resulted in publications. Staff costs that did accrue must have been close to an average salary rate since there was no obvious bias towards senior or junior staff when it came to participation in the projects. Other schemes operating under a grant umbrella must have had similar cost structures. Any variations would be within the level of grants or support. Other project-type activities have operated without the umbrella of support provided by a grant-awarding scheme. At the lowest level, individuals or small groups try out teaching innovations of their own initiative. On a somewhat larger scale, a handful of projects can form a loose alliance around a common critical friend. These projects might be unfunded or might attract a small grant from a research or other fund. The only substantial costs are the time of the participants. Again these are not a cost to teaching quality, but no doubt were opportunity costs to those involved.

Quality enhancement

The Action Learning Project did attempt to conduct an evaluation along cost-effectiveness lines. Earlier schemes for awarding grants for prospective teaching initiatives also produced evidence of demonstrable improvements in the quality of student learning. The evidence is in the form of individual projects, which are able to report changes to learning outcomes that could reasonably be attributed to the project initiatives. Gibbs (1992b) reports on a set of 10 case studies of quite diverse initiatives. Evaluation was by a similar approach across projects consisting of interviews with students about their learning approaches, plus before-and-after use of a shortened version of the Approaches to Studying Inventory (Ramsden and Entwistle, 1981) used to measure learning approaches. Gibbs' conclusion was that (p 164):

> Most of the case studies demonstrated a significant positive impact on students' approaches to studying. This was evident in scores on the Approaches to Studying questionnaire and even more evident in interviews. On most occasions where this change was identified it was also possible to demonstrate that parallel courses did not induce a similar change or that previously there had been no change.

Educational action research projects in Hong Kong that were precursors to the Action Learning Project used similar evaluation techniques together with more diverse project-focused interviews, student feedback questionnaires, classroom observation and reflective journals. The evidence from a number of the projects has been sufficient to convince journal referees that the projects have achieved something worth publishing (eg Conway and Kember, 1993; Conway et al, 1994; Davies, Sivan and Kember, 1994; Kember and Kelly, 1993; Sivan et al, 1991).

Action Learning Project evidence

The results from the questionnaire survey indicated that the participants perceived the Action Learning Project as having a marked effect upon teaching across the seven universities in Hong Kong. A significant 87 per cent of respondents agreed or strongly agreed with the statement that 'the project has led to an improvement in my teaching'. Furthermore the impact is likely to be on-going, as 82 per cent envisaged themselves doing similar action research studies into their own teaching after the completion of their current project. The project outcomes were rated as successful by 87 per cent of participants. More importantly the participants believed that their projects were having a beneficial impact upon student learning. Over 75 per cent of respondents believed that their project had led to an improvement in students' learning approaches, and 68 per cent felt that student performance had improved.

Evidence of the outcomes of the projects supported by the Action Learning Project was given in the final reports by the teams, which were collated into an edited collection (Kember *et al*, 1997). Reducing these reports to some succinct overall statement about the outcomes of the projects is far from easy. Each project had its own aims and these show great variety. The evaluations performed for the projects reflect their aims and, therefore, also show diversity in methodology, approach and questions asked. Indeed the very diversity and the level of concordance between project aims and the nature of evaluation could be seen as an indicator of success for the project. However, it does make it much more difficult to attempt any macro-level assessment.

Accepting that some neat quantitative macro-assessment is problematic, it seems reasonable to draw upon the conclusions of the independent evaluation panel. They accepted that the high level of completion of the projects was one indicator of success. They found it no easier succinctly to conclude whether the projects had, overall, met the conditions they determined for success. They determined that the projects showed varying degrees of meeting these success criteria. Clearly the overall effectiveness could have been higher if more projects had come closer to all success criteria. Though, as the independent panel concluded that the ALP represented good value for money, they presumably felt it had been reasonably effective (Biggs and Lam, 1997: 171):

> Given all the above, that valuable outcomes can be reliably associated with probably most projects (and less reliably with all completed projects), the positive outcomes are in fact considerable. If, as seems likely, most participants got *something* of value as far as their teaching was concerned, then it follows that the teaching of at least one hundred teachers, and the learning of thousands of students, were improved at a cost of . . . This seems pretty good value for money.

Quality/cost relationship

The initial return on investment of teaching grants is shown on the quality/cost graph as somewhat greater than quality-control measures. The main argument here is the degree to which effort is – or is not – diverted from teaching and research. The question of the level and cost of the staff involved in the respective types of schemes is a secondary argument.

The argument for greater returns becomes stronger as the level of investment of effort increases. There is again no reason to suspect that any plateau effect will occur, as the quality-enhancement measures are not aiming for a minimum acceptable standard. There is also no reason to expect a petering-out effect. Indeed, submissions for grants from the Action Learning Project requested far more than available funds, and in other schemes of this type demand for grants commonly exceeds funds available by a substantial margin (Committee for the Advancement of University Teaching, 1995; Gibbs, 1992b).

The relationship between quality returns and investment is unlikely to be linear. Demand for grants from the Action Learning Project exceeded available funds. Obviously criteria for awarding grants included the likelihood of success and the anticipated benefits. Assuming the selection committee did a reasonable job, it means that the projects first awarded funds tended to be those where the need was most apparent and the returns likely to be better. They could well be those with the most enthusiastic and competent staff. Hence, the more funding is increased, the more difficult it may be to find worthy projects. Alternatively, allocating greater amounts of funding to selected projects is unlikely to yield proportional benefits in quality. The divergence from a linear relationship is unlikely to be great, though, unless very substantial investments are made, since the demand for funding always seems to exceed supply by a substantial margin.

Any deviation from a linear return due to a reduction in the quality of proposals may be countered to some extent by encouragement of greater participation in the dissemination activities discussed in Chapter 7. The greater the number of projects, the greater the impact of these activities is likely to be as more will be involved.

THE LEVEL OF QUALITY ASSURANCE

Academics are currently caught up in a wave of teaching-quality assurance initiatives. The banner of greater accountability and better-quality teaching is alluring, so it would take a brave person to stand against the tide. The purpose of this chapter is not to argue that quality assurance is wrong *per se*, but to urge institutions and regulatory bodies to ensure that quality-assurance measures are yielding some quality returns and have not become mired in the plateau region – or worse still giving negative returns.

The reasons for the recent trend of establishing and expanding quality-assurance mechanisms are largely political. Even if universities become convinced that quality-control measures are not particularly effective they will still retain the schemes out of political necessity. Given the current drive for accountability, it would be politically unwise to shed quality-control systems and in many cases they are now required by regulatory bodies. UK universities, for example, are contractually required to participate in both teaching and research reviews and to have performance appraisal schemes.

Universities may be politically obliged to maintain quality-control schemes. They do, however, have considerable discretion over the intensity and nature of internal schemes. The form of operation of the schemes can usually be over a wide spectrum of intensity.

Performance appraisal, for example, can take the form of a fairly brief and informal conversation with a department head every other year. At the other extreme come formal annual reviews with much form-filling and several levels of reporting. The schemes can also range on a spectrum from developmental and formative to summative and judgemental.

Another good example is the contrast between the programme-approval mechanisms under the former two-tier higher education system in the UK and Australia, cited above. Traditional university schemes typically required little documentation and only internal approval, whereas the non-university institutions required extensive submissions and reviews by a series of panels including external members. The cost difference between extremes of the types was probably an order of magnitude of two. Where discretion is possible, a programme-approval scheme can be pitched at any point of intensity between the two extremes.

Perhaps the most important conclusion which can be drawn from the cost/quality graphs is ensuring that quality-assurance systems remain within the area in which there are appreciable returns from the investment of time and money in the quality process. Once schemes approach the plateau region it clearly becomes inefficient to continue them at the same level of intensity, let alone make them more rigorous.

A simple quality-assurance scheme is almost certainly more cost-effective than an elaborate one. The practice of many institutions has moved in the opposite direction in recent years, however. Faced by accountability pressures, quality-control systems have tended to become more comprehensive and complex rather than simpler.

A further avenue for returning to the efficient part of the curve is through less frequent monitoring. Courses are normally monitored and staff appraised at regular intervals. Increasing the frequency of this monitoring will tend to decrease the marginal quality return on the extra effort involved. Doubling the period between reviews may result in little or no difference to quality but would approximately halve the effort and cost.

FROM QUALITY ASSURANCE TO ENHANCEMENT

Another implication of the quality/cost graph might be a shift from quality assurance towards quality-enhancement measures. This suggestion is particularly appropriate for institutions that have already implemented a reasonable level of quality assurance. It is possible that these schemes are already ensuring that most courses and teaching reach some minimum acceptable level. Any further tightening of the quality-assurance monitoring could result in minimal marginal returns. The institutions would be better advised to invest in quality-enhancement initiatives.

A shift towards this end can come through empowering teachers and course teams to take responsibility for quality themselves rather than relying upon the inspection and certification of a panel or committee. Frazer (1992) asserts that years ago industry learnt that quality control through inspectors was not enough, and suggests that universities too need more sophisticated approaches. He believes that everyone in the enterprise should feel owner-ship of the system and should take responsibility for enhancing quality. Elton (1992) argued along similar lines for a shift from the quality 'A's to the quality 'E's.

It is hard to see such a shift occurring if there is an extensive reliance upon quality-assurance measures because these take responsibility for decisions on quality out of the hands of the teachers. It is the panel, or the committee, that adjudicates whether quality is adequate or how improvements might be made. The approach contributes to a sense of dependency.

What is worse, quality-assurance systems can generate a negative atmosphere since the need for such schemes implies, inadvertently or otherwise, a deficit view of teaching quality. When the deficiency is made explicit it is normally expressed as teaching not being taken sufficiently seriously because academics and universities devote too much attention to research. It is questionable whether the assertion is as applicable as the critics would have us believe – in many cases it can be interpreted as dogma becoming accepted wisdom because the mantra has been chanted so often.

A large survey of academics in six Australian universities (Ramsden and Martin, 1996) found that 95 per cent thought that teaching should be highly valued by their institution; however, only 37 per cent thought that it was. These figures can be interpreted as suggesting that teaching is taken seriously but needs greater encouragement rather than inspection. This interpretation is also consistent with answers to questions about possible measures to improve the quality of teaching. The strongly approved measures were categorized by the authors as those which rewarded good teaching and which created a better environment for academics to teach and introduce innovations. The least popular measures were those asso-ciated with compulsory evaluation and audit. Essentially, encouragement was felt more likely to be beneficial than quality control and audit schemes.

The participants in the Action Learning Project similarly saw the benefits of the quality-enhancement approach over the quality-control measures they had experienced. This was a typical response to open-ended questions:

I think this was a far-sighted initiative. It was able to support such a variety of different projects generated bottom-up, from the delivery point of instruction. It had more impact on the quality of learning than any of the top-down quality initiatives I've encountered!

An empowering shift towards ownership of responsibility for teaching quality is much more likely to arise from a more positive view of teaching quality. Such a view would be that of the large majority of academics taking their teaching seriously and keen for incentives to look for improvement. This position is not only more conducive to empowerment but is also both a reasonable and a responsible position to take.

A BALANCED PORTFOLIO

The advocacy of a shift from quality control to quality-enhancement measures should not be taken too far. There are limitations to the ambit of quality-enhancement schemes. Participation in them is voluntary. Active participants can influence the teaching of colleagues in their course team or department. However, there is no mechanism to impact upon the disinterested or pathologically disabled teacher.

This is the province of quality-assurance schemes, as they are imposed by institutional managements or regulatory bodies who have the power to make them mandatory. They do, then, have a mechanism for impacting upon the poorest teachers and courses to bring them up to an acceptable standard, though it is by no means automatic that they will succeed in this aim.

To further develop the economic analogy, a wise institution will have invested in a diversified quality portfolio. There will be a staple investment in quality-assurance schemes. This will be kept to a limited proportion of the available funds so as to ensure that returns remain appreciable and do not reach the plateau of minimal marginal returns. The remainder of funds and effort available for quality improvement would be invested in a range of quality-enhancement schemes.

The resources, energy and effort available for teaching-quality schemes in any university are finite. In recent times many have been forced to devote extra time and energy to the quality-accountability drive. There must be a limit, though, to which extra resources can be added or diverted. The question then becomes that of ensuring that available resources are used as effectively as possible. It is the contention of this chapter that, unless the available resource level is extremely low, greater benefits will accrue from a dispersed range of measures. The greater the level of resources committed, the more likely it is that quality-enhancement schemes will be more beneficial.

It could well be appropriate for institutions to thoroughly examine their quality-assurance systems. Once these are in place, they tend to be driven by their own momentum and become entrenched. It is not common for them to be examined at all and very rare for them to be subjected to questions such as:

- Are the quality-control schemes effective in improving the quality of teaching and learning?
- Do the outcomes of the measures justify their costs?
- Would simpler and less costly schemes be as effective?

With the recent drive towards quality assurance, it is likely that many institutions are positioned well along the cost axis and, therefore, in the position of low marginal returns. Worse still, many could be further along the cost axis and mired in the plateau region or getting negative returns on investment. In which case they would be well advised to shift resources out of quality control towards quality enhancement.

Among quality-enhancement measures, there also needs to be a balance. Over-investment in workshop-type schemes would not be wise as the returns start to enter the petering-out zone. A sensible policy is that of setting the level of workshop provision by market demand, which seems to have a good relationship to need. Short courses for new staff appear to be better attended than workshops on more advanced topics. It seems eminently plausible that new academics are not only more willing to admit a need for help with their teaching, but more likely to actually be in need of help.

The other type of workshops which do appear to be useful and well attended are those which cater for new issues or problems which have arisen due to changing circumstances. A good example here would be a need for workshops on postgraduate supervision in a new university, which has only recently introduced research degrees.

Once the basic level of quality assurance is satisfied and the market demand for workshops is catered for, it would appear that the best returns from investment in the quality process come from projects, if necessary supported by grants. Institutions might look to utilize remaining resources for quality enhancement for schemes of this type.

Project-type activities are definitely under-represented, compared to either quality-control measures or workshop-type activities. The Australian Government schemes (CUTSD and earlier CAUT) are probably the most extensive. They provide grants for projects following the submission of proposals under a competitive framework. The projects funded by the scheme have some similarities to those supported by the Action Learning Project. There is a greater proportion of technology-based projects, which gives the scheme a developmental emphasis, particularly as projects are limited to a duration of one year. The action research flavour of the Action Learning Project is lacking, as projects judged to have a research nature are excluded.

Other examples of initiatives operating jointly under an umbrella project have tended to follow the award of a grant to the umbrella holder (Gibbs, 1992b; Weeks and Scott, 1992). As such they have usually been transitory. There are also some teaching development grant schemes internal to universities, which in the main offer low levels of funding.

Beyond that there appears to be relatively low levels of engagement in project-type activities. Wright and Associates (1995) edited a book about 'teaching improvement practices' with chapters by many leading proponents of academic and faculty development from around the world. None of the 15 chapters dealt with project-type activities and it has to be assumed that the selection was an informed one as the book includes a wide survey of international approaches to the improvement of teaching.

Essentially, most quality portfolios are either devoid of any investment in project-type activities or underweight. In view of the arguments above about the questionable level of returns from overweight investment in quality-control measures or workshop-type activities, there is a sound argument for a substantial shift of resources towards project-type activities across the higher education sector.

National schemes

The arguments above have related to individual institutions, so refer to those aspects of quality measures that are within the ambit of the university itself. In many countries an increasing portion of the quality portfolio is determined for universities because of the requirement to comply with, and participate in, national quality-assurance schemes.

At the national level, the nature of quality-assurance schemes is a matter for policy decisions. In countries influenced by the British Commonwealth system there is usually a government-appointed body, which deals with funding and the regulatory framework for universities. These bodies have increasingly imposed quality reviews upon both research and teaching. Through various mechanisms they also influence internal university policies and practices, including those for quality assurance and enhancement of teaching.

It would take a book in itself to discuss national quality systems, and such a book would rapidly become out of date, as change is commonplace. What might perhaps be most useful is to present evidence that the trends in many national systems are along the same lines as those described above which exist in many individual universities.

Firstly, it might be noted that concern about teaching quality is growing at the national level. This appears to be a worldwide phenomenon.

Where the concern has been translated into action, at the national level it has generally led to quality assurance by review rather than any of the forms of quality enhancement. A common measure is the review of universities to ensure that they have in place adequate measures for ensuring teaching quality. The UK approach of using external examiners to directly review teaching within individual departments or disciplines is less common.

Relating these observations to the portfolio model developed in this chapter suggests that many national quality systems are heavily weighted towards quality assurance through review procedures. Many national systems directly contribute little or nothing to quality enhancement. In the UK there has been some funding of national consortia offering workshops. The teaching development grants offered by CAUT and then CUTSD in Australia are possibly the largest project-type initiative. National quality portfolios are, therefore, unlikely to be in the state of balance that this chapter has argued is most likely to achieve the best returns of quality enhancement for the level of resource invested.

There seems no doubt that these national governing bodies are concerned about teaching. That schemes for monitoring the quality of teaching have been introduced or strengthened in many countries is surely evidence that governments and their appointed bodies feel that the quality of teaching and learning should be seriously addressed by the academic community. The tendency to concentrate upon review schemes is probably a consequence of their relationship to universities. The normal way these bodies exert influence upon their constituent universities is by imposing regulations and awarding funding. It must follow naturally to use the same processes when attempting to insert leverage upon teaching quality.

However, in a number of countries there is evidence that these approaches are having unintended outcomes. If it is accepted that regulatory bodies have a genuine interest in teaching quality, one would expect academics to recognize the concern and perceive that teaching is valued as an important facet of their work – for the majority, *the* most important part of their work.

Yet from many quarters it is possible to find evidence that this is not the case. Wright and O'Neil (1995) conducted a large-scale survey of potential teaching improvements across four major countries. The top-ranked overall potential improvement, out of 36 suggestions, was for deans and heads of department to foster the importance of teaching responsibilities. For this to be cited top in three countries and second in the fourth suggests that the respondents felt that the importance of teaching responsibilities currently wasn't being fostered. It would hardly be so widely selected were it already happening.

Boyer's (1990) study in the USA asked faculty whether pressure to publish reduced the quality of teaching at their university. Thirty-five per cent agreed and a further 19 per cent were neutral. These figures hardly indicate positive support for the importance of teaching in universities.

The evaluation of the Action Learning Project did not set out to investigate how teaching was perceived in general. There was, though, evidence that the approach to quality enhancement was perceived in a far more positive way than teaching quality review exercises, which had done little or nothing to stimulate interest in teaching. Significant numbers of the participants commented on both the approach to ensuring teaching quality and the prevailing perception of the importance of teaching and research:

> Despite UGC and [other] funding, and rhetoric to the contrary, we feel that that academic work involved in providing supporting materials for students' use does not carry the same respect and value for staff development as other types of research and publication.

> I appreciate this opportunity to conduct research on teaching and learning. I would like to thank the coordinators of the Action Learning Project for their insights into the value of improving the quality of tertiary education. They have provided us a supportive environment to improve teaching and learning in the tertiary level, which has often been given lower priority to research.

In an extensive survey of Australian academics, Ramsden and Martin (1996) found that 95 per cent of staff felt that teaching should be highly valued, while only 37 per cent felt that it was highly valued by their institution. The second part of the survey asked what types of measures were most likely to improve teaching quality. The authors placed the positive responses in two categories. Firstly, there were measures that created a working environment that encouraged and provided time for staff to develop and enjoy their teaching. Secondly, there were measures that recognized good teaching through resource allocations and promotion.

Ramsden and Martin (1996) drew the conclusion that there was a marked perception gap between the academic staff who did most of the teaching, and the university administrators and heads of department. They argued that their findings suggested that teaching-quality improvement was more likely to result from measures consistent with an academic culture. They argued for research-based approaches to teaching improvement, collegial review and proper training.

These conclusions are entirely consistent with those argued throughout this book. They suggest a shift from quality assurance to quality enhancement.

The recommendations are consistent with promoting a shift in emphasis from imposed quality control to empowering academics to take responsibility for the quality of their own teaching, through evaluating or researching their students' learning and reflecting upon their own teaching.

Data from all round the world show that academics do not feel their universities treat teaching as seriously as they ought to. Governments and their regulatory bodies, though, are saying that universities and their academics should take teaching seriously. Clearly something is wrong! In rather different ways, Ramsden and Martin (1996) and this book are suggesting that the measures used to ensure good teaching are having unintended outcomes. Rather than relying upon ever more intrusive quality-assurance reviews, more positive outcomes might be ensured by re-directing resources towards quality-assurance measures which recognize the competence of academics to be their own quality monitors and developers.

Implications for educational development units

There are also implications for academic developers and academic development units. The extent to which the effects upon practice of educational developers correspond with the implications for institutions depends upon the extent to which the policies and practices of the unit and the developers are in accord with those of the institution. The staff, and particularly the head, of such units are often expected to have an advisory or advocacy role for policy on teaching issues. The framework provided in this chapter might prompt some to encourage institutional managements towards a serious examination of the balance of resource allocation to the various elements of quality assurance and enhancement.

Within academic development units themselves, there might also be consideration given to the type of activities to which the staff devote their efforts. Most units are engaged in workshop-type activities and play some role with respect to the quality-assurance processes. An increasing number act as facilitators for project-type activities. Just as an institution should examine the balance of resources devoted to each type of activity, so should academic development units and even individual academic developers.

Many academic development units feel themselves to be under-resourced, so determination of priority activities does not always take a long-term perspective and may not be examined as thoroughly as it might. When there are only a small number of academic developers, there can be a tendency to respond to those who shout loudest or engage in activities that will create an immediate impact with as many as possible. Both these concerns, and the need to keep on the right side of central management, usually dictate some involvement with quality-assurance processes. The imperative to have a short-term impact and to be seen to be doing something tend to lure units towards workshop-type activities. It can be no surprise that Moses (1985) found workshops to be the activity units engaged in most frequently by Australian educational development units.

In achieving a balanced portfolio it is likely that it is in facilitating project-type activities that academic development units are most likely to be underweight. It may be politically difficult to shift resources towards this type of activity as any evidence of outcomes and impact takes time to appear. However, in the longer run the quality return may be greater.

CONCLUSION

The most important message in this chapter, then, is to urge both institutions and academic development units to check the balance of their quality portfolio. The pressures towards accountability have undoubtedly led to more and greater intensities of quality-assurance schemes. The increase has been management-driven so the recent investment has probably been biased towards quality assurance, as it is that type of scheme that managements can impose, direct and require participation in.

To determine whether a quality portfolio is appropriately balanced needs evaluation of the constituent schemes. That evaluation should focus upon the impact of the monitoring or initiatives upon teaching and learning, rather than gathering just staff reactions. It is important that the costs of the schemes, including the time costs, are determined.

Most institutions and national systems have a preponderance of quality-assurance measures. Where this is the case, it is likely that a redirection of resources towards quality enhancement will be more effective in bringing about an improvement in teaching and learning. The balance between workshop-type activities and projects can be determined by market forces. A desire for workshops is often felt by those new to teaching but the level of need falls as experience grows since generic workshops do not deal with implementation or the individual context. Many institutional and national portfolios are underweight in project-type activities so a shift towards them might well result in greater degrees of teaching improvement for given levels of resourcing. Such a shift would undoubtedly be favoured by many academics who would prefer to be empowered by their teaching being taken more seriously and initiatives encouraged.

17

Final reflections

This chapter draws together threads and finalizes positions that have been explored in previous parts of the book. Most conclusions drawn in this chapter will be applicable widely across universities around the world.

Conclusions were based on results drawn from a triangulation of the evaluation methods. The triangulation process incorporated both multiple perspectives and multiple evaluation methods. The conclusions briefly outlined in the following sections were all derived from results substantiated by at least two evaluation methods and sources. They mostly elaborate upon issues that have been explored in previous chapters.

SECOND ROUND OF PROJECT

The Action Learning Project was itself an action research project into how to structure quality-enhancement initiatives with an action research philosophy if they are to have maximum impact. During the course of the initiative much was learnt by the coordinating team. By the end of the first phase of the project, which is discussed in this book, the team felt that they had sufficient insights to pass on to others to justify this book. We also felt that we had learnt a lot from the experience and given the chance to do it all over again would have been able to make marked improvements.

As it happens, we have in a way been given the chance to do it all over again, as a further grant has been obtained to run the Action Learning Project for a second round. Starting the second round has overlapped with the writing of this book. There are, then, some insights into whether lessons learnt about organizing the initial stages of large clusters of projects might be better formatted. In drawing these final conclusions, these experiences will be drawn upon in the form of personal reflections from the new coordinating team. More detailed comparison cannot be made until the second round reaches its conclusion and has in turn been evaluated.

It might be noted that, in moving into this second phase of operation, the project has expanded its ambit from seven to eight institutions. While grant applications were being considered the Hong Kong Institute of Education was accepted as coming under the auspices of the UGC. Although the institute was not a partner in the proposal, the management committee decided that it should be invited to participate. Institute staff were, therefore, invited to submit proposals for funding for second round grants.

Action research framework

The primary focus of this book is upon the utilization of an action research or action learning framework for conducting projects that aim to improve the quality of teaching and learning. Webb (1992, 1996) has observed that it is unusual for educational development initiatives to be underpinned by any theoretical rationale. Of the recent attempts to develop theoretical frameworks for academic development, action research has probably had the greatest number of advocates (Kember and Gow, 1992; Kember and Kelly, 1993; Kember and McKay, 1996; Schratz, 1993; Zuber-Skerrit, 1992a). Quality-assurance schemes, surprisingly, also rarely operate within any explicit theoretical model. Given that the Action Learning Project had a very explicit framework, it is obviously central to the conclusion to examine whether it was appropriate.

Virtually all of the participants themselves felt the framework was appropriate, even though the majority had no experience of action research prior to the projects. The action research framework led to participants developing abilities to evaluate and systematically reflect upon their own teaching. The majority of participants thought this would be an enduring effect. The evaluation panel readily accepted the conclusion that action research provided a suitable framework (Biggs and Lam, 1997).

The most important evidence that action research is an appropriate framework for enhancing the quality of teaching and learning is the substance of this book, showing that it can be effectively put into practice through a large-scale project. Theory that cannot be applied in practice is not useful theory.

Implications for university quality-assurance procedures follow from the establishment of action research as a viable mode of enhancing teaching quality. The previous chapter has argued that institutions should check the balance between quality-control systems and quality-enhancement initiatives. The effectiveness of existing measures ought to be evaluated and it is likely that, in many cases, a shift of resources towards project-type initiatives would be beneficial.

There are also implications for educational development units. If it is accepted that supporting educational action research projects is an effective way of improving the quality of teaching and learning, then it would seem logical to recommend that educational development units engage in the activity of supporting educational action research projects.

FROM CONTROL TO EMPOWERMENT

Not only was the project surprisingly unusual in being based upon an explicit theoretical framework, it also made quite different assumptions of academics to many other quality schemes. Efforts to improve university teaching have often been based upon implicit deficit presumptions, and imposed top-down. Quality accreditation and review procedures seek to identify sub-standard programmes and withdraw accreditation or recommend remedial measures. Evaluation through student feedback questionnaires and staff appraisal schemes target those with poor ratings who subsequently receive counselling or are not given tenure. Teaching-assistant and new-staff training programmes are designed with the assumption that the incoming academics do not currently possess well-developed teaching skills.

Clearly such initiatives have a place in bringing teaching up to an acceptable level but do little to encourage positive attitudes towards teaching or a striving for excellence. Indeed, excessive reliance upon a deficit model can lead to disillusionment with quality-assurance measures and tends to reduce the status of teaching compared to research.

The Action Learning Project took a quite different perspective, in assuming that there are academics who would be both competent and keen to engage in action research projects on some aspect of their teaching. The approach is bottom-up and the underlying philosophy is that of empowering practitioners to reflect upon and evaluate their own teaching.

The participants clearly had a strong preference for these more positive assumptions of their interest in teaching and abilities to teach. The outcomes of the projects suggest that these participants were not just competent teachers but academics capable of successfully introducing and implement-ing innovatory modes of teaching and learning. Universities and their accrediting authorities might be encouraged to take more positive views of academics' teaching by shifting some resources from quality-assurance schemes, based upon deficit assumptions, to those encouraging and empowering academics to strive for excellence.

REFLECTION VERSUS DEVELOPMENT

Chapters 10, 11 and 12 argued that the process of the teams' engaging in action research into their teaching was itself an important outcome. Indeed, it could be argued that the process is more important than any of the innovations introduced into the curriculum. Those involved in these projects will collectively face many more years of teaching. The aim of the Action Learning Project was to impact upon the teaching of participants beyond the lifetime of their projects.

By engaging in the process of action research into their own teaching, the participants should become equipped to reflect upon, regularly monitor and evaluate their own teaching. Essentially, the aim was to produce reflective practitioners (Schön, 1983).

Evidence from Chapter 13 and from numerous discussions between the coordinating team and the participants would suggest that this aim was met within most of the projects. However, the final reports were not always a good indication of reflective thinking. Many tended to write in a very impersonal style and concentrated upon successful outcomes, rather than the struggle to reach them and the wrong turnings made on the way.

We are not convinced, however, that the reports produced by the teams are necessarily reliable measures of the level of reflective thinking or the degree to which action research methodology was embraced. It seems to be widely accepted that it can be difficult to develop the abilities of students to write reflective journals (Kember *et al*, 1996a). The difficulty is that of unlearning conventions that have been assimilated over time. Students are taught to write in the third person, in a passive tone and to cite academic authorities rather than personal opinions or feelings. In reports they are taught to focus upon outcomes rather than the struggle to achieve them.

If it is hard to get students to engage in reflective writing it must be more difficult still with academics, particularly those from the more quantitative disciplines. They would have had longer to learn, observe and practice the conventions of 'academic' writing and are in their present positions because they learnt the lessons well.

We are, therefore, quite convinced that the levels of compliance with action research methodology and the extent of reflection upon teaching was higher than that indicated by the reports on the projects. From contacts between the coordinating team and the participants we were convinced that a number of projects did employ an action research approach but wrote up their projects in the writing genre to which they were accustomed.

When the final reports were reviewed, in some cases the authors were urged to be more reflective in their writing and provide more information about the developmental processes rather than concentrating exclusively upon the final outcomes. Such requests usually resulted in some changes but not always as much as might have been hoped for. Presumably the writing styles were too entrenched. It is not obvious what further steps might be taken, so there may have to be an acceptance that in similar ventures not all reports will reveal the level of reflection that took place.

There is, then, some loss, as information about what did not work can be as valuable at times as knowing what did work.

Encouraging reflection

Notwithstanding this belief that the levels of reflection upon teaching practice are always likely to be higher than that which might be deduced from final reports, it is worth examining the factors which might encourage participants in action learning projects to reflect critically upon their practice. For the second round of the Action Learning Project, the grant-awarding committee tried to weed out projects or evaluation designs incompatible with an action learning orientation. Proposals which received careful scrutiny were those which appeared to focus primarily or exclusively upon developing a product, most commonly a Web site or media package. The panel looked for evidence that initiatives were proposed in relationship to a reflective diagnosis of the current teaching situation and had a formative evaluation design, which permitted iterative progress and development.

The selection committee were convinced that the standard of proposals was significantly higher than for the first round and that it was not difficult to select proposals compatible with an action learning philosophy. This observation presumably indicates that the academic community in Hong Kong had achieved a better understanding of the action research methodology underpinning the initiative.

The coordinating team were also able to meet with teams very soon after awards were made – and in some cases even before awards were finalized. Those asked to re-write and re-submit proposals were all invited to meet with members of the coordinating team prior to re-writing. These meetings did provide the opportunity to discuss plans for the projects and ensure that any questionable elements were fully discussed.

There are also lessons for the wider context of other schemes, which offer grants for teaching development projects. If these wish to encourage reflection upon practice, the grants offered need to enable projects to last for a two-year period. Projects need at least two cycles, usually of a semester or a year each, to develop, implement and evaluate an initiative. Shorter timeframes lead to a development-only perspective. In evaluating the CAUT projects, Hayden and Speedy (1995) recommended that the one-year timeframe specified by CAUT was insufficient for projects to be implemented and evaluated. They recommended extending the period to two years for larger projects.

A further conclusion might be drawn from the fact that a significant proportion of the ALP projects that showed the least evidence of reflection upon practice were those which developed a media package. This is not to say that media development is incompatible with reflection, as many of the media projects did generate profound critical reflection, but it does suggest that teaching enhancement should not be restricted to technology-based initiatives as happens in some other schemes. Any scheme that focuses narrowly upon media-based projects is likely to develop a purely developmental perspective.

THE PROCESS AS AN OUTCOME

The encouragement of teachers to become reflective practitioners is one example of the processes undertaken by the project teams themselves being a valuable outcome. Developing both the mentality and the skills to observe, monitor, evaluate and research one's own teaching is a lasting benefit. The direct outcomes of the project, related to its aims, should have an impact for a reasonable timeframe as long as there is a reasonably stable course structure. The development of the ability to reflect upon one's own teaching can impact upon practice for a whole career.

In looking at the effectiveness of projects, the scope should be wider than whether the original objectives were obtained. The experiences of many participants suggest that in many ways the journey was more important than reaching the destination. In fact it was often those who had to struggle most on the journey because projects did not turn out as anticipated who drew the greatest benefits. Unanticipated difficulties could and did lead to a major re-consideration of deep-seated convictions about teaching practices.

NEED FOR SUPPORT

Chapter 13 put forward evidence that the support provided by the coordinating team was necessary. The independent evaluation panel also concluded that the support was needed. Universities intending to develop similar project-type initiatives should be advised that it is necessary to provide support, particularly for advice and help with evaluation.

The supporting role evolved and developed throughout the project. The Action Learning Project was itself an action research project into how to organize and support a teaching-quality enhancement initiative along action learning lines. Chapter 14 described the various facets of the support role which were provided to the teams. The 'critical friend' orientation provided a suitable level of support while still permitting ownership of projects by participants. This led to greater involvement and allowed participants to develop valuable skills and appropriate perspectives.

The development of the facilitative role by the coordinating team provides an interesting insight into the nature and portrayal of action research. The classic representation of action research is as a series of major cycles, each containing stages of planning, action, observation and reflection. This portrayal does not reveal the multiple iterations that take place within each of the cycles in our own action research project in learning to be a good action research facilitator. It would be hard to draw, but a more realistic representation would have been one of multiple, often indistinct, mini-cycles within the macro-cycles. Essentially the process is much messier than the sequential graphical diagrams commonly found in books.

Having gone through the iterative mini-cycles, the coordinating team became clearer about their role and the type of support that was useful to the project teams. In the second round the teams were contacted as early as possible. A short brochure was given to all participants, describing the operation of the project, the role of the coordinating team and the nature of the support that could be provided. This was backed by personal visits to all teams as early as possible.

TEACHING AS AN ACADEMIC ACTIVITY

The Action Learning Project was structured as a research programme. It seemed sensible to follow well-known and established procedures. Structuring the initiative in this way was also part of a bid to enhance the status of teaching and learning as a valued academic activity.

Not only was the project run along academic lines, it was run rigorously. Interim reports were only included in the collective volume if approved by two independent reviewers. The final reports were subjected to the same procedures. The support provided by the coordinating team was an effort to ensure high-quality projects. The overall project was intensively evaluated. Maintaining rigour and quality was seen as important: otherwise research on teaching and learning will be seen as an inferior form of research activity.

Maintenance of quality standards was also important in respect of the dissemination activities of the ALP. In these activities, the projects are portrayed as paradigms of good practice. If they are not, then the worth of the dissemination aspect is seriously undermined. Feedback from participants in the projects and those attending the conference and interest group meetings suggests that the dissemination activities were widely valued and quite successful in communicating ideas and lessons from the projects to a wider audience.

Whether the ALP had any success in enhancing the academic status of the teaching and learning is hard to judge. The fact that the UGC provided substantial financial support for a widely visible project, and has now awarded a further grant, must have sent a message in itself.

An indication of acceptance of the status of teaching development initiatives comes from participants' reports of support from heads of departments. Heads of department are a major determinant of tenure, contract renewal and promotion so their attitude is important. The large majority felt that they did receive support from their head (see Chapter 15), which suggests that in these departments teaching is valued. However, a quarter of the participants did not feel that they received support from the department head and a number of these made quite strong comments to this effect. As the UGC has stressed the importance of teaching, department heads who do not accept the importance of teaching are clearly undermining both the UGC's position and public statements about the significance of teaching, which have been made by all the Hong Kong universities. This is a good indication of the way in which theory in use does not always match espoused theory.

If it is accepted that quality enhancement of teaching can be pursued through action research programmes and these are best structured as academic activities, there are implications for educational developers and their units. If educational developers are to play the role of the critical friend, described in Chapter 14, in support of educational action research projects, they clearly need to be well qualified academically and granted academic status.

There is a touch of irony about the Action Learning Project in that the coordinating team, which has been advocating and implementing educational development as an academic activity, was not itself accorded academic status. The educational development unit of the host university is designated a central service unit and its staff are classified as non-academics. There is clearly an element of inconsistency here, as staff who have been instrumental in developing a more theoretically sound approach to academic development within an academic framework are not themselves accorded academic status. Non-academic status has inhibited the further development of teaching improvement through research-based activities since the staff have been prohibited from applying for internal research grants or supervising PhD students. By designating academic development units as non-academic, universities may be (probably inadvertently) sending a subtle signal that teaching is an inferior activity.

Universities could go further than this by encouraging academics to conduct research into teaching and learning on courses they teach. Measures that would support this activity include:

- according publications on teaching and learning research the same status as discipline-based research;
- accepting research on teaching and learning in staff appraisal exercises;
- considering grant proposals for teaching and learning research on an equal footing with discipline-based research;
- awarding higher-degree research scholarships and places to those who wish to do research on aspects of teaching and learning;
- introducing part-time secondment schemes for staff who wish to research some aspect of a course they teach or introduce some innovation;
- introducing grant schemes specifically targeted for educational development activities.

Many universities will be able to produce charters that show that some or indeed all of these measures are incorporated into official policy. Whether heads of department consistently apply the principles may be another matter.

VALUE OF DISSEMINATION ACTIVITIES

An aspect of the Action Learning Project that was clearly successful was the dissemination activities. The participants valued the informal networking experiences and the more formal ones through the interest group meetings. These and the conference were a valuable opportunity to pass on lessons from the projects to a wider audience of Hong Kong academics. This process surely had some impact in promoting teaching as a scholarly activity.

Introducing participants to others in a similar discipline or with related interests often resulted in the formation of supportive networks. In the initial stages particularly, mutual support among participants was valuable. Those who met unexpected difficulties particularly valued talking to others as they soon learnt that projects that proceed precisely according to plan are the exception rather than the rule.

The recommendation derived from this conclusion is simply that of ensuring that quality-enhancement initiatives do include a dissemination component. The project teams awarded grants in the Action Learning Project were asked to sign an initial agreement, which included the requirement of participating in meetings and the conference, and producing a final report. It seems sensible to incorporate these obligations in a written agreement, though it must be said that the participants saw the dissemination activities as events they wished to participate in rather than things they were forced to do. Similarly the production of reports was accepted as a necessary final outcome, though some teams did seem to find difficulty meeting the deadlines.

EVALUATION DESIGN

There are two points about the evaluation design that are worth making. Firstly, it is significant that the Action Learning Project was evaluated at all. Quality schemes need to be evaluated and, furthermore, evaluated for cost-effectiveness, but rarely are. The cost/benefit analysis on the Action Learning Project may not have been precise, in that effectiveness is hard to measure. However, the evaluation of the project was conducted in sufficient depth that the independent evaluation panel were able to reach a conclusion on cost-effectiveness and concluded that the ALP was good value for money.

The evaluation design of the Action Learning Project itself may be instructive to other large projects. The design featured multiple levels, multiple perspectives and multiple methods. The action research philosophy was followed, by requiring participants to evaluate their own projects and having the coordinating team evaluate procedural and organizational aspects of the overall project. The employment of an independent evaluation panel, though, added the objectivity and credibility important for such a substantial project.

OVERALL CONCLUSIONS

Quality assurance is one of the most topical issues currently facing higher education. Governments and accrediting authorities are becoming increasingly concerned that universities are cost-effective and accountable for the quality of education provided. There are numerous schemes for quality assurance, though few are based on any articulated theoretical justification and a surprisingly small proportion are evaluated for cost-effectiveness.

This book reports on a large project across seven universities, which was based upon a theoretical framework derived from action research. The implementation of the project was itself an action research project, which has yielded valuable insights into how similar initiatives might be conducted elsewhere.

The theoretical framework for the initiative has been expounded. The implementation of the framework has been described in detail and the lessons learnt through iterative development have been discussed. The project has been evaluated thoroughly, through multiple voices and multiple methods examining aspects appropriate to their involvement. Most universities should be able to learn something from this book about enhancing the quality of teaching and learning within courses they offer. It may not be possible to match the scale of the Action Learning Project, but appropriately sized versions are likely to be as effective. Accreditation or state authorities might consider supporting similar collaborative ventures, as there do seem to be benefits from collaborating across institutions.

References

Argyris, C and Schön, D (1978) *Organisational Learning: A theory-of-action perspective*, Addison Wesley Longman, Reading, MA

Barnett, R (1992) *Improving Higher Education: Total quality care*, Society for Research into Higher Education, Open University Press, Buckingham

Biggs, J and Lam, R (1997) in *Action Learning Project: Final evaluation report*, eds D Kember *et al*, Action Learning Project, Hong Kong

Biggs, J (1987) *Student Approaches to Learning and Studying*, Australian Council for Educational Research, Melbourne

Biggs, J (1992) *Why and How Do Hong Kong Students Learn? Using the Learning and Study Process Questionnaires*, Hong Kong University, Hong Kong

Biggs, J B and Collis, K F (1982) *Evaluating the Quality of Learning: The SOLO taxonomy*, Academic Press, New York

Bowden, J (1988) Achieving change in teaching practices, in *Improving Learning*, ed P Ramsden, Kogan Page, London

Boyer, E L (1990) *Scholarship Reconsidered: Priorities of the professorate*, The Carnegie Foundation for the Advancement of Teaching, San Francisco

Boyes, W J, Happel, S K and Hogan, T D (1984) Publish or perish: Fact or fiction, *Journal of Economics Education*, **15**, pp 136–41

Brinko, K T (1993) The practice of giving feedback to improve teaching: What is effective?, *Journal of Higher Education*, **64** (5), pp 575–93

Bryman, A, Haslam, C and Webb, A (1994) Performance appraisal in UK universities: A case of procedural compliance?, *Assessment and Evaluation in Higher Education*, **19** (3), pp 175–87

Busher, H (1989) Bringing out a new publication – the role of the catalyst in the micropolitics of the management of institutional change in education, *British Educational Research Journal*, **15** (1), pp 77–87

Candy, P C (1989) Alternative paradigms in educational research, *Australian Educational Researcher*, **16** (3), pp 1–11

Carr, W and Kemmis, S (1986) *Becoming Critical: Education, knowledge and action research*, Falmer Press, Brighton, Sussex

Champagne, A B, Gunstone, R F and Klopfer, L E (1985) Effecting changes in cognitive structures among physics students, in *Cognitive Structure and Conceptual Change*, eds L H T West and A L Pines, Academic Press, New York

Clark, R E (1983) Reconsidering research on learning from media, *Review of Educational Research*, **54** (4), pp 445–60

Clark, R E (1985) Confounding in educational computer research, *Journal of Educational Computing Research*, **1** (2), pp 28–42

Committee for the Advancement of University Teaching (1994) *Annual Report 1994*, Australian Government Publishing Services, Canberra

Committee for the Advancement of University Teaching (1995) *Improving University Teaching: National teaching development grant projects 1996*, Committee for the Advancement of University Teaching, Canberra

Conway, R and Kember, D (1993) Effecting changes in the teaching of practice management, *Optometric Education*, **18** (4), pp 119–23

Conway, R *et al* (1994) Making departmental changes through action research, based on adult learning principles, *Higher Education*, **28** (2), pp 265–82

Cook, T (1998) The importance of mess in action research, *Educational Action Research*, **6** (1), pp 93–108

Craft, A (ed) (1992) *Quality Assurance in Higher Education*, Falmer Press, London

Craft, A (ed) (1994) *International Developments in Assuring Quality in Higher Education*, Falmer Press, London

Cross, K P (1996) *Classroom Research: Implementing the scholarship of teaching*, Jossey-Bass, San Francisco

Dahlgren, L O (1978) Qualitative differences in conceptions of basic principles in economics. Paper read to the *4th International Conference on Higher Education* at Lancaster, August/September 1978

Dahlgren, L O (1984) Outcomes of learning, in *The Experience of Learning*, eds F Marton, D Hounsell and N Entwistle, Scottish Academic Press, Edinburgh

Daly, W T (1994) Teaching and scholarship: Adapting American higher education to hard times, *Journal of Higher Education*, **65** (1), pp 45–57

Dart, B and Boulton-Lewis, G (eds) (1998) *Teaching and Learning in Higher Education*, Australian Council for Educational Research, Melbourne

Davies, H, Sivan, A and Kember, D (1994) Helping Hong Kong business students to appreciate how they learn, *Higher Education*, **27**, pp 367–78

Eisner, E W (1991) *The Enlightened Eye: Qualitative inquiry and the enhancement of educational practice*, Macmillan Publishing, New York

Eison, J and Stevens, E (1995) Faculty development workshops and institutes, in *Teaching Improvement Practices*, eds W A Wright and Associates, Anker, Boston, MA

Elliott, J (1985) Facilitating educational action-research: Some dilemmas, in *Field Methods in the Study of Education*, ed R Burgess, Falmer Press, London

Elliott, J (1991) *Action Research for Educational Change*, Open University Press, Milton Keynes

Elton, L and Partington, P (1991) *Teaching Standards and Excellence in Higher Education: Developing a culture for quality*, Committee of Vice-Chancellors and Principals, Occasional Green Paper No. 1, Sheffield

Elton, L (1992) Quality enhancement and academic professionalism, *The New Academic*, **1** (2), pp 3–5

Frazer, M (1992) Quality assurance in higher education, in *Quality Assurance in Higher Education*, ed A Craft, Falmer Press, London

Gibbs, G (1992a) *Creating a Teaching Profile*, Technical and Educational Services, Bristol

Gibbs, G (1992b) *Improving the Quality of Student Learning*, Technical and Educational Services, Bristol

Gibbs, G (1995) Models of staff development, *The New Academic*, **4** (3), pp 15–17

Goldhammer, R, Anderson, R H and Krajewski, R J (1980) *Clinical Supervision: Special methods for the supervision of teachers*, 2nd edn, Reinhart and Winston, New York

Gow, L and Kember, D (1990) Does higher education promote independent learning?, *Higher Education*, **19**, pp 307–22

Gow, L and Kember, D (1993) Conceptions of teaching and their relationship to student learning, *British Journal of Educational Psychology*, **63**, pp 20–33

Gow, L, Kember, D and Sivan, A (1992) Lecturers' views of their teaching practices: Implications for staff development needs, *Higher Education Research and Development*, **11** (2), pp 135–49

Habermas, J (1972) *Knowledge and Human Interests*, tr J J Shapiro, Heinemann, London

Habermas, J (1974) *Theory and Practice*, tr J Viertel, Heinemann, London

Halsey, G T (1980) *Higher Education in Britain – A study of university and polytechnic teachers*, Final Report on SSRC Grant

Hayden, M and Speedy, G (1995) *Evaluation of the 1993 National Teaching Development Grants*, Report commissioned by the Committee for the Advancement of University Teaching

Ho, A S P (1998a) A conceptual change staff development programme: Effects as perceived by the participants, *International Journal of Academic Development*, **3** (1), pp 24–38

Ho, A S P (1998b) *Changing Teachers' Conceptions of Teaching as an Approach to Enhancing Teaching and Learning in Tertiary Education*. Unpublished PhD thesis, University of Hong Kong

Hong Kong Government Publications (1996) *1995 Hong Kong Yearbook*, Hong Kong Government Publications, Hong Kong

Hook, C (1981) *Studying Classrooms*, Deakin University Press, Victoria

Kember, D (1991) A curriculum development model based on deforestation and the work of Kafka, *Higher Education Review,* **24** (1), pp 7–13

Kember, D (1996) The intention to both memorise and understand: Another approach to learning?, *Higher Education,* **31**, pp 341–51

Kember, D (1997) A reconceptualisation of the research into university academics' conceptions of teaching, *Learning and Instruction,* **7** (3), pp 255–75

Kember, D and Gow, L (1991) A challenge to the anecdotal stereotype of the Asian student, *Studies in Higher Education,* **16** (2), pp 117–28

Kember, D and Gow, L (1992) Action research as a form of staff development in higher education, *Higher Education,* **23** (3), pp 297–310

Kember, D and Gow, L (1994) Orientations to teaching and their effect on the quality of student learning, *Journal of Higher Education,* **65** (1), pp 58–74

Kember, D *et al* (1996a) Developing curricula to encourage students to write reflective journals, *Educational Action Research,* **4** (3), pp 329–48

Kember, D *et al* (1996b) Encouraging critical reflection through small group discussion of journal writing, *Innovations in Education and Training International,* **33** (4), pp 203–12

Kember, D and Kelly, M (1993) *Improving teaching through action research,* Green Guide No. 14, Higher Education Research and Development Society of Australasia, Campbelltown, NSW

Kember, D and Kwan, K P (in press) Lecturers' approaches to teaching and their relationship to conceptions of good teaching, in *Teacher Thinking, Beliefs and Knowledge in Higher Education,* eds N Hativa and P Goodyear, Kluwer Academic Publishers, Dordrecht, The Netherlands

Kember, D *et al* (1997) *Case Studies of Improving Teaching and Learning From the Action Learning Project,* Action Learning Project, Hong Kong

Kember, D and McKay, J (1996) Action research into the quality of student learning: A paradigm for faculty development, *Journal of Higher Education,* **67** (5), pp 528–54

Kemmis, S (1988) Action Research, in *Educational Research, Methodology, and Measurement: An international handbook,* ed J P Keeves, Pergamon Press, London

Kolitch, E and Dean, A V (1999) Student ratings of instruction in the USA: Hidden assumptions and missing conceptions about 'good' teaching, *Studies in Higher Education,* **24** (1), pp 27–42

Krajewski, R (1993) The observation cycle: A methodology for coaching and problem solving, in *Clinical Supervision: Coaching for higher performance,* eds R H Anderson and K J Snyder, Technomic, Lancaster, Basel

Kuhn, T S (1970) *The Structure of Scientific Revolutions,* The University of Chicago Press, Chicago, IL

Labaree, D F (1998) Educational researchers: Living with a lesser form of knowledge, *Educational Researcher*, **27** (8), pp 4–12

Levie, W H and Dickie, K (1973) The analysis and application of media, in *Second Handbook of Research on Teaching*, ed R M W Travers, Rand McNally, Chicago, IL

Levinson-Rose, J and Menges, R F (1981) Improving college teaching: A critical review of research, *Review of Educational Research*, **51** (3), pp 403–34

Lewin, K (1946) Action research and minority problems, *Journal of Social Issues*, **2**, pp 34–46

Lewin, K (1952) Group decision and social change, in *Readings in Social Psychology*, eds G E Swanson, T M Newcomb and F E Hartley, Holt, New York

Loder, C P J (1990) *Quality Assurance and Accountability in Higher Education*, Kogan Page, London

Marsh, H W (1981) The use of path analysis to estimate teacher and course effects in student ratings of instructional effectiveness, *Applied Psychological Measurement*, **6**, pp 47–60

Marsh, H W (1987) Students' evaluations of university teaching: research findings, methodological issues, and directions for future research, *International Journal of Educational Research*, **11**, pp 253–388

Marsh, H W and Roche, L (1993) The use of students' evaluations and an individually structured intervention to enhance university teaching effectiveness, *American Educational Research Journal*, **30** (1), pp 217–51

Martin, E and Ramsden, P (1992) *An Expanding Awareness: How lecturers change their understanding of teaching*. Paper presented at the HERDSA Conference, Gippsland

Marton, F and Säljö, R (1976) On qualitative differences in learning, outcome and process I, *British Journal of Educational Psychology*, **46**, pp 4–11

Marton, F, Hounsell, D and Entwistle, N (eds) (1984) *The Experience of Learning*, Scottish Universities Press, Edinburgh

McGill, I and Beaty, L (1995) *Action Learning: A guide for professional, management and educational development*, 2nd edn, Kogan Page, London

McKay, J (1995) *Promoting Reflection Within Teaching: A case study in educational change within a department*. Unpublished PhD Dissertation, Hong Kong Polytechnic University, Hong Kong

McKay, J and Kember, D (1997) Spoonfeeding leads to regurgitation: A better diet can result in more digestible learning outcomes, *Higher Education Research and Development*, **16** (1), pp 55–67

McKernan, J (1991) *Curriculum Action Research*, Kogan Page, London

McNiff, J (1992) *Action Research: Principles and practice*, Routledge, London

McTaggart, R and Garbutcheon-Singh, M (1987) A fourth generation of action research: Notes on the Deakin seminar, in *The Action Research*

Reader, eds S Kemmis and R McTaggart, Deakin University Press, Geelong, Victoria

Mezirow, J (1981) A critical theory of adult learning and education, *Adult Education*, **32** (1), pp 3–24

Moses, I (1985) Academic development units and the improvement of teaching, *Higher Education*, **14**, pp 75–100

National Committee of Inquiry into Higher Education (1997) *Higher Education in the Learning Society* (The Dearing report), HMSO, London

O'Neill, G P (1990) Publish or perish: Dispelling the myth, *Higher Education Review*, **23** (3), pp 55–62

Owens, R (1982) Methodological rigor in naturalistic inquiry: some issues and answers, *Educational Administration Quarterly*, **18** (2), pp 1–21

Parlett, M and Hamilton, D (1976) Evaluation as illumination: A new approach to the study of innovatory programs, in *Curriculum Evaluation Today: Trends and implications*, ed D A Tawney, Macmillan Education, London

Parlett, M and Hamilton, D (1977) Evaluation as illumination: a new approach to the study of innovatory programmes, in *Beyond the Numbers Game*, eds D Hamilton *et al*, Macmillan Education, London

Polytechnics and Colleges Funding Council (1990) *Teaching Quality*. Report of the Committee of Enquiry appointed by the Council

Pratt, D (1992) Conceptions of teaching, *Adult Education Quarterly*, **42** (4), pp 203–20

Pratt, J (1991) Expansion and quality: Killing the golden goose, *Higher Education Review*, **24** (1), pp 3–6

QSR NUD•IST (1997) Qualitative Solutions and Research Pty Ltd, La Trobe University, Victoria

Ramsden, P (1992) *Learning to Teach in Higher Education*, Kogan Page, London

Ramsden, P (1994) Describing and explaining research productivity, *Higher Education*, **28**, pp 207–26

Ramsden, P and Entwistle, N J (1981) Effects of academic departments on students' approaches to studying, *British Journal of Educational Psychology*, **51**, pp 368–83

Ramsden, P and Martin, E (1996) Recognition of good university teaching: Policies from an Australian study, *Studies in Higher Education*, **21** (3), pp 299–316

Rapoport, R N (1970) Three dilemmas in action research, *Human Relations*, **23** (6), pp 499–513

Reigeluth, C M and Stein, F S (1983) The elaboration theory of instruction, in *Instructional Design Theories and Models: An overview of their current status*, ed C M Reigeluth, Erlbaum, Hillsdale, New Jersey

Richards, T J and Richards, L (1991) The NUD•IST qualitative data analysis system, *Qualitative Sociology*, **14** (4), pp 307–24

Robinson, J (1989) A second pair of eyes: A case study of a supervisor's view of clinical supervision, in *Case Studies in Clinical Supervision*, ed W J Smith, Deakin University, Victoria

Rust, C (1998) The impact of educational development workshops on teachers' practice, *International Journal of Academic Development*, **3** (1), pp 72–80

Samuelowicz, K and Bain, J D (1992) Conceptions of teaching held by academic teachers, *Higher Education*, **24**, pp 93–111

Schön, D A (1983) *The Reflective Practitioner: How professionals think in action*, Basic Books, New York

Schram, W (1977) *Big Media, Little Media*, Sage Publications, Beverly Hills, CA

Schratz, M (1993) Crossing the disciplinary boundaries: Professional development through action research in higher education, *Higher Education Research and Development*, **12**, pp 131–42

Schulman, L S (1988) Disciplines of Inquiry: An Overview, in *Complementary Methods for Research in Education*, ed R M Jaeger, American Educational Research Association, Washington, DC

Scriven, M (1991 *Evaluation Thesaurus*, Sage Publications, US

Seldin, P (1993) *Successful Use of Teaching Portfolios*, Anker, Boston, MA

Simon, H (1987) *Getting to Know School in a Democracy*, Falmer Press, London

Sivan, A, Leung, R W, Gow, L and Kember, D (1991) Towards more active forms of teaching and learning in hospitality studies, *The International Journal of Hospitality Management*, **10** (4), pp 369–79

Stake, R E (1976) *Evaluating Educational Programmes: The need and response*, Center for Educational Research and Innovation, Urbana-Champagn, IL

Stenhouse, L (1975) *An Introduction to Curriculum Research and Development*, Heinemann Education, London

Strike, K A and Posner, G J (1985) A conceptual change view of learning and understanding, in *Cognitive Structure and Conceptual Change*, eds L H T West and A L Pines, Academic Press, New York

Trigwell, K and Prosser, M (1996a) Changing approaches to teaching: A relational perspective, *Studies in Higher Education*, **21** (3), pp 275–84

Trigwell, K and Prosser, M (1996b) Congruence between intention and strategy in university science teachers' approaches to teaching, *Higher Education*, **32**, pp 77–87

Trigwell, K, Prosser, M and Lyons, F (1997) *Defining Good Teaching: Relations between teachers' approaches to teaching and student learning*. Paper presented at the 7th Conference of the European Association for Research in Learning and Instruction, Athens, August 1997

Walberg, H J and Haertel, G D (eds) (1990) *The International Encyclopaedia of Educational Evaluation*, Pergamon Press, Oxford

Watkins, D (1998) Assessing approaches to learning: A cross-cultural perspective, in *Teaching and Learning in Higher Education*, eds B Dart and G Boulton-Lewis, Australian Council for Educational Research, Melbourne

Watkins, D and Biggs, J B (eds) (1996) *The Chinese Learner: Cultural, psychological and contextual influences*, Australian Council for Educational Research, Melbourne and the Comparative Education Research Centre, University of Hong Kong, Hong Kong

Webb, G (1992) On pretexts for higher education development activities, *Higher Education*, **24**, pp 351–61

Webb, G (1996) *Understanding Staff Development*, Society for Research into Higher Education, Open University Press, Buckingham

Weeks, P and Scott, D (eds) (1992) *Exploring Tertiary Teaching: Papers from the TRAC (teaching, reflection and collaboration) project*, University of New England, Armidale

Weimer, B and Lenze, L F (1991) Instructional interventions: A review of the literature on efforts to improve instruction, in *Higher Education: Handbook of theory and research*, ed J C Smart, Agathon Press, New York

Williams, I and Gillard, G (1986) Improving satellite tutorials at the University of the South Pacific, *Distance Education*, **7** (2), pp 261–74

Williams, R (1988) *Keywords: A vocabulary of culture and society*, Fontana Press, London

Williams, R (1991) Evaluating self reports of action research in changing educational institutions: A response to Hugh Busher, *British Educational Research Journal*, **17** (3), pp 237–47

Woodhouse, D (1995) Efficient quality systems, *Assessment and Evaluation in Higher Education*, **20** (1), pp 15–24

Worthen, B R and Sanders, J R (1987) *Educational Evaluation: Alternative approaches and practical guidelines*, Longman, New York

Wright, W A and O'Neil, M C (1995) Teaching improvement practices: International perspectives, in *Teaching Improvement Practices*, eds W A Wright and Associates, Anker, Boston, MA

Wright, W A and Associates (eds) (1995) *Teaching Improvement Practices*, Anker, Boston, MA

Zuber-Skerritt, O (1992a) *Professional Development in Higher Education: A theoretical framework for action research*, Kogan Page, London

Zuber-Skerritt, O (1992b) *Action Research in Higher Education: Examples and reflections*, Kogan Page, London

Appendix A

QUESTIONNAIRE FOR PARTICIPANTS IN THE ACTION LEARNING PROJECT

Please answer the following questions by marking the appropriate response on the red 'general purpose survey/answer sheet'. For questions 1 to 55 please use the following letter codes:

A = strongly agree
B = agree
C = disagree
D = strongly disagree

In this questionnaire 'this/our project' refers to the project conducted by you and your team. 'Action Learning Project' refers to the overall project funded by the UGC.

Motivation for participation

1. I had no previous experience of action research before participating in this project.
2. I was motivated to participate in this project because I could obtain a grant.
3. I was motivated to participate in this project because I wanted to improve the quality of my teaching.
4. I was motivated to participate in this project because I wanted to improve the quality of my students' learning.
5. I was motivated to participate in this project because I thought it would lead to publications.
6. I was motivated to participate in this project because it is a way of doing research into teaching.
7. I was motivated to participate in this project because I wanted to influence the teaching on my course or in my department.

Framework

8. Action research provided a suitable framework for conducting the project.
9. Action Learning Project grants are accorded high status in our university.
10. The Action Learning Project can contribute to improving teaching and learning in my university.
11. The Action Learning Project is an effective means to improve university teaching and learning in the context of Hong Kong.
12. Evidence gathered from our project has been used to convince departmental colleagues to modify their practices.
13. Lessons from our project can be passed on to other teams which desire to conduct action learning projects.

Teamwork experience

14. Coordination and cooperation among team members was difficult.
15. Teamwork is important to the success of the project.
16. Employing an RA was essential to the success of the project.
17. Our students were aware that the project was taking place.
18. Our students played an integral part in the project.

Process

19. Our project was carried out as originally scheduled.
20. We stuck closely to our original design for our project.
21. It was hard to recruit a suitable research assistant.
22. Students were happy to meet the requirements our project imposed upon them.
23. We ended up with far more data than we could analyse.

Support

24. We received support from our departmental head to participate in the project.
25. We received support from our departmental colleagues to participate in the project.
26. We received support from our students to participate in the project.

Outcomes

27. My expectations of our project as a whole were realized.
28. The evaluation of our project we conducted has been very effective.
29. Conducting this project will have a lasting effect on my teaching.
30. Conducting this project will have a lasting effect on the course I teach.
31. Our project was successful.
32. We found it very difficult to carry out our project.
33. I think I will do similar types of action research into my own teaching after this project.
34. Having conducted this project, I have a greater awareness of important factors affecting the quality of teaching.
35. Having conducted this project, I have a deeper understanding of educational research in general.
36. Conducting the project has improved my research ability.
37. Similar work will continue after the end of this academic year.
38. If I could obtain another grant from the Action Learning Project I would continue this project.
39. If I could obtain another grant from the Action Learning Project I would do another project.
40. This project has strengthened my belief in the value of research into teaching.
41. Having conducted this project, I have become more reflective about my teaching.

Influence on teaching and learning

42. The project has led to an improvement in students' performance.
43. The project has led to an improvement in students' learning approaches.
44. The project has led to an improvement in students' attitude.
45. The project has led to an improvement in teacher–student relationships.
46. The project has led to an improvement in my teaching.
47. The project has led to an improvement in the teaching of others in my department.

Events

48. The seminar series on research into teaching and learning in tertiary education was interesting.
49. The workshops on evaluation of teaching were valuable.

50. The interest group meeting was a valuable opportunity to learn from others.
51. The conference is a necessary part of the Action Learning Project.

Organization

52. The Action Learning Project was organized efficiently.
53. The Action Learning Project staff were helpful.
54. Communication was too slow.
55. There was too much bureaucracy.

Need for support

Please rate your need for the following types of support.
    For questions 56 to 64 please use the following letter codes:

A = very necessary
B = necessary
C = not very necessary
D = definitely not necessary

56. Advice on writing a proposal.
57. Advice on evaluating the project.
58. Advice on writing up the outcomes.
59. Advice on action research methodology.
60. Prompting to stick to deadlines.
61. Arranging contact with others doing similar projects.
62. Help with data analysis.
63. Advice on collecting data.
64. Help with training a research assistant.

Quality of support

Please rate the quality of the following types of support.
    For questions 65 to 73 please use the following letter codes:

A = very good
B = good
C = poor
D = very poor
E = not provided

65. Advice on writing a proposal.
66. Advice on evaluating the project.
67. Advice on writing up the outcomes.
68. Advice on action research methodology.
69. Prompting to stick to deadlines.
70. Arranging contact with others doing similar projects.
71. Help with data analysis.
72. Advice on collecting data.
73. Help with training a research assistant.

OPEN-ENDED QUESTIONS FOR ACTION LEARNING PROJECT PARTICIPANTS

A. Do you think your project was successful, and if so what were the important factors in its success or lack of success?
B. Has your project had any impact on teaching and learning?
C. Do you have any comment on the organization and support of the Action Learning Project staff?
D. Are there any other comments you would like to make?

Thank you for completing this questionnaire

Appendix B

INTERVIEW SCHEDULE

The questions listed below were used as a rough guide for the interviewer. In practice most interviews developed as a conversation between the interviewer and the focus group, which equated to the project team. The questions were mainly used to ensure that relevant topics were covered. Possible prompts are shown indented.

What stimulated you to start your project? What particular things were you concerned about?

How did the members of your team come together to generate an idea for your project?

To what extent do you feel that your expectations of your project as a whole are being realized?

> Were there any outcomes from the project that were unexpected (positive or negative)?

Do you think your project has been successful?

Has your project had any influence on teaching and learning?

> Students' learning/your teaching/colleagues' teaching?
> A deeper understanding of educational research in general?
> Any other benefits?
> Have students taken an active part in the development of the project?

Will the project influence the behaviour of you and your departmental colleagues in the future?

Assuming you performed the project with a group of people, how did you find this experience?

Coordination and cooperation among team members?
To what extent do you think such experience is important to the success of the project?

Would you mind sharing your experience on the variables which affect the success of your project?

Factors influencing success
Factors giving rise to difficulties

In the light of your experience, are there any issues or general concerns relating to the Action Learning Project which you would like to see addressed?

In what way do you think the Action Learning Project could be improved?

Has participating in the project benefited you?

Publications etc.

Okay, you've been very helpful. We'd be very interested in any other feelings and thoughts you'd like to share with us to help us understand your experience of the project and how it affected you.

Appendix C

TITLES OF PROJECTS

The projects are grouped under headings showing the interest groups.

Assessment

Effect of assignment expectations on student learning approaches;

Fostering the students' development of clinical competence through objective structured clinical assessment;

Implementing peer-assessment to improve teaching and learning;

Investigating peer- and self-evaluation in enhancing postgraduate student performance in oral presentations and discussions in English;

Students' strategies in interpreting examination questions and in organizing answers.

Case studies or projects

Enhancing student learning in engineering analysis and design;

Using a case-album approach to enhance critical thinking and daily-life application in a psychology course.

Curriculum restructuring

Application of the action learning methodology to improve teaching of the module quantum and solid-state physics;

Enhancing teaching performance in the faculty of social sciences;

Integrating theory and practice in marketing education;

Restructuring the English foundation programme for part-time students;

The integration of technology and commerce in maritime transport education.

Experiential learning

'Speaking in English? I'd be seen by my classmates and there'll be public opinions': developing opportunities for speaking English;

Applying team learning and effective management skills to learning;

Development of a professional development programme and recording system for information systems undergraduates in an action learning environment;

Enhancing the teaching–learning process for postgraduate and post-experience courses with students from multi-professional background;

Learning through experience;

The adaptation of 'the looking glass' to Hong Kong students;

Visualization of structural engineering behaviour.

Multimedia

Action learning in robotics education: a distributed hypermedia environment;

An experimental investigation on the effectiveness of using an interactive multimedia teaching-support system in enhancing students' learning ability;

Computer-based support for foreign language learning in the university;

Development of multimedia action learning programme for social science;

Learning computer communication networks through software-based experiments;

Lecturing technology – a future with multimedia;

Multimedia-based learning system for database modelling and design;

Self-motivated learning systems in engineering education;

The enhancement of teaching through computer-aided 3-D instruction;

Using multimedia to promote and support problem-based learning in construction technology;

Problem-based or student-centred learning;

A self-directed English course through English centre self-access: analysing teacher–student interaction in self-access consultation;

Active learning in the general practice clerkship;

Assessment of problem-based learning in information systems;

Introducing problem-based learning to conventional building services engineering curriculum;

Teaching and learning in physiology and pathology: an active approach;

The systems approach and the enhancement of problem-solving skills;

Utilizing experience mix as a resource in implementing student-centred learning strategies.

Reflective practice

Critically reflective community work education: a social work curriculum addressing social deprivation and poverty;

Enhancing reflection and collaborative learning of communication tasks;

Enhancing the quality of fieldwork instruction through student–teacher partnership in action research;

Promoting reflective learning and practice for the education of profess-ionals;

Promoting the application of theoretical holistic health concepts to the day-to-day professional practice among registered nurses;

Promoting the integration of theory and practice, and partnership between teachers and students in the education of registered nurses;

The process of integrating experience with learning of first-year social work students.

Tutorials or small group teaching

Action learning in anatomy and English;

An investigation into the efficiency of, and optimizing alternatives for, tutorial sessions in behavioural sciences courses within the bachelor of nursing programme;

Enhancing the participation of law students in academic tutorials;

Enhancing the quality of thesis writing: a structured workshop programme for research postgraduates;

Exploring strategies for stimulating and fostering English language use in small group work in monolingual Cantonese classes of year-one engineering students;

The improvement of participation of students during tutorials;

Training independent writers of business English through interactive feedback in a course offered to science and engineering students.

Index

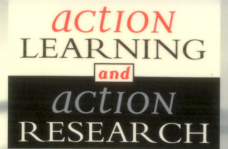

action LEARNING and action RESEARCH

The issue of quality in learning is of the highest importance. Institutions around the world are increasingly moving to new models of funding, scrutiny and accountability. As a result, those with an interest in, or responsibility for, effective and high-quality teaching and learning must pay greater attention to improving the quality of learning within this challenging and changing environment. This fascinating and stimulating book presents the methods used across a range of institutions to acclaimed effect.

Action research is a widely acknowledged and understood technique in education, and its benefits are widely supported. However, it has received less attention as a tool for improving education itself. In *Action Learning and Action Research*, David Kember and his colleagues present their own experiences in Hong Kong universities, where they pioneered the use of action learning methods for the improvement of teaching and learning. This book is based on experiences within the Action Learning Project, an inter-institutional initiative which supported 90 action research projects in eight universities in Hong Kong.

Opening with a detailed consideration of the theory of action learning, the book then presents a detailed, step-by-step route through the use of the technique. In doing so, it equips the reader with a practical guide to the issues and background to establishing projects, and their potential benefits. The book ends with an extensive conclusion and reflection on the lessons of the project, which will be of great value to researchers and all those needing to take practical measures in educational development. More than simply the results of the project, the book explores in detail approaches to enhancing education and will act as an indispensable guide for anyone wishing to use this technique in his or her own work.

David Kember was the Coordinator of the Action Learning Project when this book was written. He is currently Assistant Director of the Educational Development Unit at the Hong Kong Polytechnic University. Previously he worked in a variety of educational development positions in Britain, Fiji, Papua New Guinea and Australia. His research interests include student learning, action research and lifelong learning.

This book also includes contributions from the former Associate Coordinators of the Action Learning Project: Tak Shing Ha, Bick-har Lam, April Lee, Sandra Ng, Louisa Yan and Jessie C K Yum.

Kogan Page
120 Pentonville Road

£19.99

ISBN 0-7494-3113-X